Recovering Berryman

Recovering Berryman

ESSAYS ON A POET

Edited by
Richard J. Kelly and Alan K. Lathrop

Ann Arbor
THE UNIVERSITY OF MICHIGAN PRESS

Copyright © by the University of Michigan 1993
All rights reserved
Published in the United States of America by
The University of Michigan Press
Manufactured in the United States of America

1996 1995 1994 1993   4 3 2 1

Library of Congress Cataloging-in-Publication Data

Recovering Berryman : essays on a poet / edited by Richard J. Kelly
   and Alan K. Lathrop.
        p.   cm.
   Includes bibliographical references and index.
   ISBN 0-472-10419-5 (alk. paper)
   1. Berryman, John, 1914–1972—Criticism and interpretation.
   I. Kelly, Richard J.   II. Lathrop, Alan K., 1940–   .
   PS3503.E744Z86   1993
   811'.54—dc20   92-46724
                                                   CIP

A CIP catalogue record for this book is available from the British Library.

We gratefully acknowledge the following: Cleanth Brooks, for permission to
Charlotte Beck to quote from his letters to John Berryman; John Burt, for
permission to Charlotte Beck to quote from Robert Penn Warren's letters to
John Berryman; Kate Donahue, for nonexclusive, one-time use of the previ-
ously unpublished *Cleopatra: A Meditation,* copyright retained in her name;
Kate Donahue, for permission to Charlotte Beck to quote from John Berry-
man's letters to the editors of the *Southern Review;* Farrar, Straus & Giroux, to
reprint "Parting as Descent" and excerpt from "The Song of the Tortured Girl"
from *Collected Poems, 1937–1971* by John Berryman, copyright © 1989 by Kate
Donahue Berryman, and Dream Song 177, from *The Dream Songs* by John
Berryman, copyright © 1967, 1968, 1969 by John Berryman, reprinted by
permission of Farrar, Straus & Giroux, Inc.; Lewis Hyde, for permission to
reprint "Alcohol and Poetry: John Berryman and the Booze Talking." Copy-
right © 1975, 1986, and 1993, Lewis Hyde. This essay first appeared in the
American Poetry Review. It is also available as a pamphlet from Dallas Institute
Publications, 2719 Routh St., Dallas, TX 75201; David Higham Associates,
for permission to reprint "The Sirens," from *Selected Verse,* by John Manifold;
and University Press of New England, for permission to reprint "Sonnet,"
from Donald Justice, *The Summer Anniversaries,* revised edition, copyright ©
1981 by Donald Justice. "Mine Own John Berryman," by Philip Levine and
"Lowell on Berryman on Lowell," by Paul Mariani were first published in the
Autumn 1991 issue of the *Gettysburg Review,* reprinted here by permission of
the editor and authors. Portions of Peter Stitt's essay, "John Berryman: His
Teaching, His Scholarship, His Poetry," appeared in an earlier form in the
Southern Review and *John Berryman Studies.*

Acknowledgments

The editors wish to thank all of the participants in John Berryman: His Life, His Work, His Thought, a national conference held at the University of Minnesota, 25–27 October 1990, where the papers selected for inclusion in this collection originated. For their extraordinary contributions to the success of the conference, we are grateful to Leslie Denny and her staff in the Department of Professional Development and Conference Services at the University of Minnesota; to Professor Michael Dennis Browne, Director of the Creative and Professional Writing Program at the University of Minnesota; to Thomas L. Trow, of the College of Liberal Arts Dean's Office, University of Minnesota, and to the other members of the conference planning committee. We would also like to thank administrators and colleagues in the University of Minnesota Libraries for their support throughout this project. Our sincere gratitude, too, to Kate Donahue (Mrs. John Berryman), for permission to publish, for the first time, *Cleopatra: A Meditation,* and for her generous cooperation in many aspects of the preparation of this volume. A special word of thanks, as well, to George Swan for his patience and expertise in typing the introductory materials and other editorial aspects of this book. Finally, our sincere appreciation to LeAnn Fields at the University of Michigan Press for her commitment to this volume and for her resourceful editorial assistance throughout its preparation.

Contents

Chronology

1914	Born John Allyn Smith, Jr., 25 October, in McAlester, Oklahoma; the first son of John Allyn Smith and Martha (Little) Smith.
1919	Brother, Robert Jefferson, born.
1925	Smith family moves to Clearwater, Florida.
1926	JB's father commits suicide. His mother marries John Angus McAlpin Berryman, who formally adopts her two sons and gives them his name.
1927	Family moves to Jackson Heights, New York, where JB attends P.S. 69.
1928–32	Attends South Kent School, a small Episcopal boarding school, in Connecticut.
1932	Enters Columbia University. Mark Van Doren becomes his mentor.
1936	Graduates Phi Beta Kappa, B.A. Engaged to Jean Bennett. Receives Euretta J. Kellett Fellowship to study in England. Enters Clare College, Cambridge.
1937	Engaged to Beryl Eeman. Wins Charles Oldham Shakespeare Scholarship.
1938	Returns to New York City.
1939	Becomes poetry editor for the *Nation*. Appointed Instructor in English, Wayne State University, Detroit.
1940	Appointed Instructor in English, Harvard University. "Twenty Poems" published in *Five Young American Poets*.
1942	First individual collection, *Poems,* one in a series of poetry pamphlets, published by New Directions. Marries Eileen Patricia Mulligan.

1943   Appointed Instructor in English at Princeton (where he
        held various positions until 1953).

1944   Awarded Rockefeller Foundation Research Fellowship to
        work on a critical edition of *King Lear.*

1945   *Kenyon Review*-Doubleday Doran Award, first prize, for
        the short story "The Imaginary Jew."

1947   Affair with "Lise," which is recounted in *Berryman's Son-
        nets* (1967).

1948   *The Dispossessed.*

1949   Wins Guarantors Prize (*Poetry*) and Shelley Memorial
        Award (Poetry Society of America).

1950   Publishes critical biography, *Stephen Crane.* Wins Levinson
        Prize (*Poetry*). American Academy Award for poetry and
        Stephen Crane. National Institute of Arts and Letters
        Award.

1952   Appointed Elliston Professor of Poetry, spring semester,
        University of Cincinnati. Awarded Guggenheim Fellow-
        ship for critical study of Shakespeare and for creative writ-
        ing.

1953   "Homage to Mistress Bradstreet" first published in *Partisan
        Review.* Spends summer with Eileen in Europe. Separated
        from Eileen upon their return and spends several months
        in New York City.

1954   Teaches one semester of poetry and creative writing at the
        Writers' Workshop, University of Iowa (Iowa City), and
        is dismissed following arrest for intoxication, profanity,
        and disturbing the peace.

1955   Appointed as lecturer in Humanities Department, Univer-
        sity of Minnesota (where he held various positions until
        his death in 1972).

1956   Divorced from Eileen. Married to Elizabeth Ann Levine.
        Homage to Mistress Bradstreet published as book. Wins
        Rockefeller Fellowship in poetry from *Partisan Review.*

1957   Awarded Harriet Monrose Poetry Prize, University of
        Chicago. Son Paul is born. Spends two months lecturing
        in India for United States Information Service (State De-
        partment).

1958   *His Thought Made Pockets & The Plane Buckt.*

1959 Divorced from Ann. *Homage to Mistress Bradstreet and Other Poems*, first book of poems to be published in England.

1960 Receives Brandeis University Creative Arts Award. *The Arts of Reading*, an anthology with commentary, co-authored with Ralph Ross and Allen Tate.

1961 Married to Kathleen (Kate) Donahue, his third and last wife.

1962 Writer-in-Residence at Brown University (1962–63). First daughter, Martha, born.

1964 *77 Dream Songs*. Receives Russell Loines Award (National Institute of Arts and Letters).

1965 Awarded Pulitzer Prize for *77 Dream Songs*. Receives Guggenheim Fellowship (1966–67).

1966 Lives with family in Dublin (1966–67).

1967 Academy of American Poets Award. National Endowment for the Arts Award. *Berryman's Sonnets* and *Short Poems* published.

1968 *His Toy, His Dream, His Rest.*

1969 Wins National Book Award and Bollingen Prize in Poetry for *His Toy, His Dream, His Rest*. Publishes *The Dream Songs* (complete edition). Appointed Regents' Professor of Humanities at the University of Minnesota.

1970 *Love & Fame.*

1971 Works on *Recovery* and *Delusions, Etc.* Second daughter, Sarah Rebecca, is born. Mother comes to live in Minneapolis. Awarded a Senior Fellowship, National Endowment for the Humanities.

1972 Commits suicide, 7 January. Given Catholic funeral and buried in Resurrection Cemetery, Mendota Heights, St. Paul

Posthumous Publications

1972 *Delusions, Etc.*
1973 *Recovery.*
1976 *The Freedom of the Poet*
1977 *Henry's Fate & Other Poems, 1967–1972* (edited by John Haffenden).

Richard J. Kelly

Introduction

He flung to pieces and they hit the floor.
—Dream Song 147

The world breaks everyone and afterward many are strong in the broken places.
—Ernest Hemingway, A Farewell to Arms

Near the end of his life John Berryman commented in a *Paris Review* interview: "The artist is extremely lucky who is presented with the worst possible ordeal which will not actually kill him. At that point he's in business." Then, looking ahead, in a brave if—as he later admitted—deluded moment, he added: "I hope to be nearly crucified." Talent and ambition aside, it was precisely his ability to transform his suffering into art, to universalize it in a way that touches others as well, that gave his work such authenticity and force.

Readers of Berryman's unmistakably personal verse will know that behind his career-long tragic cast of mind lay earlier and unelected sufferings. He was born John Allyn Smith on 25 October 1914 in McAlester, Oklahoma. Named after his father, he was the first of two sons born to John Allyn Smith, a banker, and Martha Little (Smith), a schoolteacher. A second son, Robert Jefferson, was born five years later. Over the ensuing decade Smith held banking positions in several small Oklahoma towns, but in 1925, owing to personal difficulties, was forced to resign as vice president and loan officer at the First State Bank in Anadarko. Toward the end of 1925 the Smiths moved to Tampa to try their business prospects in the then booming Florida economy. The boom quickly went bust, however, and financial disaster was accompanied by growing domestic turmoil for the Smiths. Ultimately, on 26 June 1926, John Allyn Smith "shot out his heart in a Florida dawn," as Berryman later wrote—an act that would haunt Berryman for the rest of his life.

Ten weeks later, the future poet was provided with the name the world would come to know him by when his mother married her landlord, John Angus McAlpin Berryman, who adopted the two boys. John Angus soon moved the family to New York City and began work on Wall Street as a bond salesman. In the fall of 1927, the twelve-year-old John Berryman entered eighth grade at P.S. 69 in Jackson Heights, and he graduated in June with an *A* in both scholastic record and conduct. Further unsettling changes lay ahead, however.

In September 1928, the gawky, unathletic and already bookish adolescent was packed off to South Kent School, a Connecticut prep school in the foothills of the Berkshires where, with its strong emphasis on competitive sports, he was, as might have been predicted, grievously misplaced. Over the next four years he was subjected to frequent bullying and once threw himself into the path of an oncoming train, only to be pulled off by three upper-formers who had, moments earlier, ganged up on him. Nonetheless, he did manage to impress many of his teachers with his braininess, wrote articles for the school paper, the *Pigtail,* grew increasingly interested in literature, and became the first boy in the history of the school to bypass the sixth form and go directly from the fifth into college.

In the more agreeable environs of Columbia University he rapidly metamorphosed into a highly attractive figure, admired for his intelligence and social adeptness. While there he fell under the influence of Mark Van Doren, who became his mentor, and he began to write and publish reviews and poems in the *Columbia Review.* Under Van Doren's tutelage he also developed a fascination with William Butler Yeats, a passion for Shakespeare, and eventually won a Kellett Fellowship to study for two years in England.

At Cambridge University he became only the second American to win the prestigious Oldham Shakespeare Scholarship. He also managed to meet his hero, Yeats, as well as Dylan Thomas and W. H. Auden. During this time Berryman continued his apprenticeship as a poet, tried his hand at writing plays, and encouraged by Robert Penn Warren and Cleanth Brooks, had a group of four poems published in the *Southern Review.* Toward the end of his first lonely year at Cambridge, he met a charming young Newnham College student, Beryl Eeman, and before long they were engaged.

Upon his return to the United States in 1938 he spent a stressful year, unable to find a job, while he continued to write poems, book reviews, and a few more plays. He renewed his acquaintance with Allen Tate, whom he had met in 1935, and the respected older poet invited him for a ten-day visit at his home in West Cornwall, Connecticut and became something of a father figure to him. In 1939 he was appointed poetry editor for the *Nation* for a year, found a teaching position at last at Wayne State University, and formed close friendships with fellow poets Bhain Campbell and Delmore Schwartz.

For the next two years he taught in the English Department at Harvard University, and in 1942, following the dissolution of his engagement to Beryl Eeman, he married Eileen Patricia Mulligan. His first two collections of poems—"Twenty Poems," in *Five Young American Poets* (1940) and *Poems* (1942)—were both published during this time by New Directions. Heavily influenced by Yeats and Auden, most of these early poems demonstrated a technical mastery, but were lacking an individual voice.

In 1943 another of Berryman's early heroes, R. P. Blackmur, offered him a four-month appointment at Princeton as an instructor in the English Department. As it turned out, he remained at Princeton for the next decade and there befriended not only Blackmur, but Robert Lowell, Jean Stafford, Louis MacNeice, and Randall Jarrell. With the poems in *The Dispossessed* (1948) and *Berryman's Sonnets* (written in 1947, but not published until 1967), he began to develop a unique and compelling voice and style that laid the groundwork for his masterworks. Ultimately, with the appearance of *Homage to Mistress Bradstreet* (published in the *Partisan Review* in 1953 and by Farrar, Straus and Cudahy in 1956), it was clear that a powerful and original talent had arrived. Edmund Wilson called it "the most distinguished long poem since *The Waste Land.*"

The circumstances occasioning *Berryman's Sonnets* also marked a watershed in Berryman's personal life. This sequence of 117 Petrarchan sonnets was largely written in 1947, during the course of a tempestuous affair with a married woman, called "Lise" in the first published version of the poem. The experience recounted in the poems jolted Berryman psychologically and initiated the heavy drinking that would increasingly plague him for the rest of his life. Many of the emotions released by this, for him, fatal attraction—joy, lust, anxiety, remorse, despair, retribution—would be carried over from *Berryman's Sonnets* to even better effect in his first major work, *Homage to Mistress Bradstreet,* wherein the modern day demon-lover poet attempts to seduce the first poet of New England across time and space.

Early in his academic career, before he had made his mark as a poet, Berryman earned recognition as a formidable scholar. His complex psychoanalytical study of *Stephen Crane* (1950) continues to stir both admiration and hostility from Crane scholars. Written during the period when he began *Homage to Mistress Bradstreet,* the critical biography reflects a strong identification by Berryman with many of Crane's psychological problems. His lifelong textual and biographical work on Shakespeare, only a fraction of which has so far been published, is impressive for its scholarship and perceptiveness alike. And *The Freedom of the Poet* (1976), the brilliant posthumous collection of his critical essays and reviews written between 1936 and 1967, bristles throughout with intelligence, wit, and learning.

Berryman and Eileen were separated in August 1953. A year later and jobless once more, he was again rescued by Allen Tate, who was then at the University of Minnesota. Tate found him a job teaching courses on the history of Western civilization in the Humanities Program at Minnesota, where Berryman also solidified his friendship with Saul Bellow, whom he had met earlier at Princeton. Early in his Minneapolis years he married Elizabeth Ann Levine, with whom he had a son, Paul, in 1957. After two troubled years, they were divorced. In 1961 he married Kathleen (Kate) Donahue, his third and last wife, with whom he would experience a period of relative domestic stability and artistic productivity, and have two daughters, Martha, in 1962, and Sarah, in 1971.

Soon after coming to Minnesota, Berryman had begun writing a new kind of poem which would obsess him for the next dozen years and become his major achievement. With *77 Dream Songs* (1964) and *His Toy, His Dream, His Rest* (1968), he invented a fresh stanza form, a diction, a syntax, a relation between characters (or between different aspects of the same character), and an entire realm of consciousness distinctively his own. The publication of these volumes won him numerous honors—including the Pulitzer Prize, the National Book Award, and the Bollingen Prize.

Despite his hard-won artistic triumphs, however, the movement of his life accelerated toward personal tragedy. The private man was increasingly at the mercy of the public man. Bouts of working himself into a state of exhaustion on *Love & Fame* (1970), and on *Delusions, Etc.* (1972)—both written in a new and disarmingly simple style—were followed by excessive drinking, insomnia, and, more and more, alarmingly poor health. Worn out and lacking the strength to fulfill the projects that still teemed in his brain, he lost heart in his writing and suffered a concomitant loss of confidence in his teaching. Finally, sober for nearly a year to little avail, his anguish had become more than he could either bear or transform in his work—and on the bitter Minneapolis morning of 7 January 1972, he ended it with a sad and desperate leap from the Washington Avenue Bridge, which spans the Mississippi River, to the frozen embankment below.

Eight days earlier, in the last known entry found in the three thousand volumes of his personal library, he had marked and dated in his copy of Saul Bellow's early novel *Dangling Man* (1944), a passage written by his old friend, which must have closely reflected his own psychological makeup during those last harrowing days: "I feel I am a sort of human grenade whose pin has been withdrawn. I know I am going to explode and I am continually anticipating the time, with a prayerful despair crying 'Boom!' but always prematurely."

That Berryman was able to draw lavishly on his suffering to the benefit of his work, however great the cost to his life, there can be little doubt. In John Haffenden's biography, a colleague at Princeton recalls that Berryman was referred to half seriously as Prometheus and, delving deeper, perhaps sums him up best: "The point is, I suppose, that he struck some of us . . . in something the same way that Byron must have struck his contemporaries: as the walking archetype of the brilliant, erratic, guilt-laden poet. Beneath all the posturing he was somehow the real thing."

Though fame arrived late in his career, by the time of his death in 1972 John Berryman was widely recognized as one of the most powerful and original poets of his generation. In the two decades since then, critical and biographical interest has continued at an impressive rate. Despite all of the scholarly and public attention he has received, however, Berryman's reputation remains far from fixed. Thus, the time is ripe for a fresh look, from a variety of critical perspectives, at the man and his work. The essays selected for inclusion in this volume originated in a national conference on John Berryman, held at the University of Minnesota in October 1990. Newly revised, they are grouped in four sections, reflecting particular areas of emphasis, though each essay often intersects with, and illuminates, those in other sections as well.

The essays in Part 1, "Berryman in Relation to Other Writers," examine different facets of Berryman's kinship with other writers—as teacher, mentor, colleague, friend, poet, critic. They also consider his engagement with some of those writers of the past whose work he both learned from and taught.

The initial essay, by Philip Levine, makes clearer than anything previously written on the topic, why Berryman was such a significant and influential teacher in the lives of so many of his students. Levine was enrolled in the remarkably talented Iowa Writer's Workshop classes, which included Donald Justice, W. D. Snodgrass, Paul Petrie, Jane Cooper, Robert Dana, and Henri Coulette, taught by Berryman in the winter and spring of 1954. In contrast to Robert Lowell, who was also teaching at Iowa at that time, Berryman manifested a deep and genuine interest in his students while feverishly transmitting his excitement about literature to the class. Levine testifies that Berryman's lectures possessed such passionate intensity and conviction that they "not only changed our poetry, they changed our vision of what it meant to write poetry in America, what it meant to be an American, to be human."

Peter Stitt recalls a slightly older Berryman, in 1961, teaching a course called "The European Heritage" in the Humanities Program at the University of Minnesota. Like Levine, he found Berryman to be a teacher "whose brilliance remains unsurpassed in my experience," and one who "took us seriously. He was interested in our minds." Stitt also maintains that some of the same qualities that made Berryman such an effective teacher—"attention to detail, an authoritative voice, the willingness to do his homework"—made him the outstanding literary critic who speaks to us in the critical essays gathered in *The Freedom of the Poet*. Finally, in examining Berryman's poetry in the light of his criticism, he demonstrates how both types of writing are dominated by voice and personality.

Paul Mariani provides an illuminating account of the long relationship between Berryman and Lowell and the influence they had on each other's work, which also adds considerable context to Philip Levine's observations on Berryman and Lowell at Iowa. In doing so, Mariani offers a fresh reading of Dream Song 177—wherein Lowell figures as that eighteenth-century arbiter of taste, Joseph Addison—which he convincingly argues was Berryman's wounded response to Lowell's mixed review of 77 *Dream Songs* in the *New York Times Book Review*. Mariani makes clear how much Lowell's own late style, with its "fits and starts and anacolutha," owed to Berryman. He notes that in Lowell's memoir of Berryman, written after the latter's death, he revised his early assessment of the Dream Songs, admitting that he had misjudged Berryman's achievement in the early Songs, and adding that, with them, his friend "had in fact permanently altered the poetic landscape."

In Part 2, "Berryman's Development as a Writer," four essayists examine the influence of Berryman's work in other forms (the play and the short story) on his verse, his early and significant relationship with the *Southern Review,* and his struggles to discover and cultivate his own poetic voice.

Charles Thornbury concentrates on Berryman's earliest poetry and the first of his numerous attempts at writing a play. Thornbury demonstrates how Berryman edged toward entering into a dialogue with the ghost of his father, which both proved important in his development as a poet and enabled him to complete his first dramatic effort, *The Architect* (1936). Writing the play, Thornbury notes, also forced Berryman to come to terms with "the function of language in a dramatic context," with "the relationship of the author to his work," and ultimately with "becoming a voice of and for voices, the speaker for others and himself."

Another significant early moment in Berryman's poetic apprenticeship that has not received much attention until now, his relationship with the *Southern Review* between 1937 and 1941, is considered by Charlotte H. Beck. Tracing the correspondence between Berryman and the *Review*'s editors, Robert Penn Warren, Cleanth Brooks, and John Palmer, Beck makes clear that the criticism and encouragement provided by the three was, at first, beneficial to the young poet's development, if ultimately frustrating in the often dilatory and chaotic communication they dispensed. Beck also notes that the editors' judgments of the poems Berryman submitted to the *Southern Review* were fallible enough to allow for the rejection of poems

of relative permanence, such as "Winter Landscape," and the accep-
tance of others, such as "Film," which have been virtually forgotten.

In her reflection on Berryman's short story, "Wash Far Away,"
begun in 1947, Lea Baechler points to the "elegy's function as an
active work in the process of mourning" throughout the poet's work.
She notes how the story's "integration of a subtextual reading of
'Lycidas' . . . with the early death of [Berryman's friend] Bhain
Campbell, crystallized Berryman's relationship to the elegiac tradi-
tion," from which we can follow the development of the elegiac in
his poems, from early to late. Ultimately, Baechler locates the culmi-
nation of the elegiac Berryman in the twelve poem Dream Song
sequence for Delmore Schwartz, in which he was able to apply all
that he had learned "critically, aesthetically, and intuitively."

It has become a cliché of Berryman scholarship that his rejection
of T. S. Eliot's dictum about "the impersonality of poetry" is central
to the younger poet's own development and individuality. Sharon
Bryan takes issue with Berryman's criticisms of Eliot's poetics on this
count, however, and listening to Berryman's poems for herself,
"hears echoes of and resemblances to Eliot" throughout his work.
Pointing to the similarities of temperament in the two poets, Bryan
notes that both mastered "the use of a range of voices in their poems
as a means to discover and construct their own poetic voices." She
goes on to trace the distinctive Berryman voice, found primarily in
individual lines and passages of the early poems, through its fuller
realization in the *Sonnets,* its mastery in *Homage* and, ultimately, in
The Dream Songs, which she tellingly finds "both more private and
lonelier than in the early poems."

Part 3 gathers together essays on "Psychological Issues in Berry-
man's Work." All four are concerned, in one way or another, with
the way he thinks, the patterns found in his work, and his psycho-
logical responses to the world. The first two essays, by Benfey and
Mancini, deal with aspects of the feminine in Berryman's life and
work, a hitherto largely neglected area of Berryman scholarship. The
last two, by Clendenning and Martin (see Altimont in Part 4, as
well), examine the therapeutic nature of Berryman's work.

Christopher Benfey begins with the premise that both Berryman
and Randall Jarrell were poets whose primary lyric impulse was auto-
biographical, and proposes that those poems in which they assume a
woman's identity are a "probing of repressed and evaded aspects of

the poet's own gender identity." Benfey compares Jarrell's relatively superficial use of woman's voice with Berryman's more ambitious experiments—especially in the child-birth scene in *Homage to Mistress Bradstreet*. He contends that the predominantly masculine social climate of the fifties forced Berryman to find a somewhat "disguised means of expression for aspects of himself that he considered effeminate." Thus, while recognizing the poetic achievement of Berryman and Jarrell, he cautions against a too-ready acceptance of "their confining notions of woman's voice and female desire." He also encourages readers to historicize this particular moment in American lyric poetry to help them understand its limits.

Using Nor Hall's Jungian archetypal analysis of the couvade phenomenon, Joseph Mancini, Jr., explores Berryman's ability to tap the "mothering energy inside and outside himself." Mancini argues that while Berryman was unable to sustain "couvade consciousness" in his own life, he succeeded in his mature art, especially in *Homage to Mistress Bradstreet* and *The Dream Songs*—which enabled him, among other things, to "empathize acutely with and so fully enflesh and give birth to characters like Anne Bradstreet." He also provides an insightful account of Berryman's masterful use of a "voicing technique" in *Homage*, by means of which "he is speaking the entire poem, including Anne's words."

Jerold M. Martin moves us away from the consideration of the feminine in Berryman's life and work to explore the connections between structuralist thought and Berryman's content—namely Henry's psyche—in *The Dream Songs*, with its 385 fragments. Working from the interpretive framework developed by Heinz Kohut and his followers, called *self-psychology*, Martin argues that Henry suffers from what Kohutians would call *disintegration anxiety*, the feeling that the self is breaking apart. This condition is believed to occur when such *selfobjects* as parental figures are "improperly structured or absent altogether, leaving the developing self without the necessary mirror response." It is further manifested in a tendency toward perverse or exaggerated sexual behavior and addictions to such substances as cigarettes and alcohol. Martin views Berryman's creation of *The Dream Songs* as an act of "concrete symbolization," in which poetry acted for him both as a structuralizing agent and "a heroic act of self-preservation."

Another aspect of the keenly therapeutic nature of Berryman's work is taken up by John Clendenning. Analyzing Berryman's biography of Stephen Crane, he finds it to be "substantially a self-portrait," and an effort to "work through personal torment, to seek his own rescue through Crane." Clendenning credits Berryman with being the first to notice Crane's puzzling habit of "a repetitive structuring of plots based on thwarted rescues," but believes him to be overly disposed toward discovering correspondences between their lives, including a "primal scene" in Crane's childhood similar to his own. Ultimately, he judges Berryman's *Crane* to be "a work of penetrating brilliance, yet still a maze of mirrors."

Part 4, "Berryman and Alcoholism," is much more deliberately dialectic than the other sections. Using Lewis Hyde's 1975 essay "Alcohol and Poetry: John Berryman and the Booze Talking" as a point of departure, the section includes three new essays that discuss alcoholism as a factor in Berryman's work and then concludes with a revisiting of the topic "with fresh eyes" by Hyde himself.

Given the perspective of seventeen years, Hyde's seminal essay can be reread now with profit for the insights it provides into the relationship between alcohol and poetry as well as for its anticipation of an aspect of literary study worthy of further scholarly attention. At the same time it is helpful to acknowledge, as Hyde now does, those judgments in the essay—that Dream Song 29 in particular and the Dream Songs in general were "written by the spirit of alcohol, not John Berryman," for example—that are overly categorical and reductive. Thanks to Lewis Hyde and others we understand more about the topic now, and yesterday's answers will not suffice.

George Wedge notes a distortion in Hyde's approach to Berryman, caused by "a built-in prejudice against the possibility that an alcoholic could write truthfully," and he "shudder[s] at the cost of this prejudice in whole canons of much loved and highly honored authors"—London, Fitzgerald, Faulkner, Lowry, Cheever, and others. Taking up Hyde's analysis of Dream Song 29, as "the booze talking," Wedge sees the poem as lacking "only a detail or two from being a clinical description" of Henry's alcoholism problem, and a sign of Berryman's growing self-awareness in this regard. He argues that here and elsewhere the poet remains in control and underscores the dramatic shift in Berryman's style that coincided with the onset of his alcoholic drinking about 1947. Certainly, Berryman's best work was to follow. Thus, Wedge raises the possibility that rather than causing him to lose control of his poetry, the loss of inhibitions brought about by Berryman's drinking, at least for a time, "freed him to write the way he wanted to and about the subjects he wanted to treat."

Roger Forseth approaches Berryman's unfinished novel, *Recovery*, as a work about "the education of the feelings," whose chief objective is to dramatize the "achievement of spirituality through ordeal." Opposing the view of the novel as a largely unvarnished autobiographical account of the author's strivings for alcoholic rehabilitation, he finds it to be a work of artistic integrity in which Berryman was able, with some success, to "objectify this experience and authentically render it . . . through the establishment of ironical distance between himself and his fictional protagonist." In this regard, Forseth's reading of *Recovery* accords with Wedge's view of the Dream Songs as a sign of Berryman's continuing struggle for distance in the interest of self-awareness and for an artistic statement useful to others.

Taking issue with Hyde's (and many others') assumptions about the therapeutic effects of poetic composition, Alan Altimont maintains that Berryman's alcoholism was subsidiary to a longer-standing psychological problem—what psychotherapists now call "fear of intimacy with a woman," which manifested itself in his use of work and fame as a substitute for love and a personal life. Beginning with Berryman's short story, "The Lovers" (1945), and continuing in *The Dream Songs*, *Love & Fame*, and *Recovery*, Altimont notes a growing tendency toward self-representation and toward a depiction of life as a struggle to obtain two mutually exclusive objectives: "to have both a personal life and also make a significant contribution to society." Altimont advances the argument that Berryman's abandonment of *Recovery* might be viewed as a positive move, since it marked his realization that, like his drinking, his writing projects had themselves become self-destructive and "part of his arsenal deployed against those who loved him."

Concluding the section, Lewis Hyde rejoins the dialogue with some further thoughts on alcohol and poetry. Noting the "marvelous complexity" of the discussion now, he recalls the "large silence" that surrounded the topic seventeen years ago and characterizes his own anger at Berryman for his drinking as "the anger of the young who want much from their elders and are necessarily betrayed." He concedes that "Wedge is right to find more truth telling in *The Dream Songs* than I allowed for in my old essay," but dissents from the idea that "the poet remains in control—even when drunk." Hyde approves of Forseth's formulation of *Recovery* as "a work about the education of the feelings." He also concurs with Altimont's "valuable widening of how we might read the links between Berryman and alcoholism," but cautions against cleaving "too fully to the psychological." In discovering considerable common ground between himself and the other essayists, Hyde observes: "It is fitting from this distance in time that greater generosity and nuance should mark our reading of Berryman's work."

The volume ends with the text of John Berryman's one-act play, "Cleopatra: A Meditation," the second of his plays to be written and now the first to be published. Completed in 1937 while he was at Cambridge, this three-character, Noh-like play was intended as a vehicle for his fiancée-to-be, Beryl Eeman, a young student-actress. It is, as Charles Thornbury points out in his introduction, the first of Berryman's numerous attempts at writing plays to have reached completion (only one other was completed). As such, it may be read simply as an example of juvenilia, but it should also be considered as a work that Berryman himself attempted to have produced and published, and one that provides insights into his development as a poet, his creation of a powerful female figure, and his mastery of the dramatic element in verse. Thornbury shows how the play foreshadows (and is a rehearsal for) *Homage to Mistress Bradstreet,* both in dramatic construction and in the creation of action, character, and poetry.

Taken together, the wide-ranging, ardent, and thoughtful essays in this volume affirm that Berryman's ability to "terrify and comfort" us has not diminished in the twenty years since his death. They also remind us, again and again, that his three careers as poet, critic, and teacher were all of a piece, bound together by his belief in the power of literature to transform both writer and reader. No doubt Berryman's work will endure to engage new generations of readers as well, for, as he said of Whitman's, it will continue to "do us good as long as our language persists and the human race is capable of interest in such things."

Abbreviations

CP	John Berryman. *Collected Poems 1937–1971*. Ed. Charles Thornbury. New York: Farrar, Straus and Giroux, 1989.
DH	*We Dream of Honour: John Berryman's Letters to His Mother*. Ed. Richard J. Kelly. New York: W. W. Norton, 1988.
DS	John Berryman. *The Dream Songs*. New York: Farrar, Straus and Giroux, 1969.
FP	John Berryman. *The Freedom of the Poet*. Preface by Robert Giroux. New York: Farrar, Straus and Giroux, 1976.
JB Papers	John Berryman Papers, Manuscripts Division, University of Minnesota Libraries, St. Paul.
JH	John Haffenden. *The Life of John Berryman*. London: Routledge and Kegan Paul, 1982.
PM	Paul Mariani. *Dream Song: The Life of John Berryman*. New York: William Morrow, 1990.
R	John Berryman. *Recovery*. Foreword by Saul Bellow. New York: Farrar, Straus and Giroux, 1973.
SC	John Berryman. *Stephen Crane: A Critical Biography*. New York: William Sloane Associates, 1950.

Part 1
Berryman in Relation to Other Writers

Philip Levine

Mine Own John Berryman

I can't say if all poets have had mentors, actual living breathing masters who stood or sat before them making the demands that true mentors must make if the fledgling is ever to fly. Some poets seem to have been totally self-starting, like the cars they used to build in Detroit; I'm thinking of such extraordinary examples as Emily Dickinson and Walt Whitman, who over a hundred years ago created not only their own gigantic works but the beginnings of something worthy enough to be American poetry, and they did it out of their imaginations and their private studies and nothing more. But then they had the advantage of being geniuses. And neither was from Detroit. I think also of those poets who had to be poets, whom no one or nothing could have derailed from their courses—Dylan Thomas, John Keats, Arthur Rimbaud—and who outstripped their mentors before they even got into second gear. There are those who were lucky enough to find among their peers people of equal talent and insight to help them on their way—poets like William Carlos Williams and Ezra Pound who for the crucial early years of their writing careers ignited each other. (Though of course Williams tells us in the "Prologue" to *Kora in Hell* that Ezra benefited from the scathing criticism of Williams's father William George. What in heaven's name had Ezra "meant by 'jewels' in a verse"? These jewels, rubies, sapphires, amethysts and whatnot, Pound went on to explain with great determination and care, were the backs of books as they stood on a man's shelf. "'But why in heaven's name don't you say so then?' was my father's triumphant and crushing rejoinder," writes Williams. And Pound himself tells us how he showed Ford Madox Ford some early verse, serious stuff, and Fordie laughed so hard upon reading the work he actually fell on the floor and "rolled around on it squealing with hilarity at the poems. Pound said that Ford's laughter saved him two years of work in the wrong direction.") Hideous conditions have driven others to take up the pen in an effort to write one's way out of the deepest nightmares imaginable—Wilfred Owen in the trenches, Edward Thomas in his melancholia, Hart Crane in the slough of Cleveland.

In some cases it worked. As for those of us here in the United States of America in the second half of the twentieth century, we have developed something called creative writing, a discipline that flourishes on hundreds of campuses and has even begun to invade the public schools and in the long run produces most of the poets—for better or worse—now writing in the country. One can only regard it as one of the most amazing growth industries we have, and since the death of anticommunism perhaps the chief one to haul into the next millennium, that is if prudery, right-wing hysteria, and censorship don't render it obsolete. Thus at the same time as we've made our society more racist, more scornful of the rights of the poor, more imperialist, more elitist, more tawdry, money driven, selfish, and less accepting of minority opinions, we have democratized poetry. Today anyone can become a poet: all he or she need do is journey to the nearest academy of higher learning and enroll in Beginning Poetry Writing and then journey through the dozen stages of purgatory properly titled Intermediate Poetry Writing, Semi-Advanced Poetry Writing, all the way to Masterwork Poetry Writing, in which course one completes her epic on the sacking of Yale (not Troy), or his sonnet cycle on the paintings of Edward Hopper, or their elegies in a city dumpster and thus earns not only an M.F.A. but a crown of plastic laurel leaves. Do I sound skeptical? Let me sound skeptical.

Skeptical as I may sound let me in fairness add that it is impossible for me to imagine myself as the particular poet I have become—again for better or for worse—without the influence of a single teacher, my one great personal mentor, and amazingly enough I found him at the head of a graduate class at that most unfashionable of writing industries, the much maligned Iowa Writers' Workshop. He was, of course, John Berryman, not yet forty years old but soon to be so, with one full-sized book of poems to his credit, and stuck with the job of teaching poetry writing for the first time in his life and for the last.

I did not go to the University of Iowa to study with John Berryman; in 1953 his reputation was based on *The Dispossessed,* that first book, and it was no larger than it should have been. The poem "Homage to Mistress Bradstreet" had not yet appeared in the *Partisan Review,* though it soon would and would create shock waves through the then tiny world of American Poetry. The attraction at Iowa was Robert Lowell, whose second book, *Lord Weary's Castle,* had received the Pulitzer Prize and whose singular voice had excited young poets as far away as Michigan. I among them journeyed to Iowa and enrolled in Lowell's writing workshop and audited his seminar in modern poetry; this was the fall of '53, America under Eisenhower ("Wide empty grin that never lost a vote," Berryman would later write) transforming itself into America under Joe McCarthy.

To say I was disappointed in Lowell as a teacher is an understatement, although never having taken a poetry workshop I had no idea what to expect. But a teacher who is visibly bored by his students and their poems is hard to admire. The students were a marvel: we were two future Pulitzer Prize winners, one Yale winner, one National Book Critics Circle Award winner, three Lamont Prize winners, one American Book Award winner, and among the thirteen of us twelve who would go on to publish at least one book of poetry. Some names: Donald Justice, W. D. Snodgrass, Jane Cooper, William Dickey, Robert Dana, Paul Petrie, Melvin Walker LaFollette, Henri Coulette, Donald Petersen, and an extraordinarily gifted woman named Shirley Eliason who soon turned to the visual arts and became a master. And your present speaker. I am sure there were others among the thirteen who were excited by Lowell as a teacher, for Lowell was one to play favorites. No matter how much they wrote like Lowell some of the poets could do no wrong; in all fairness to Lowell he praised them even when they wrote like Jarrell. Needless to say, I could write nothing that pleased Lowell, and when at the end of the semester he awarded me a *B,* I was not surprised. Along with the *B* he handed me a little card with scribbled notes regarding my poems and then told me I had made more progress than anyone else in the class. "You have come the farthest," he drawled, which no doubt meant I had started from nowhere. "Then why the *B*?" I asked. "I've already given the *A*s out," he said. This was at our second and last fifteen-minute conference, which did not irritate me nearly as much as our first, when he accused me of stealing my Freudian in-

sights and vocabulary from Auden. "Mr. Lowell," I had responded
(I never got more intimate than Mister and he never encouraged me
to do so), "I'm Jewish. I steal Freud directly from Freud; he was one
of ours." Mr. Lowell merely sighed.

Lowell was, if anything, considerably worse in the seminar. We
expected him to misread our poems—after all most of them were
confused and with very few exceptions only partly realized, but to
see him bumbling in the face of "real poetry" was discouraging. The
day he assured the class that Houseman's "Loveliest of Trees, the
Cherry Now" was about suicide, Melvin LaFollette leaned over and
whispered in my ear, "We know what he's thinking about." His
fierce competitiveness was also not pleasant to behold: with the ex-
ceptions of Bishop and Jarrell he seemed to have little use for any
practicing American poets, and he once labeled Roethke "more of an
old woman than Marianne Moore." He was eager too to ridicule
many of our recent heroes, poets I for one would have thought him
enamored of: Hart Crane and Dylan Thomas. Still, he was Robert
Lowell, the master of a powerful and fierce voice that all of us re-
spected, and though many of us were disappointed, none of us turned
against the man or his poetry. As Don Petersen once put it, "Can you
imagine how hard it is to live as Robert Lowell, with that inner life?"

During the final workshop meeting he came very close to doing
the unforgivable: he tried to overwhelm us with one of his own
poems, an early draft of "The Banker's Daughter," which appeared
in a much shorter though still hideous version six years later in *Life
Studies*. Someone, certainly not Lowell, had typed up three-and-a-
half single-spaced pages of heroic couplets on ditto masters so that
each of us could hold his or her own smeared purple copy of his
masterpiece. He intoned the poem in that enervated voice we'd all
become used to, a voice that suggested the least display of emotion
was déclassé, the genteel Southern accent he then affected even
stronger than usual. I sat stunned and horrified by the performance,
but my horror swelled to near unmanageable proportions when sev-
eral of my classmates leaped to praise every forced rhyme and obscure
reference. (The subject was Marie de Medici, about whom I knew
nothing and could care less.) No one suggested a single cut, not even
when Lowell asked if the piece might be a trifle too extended, a bit
soft in places. Perish the thought; it was a masterpiece! And thus the
final class meeting passed with accolades for the one person present

who scarcely needed praise and who certainly had the intelligence and insight to know it for what it was: bootlicking.

His parting words were an unqualified review of his successor, John Berryman, not as poet but as one of the great Shakespearean scholars of the age. And then he added that if we perused the latest issue of the *Partisan* we would discover the Mistress Bradstreet poem, clear evidence that Berryman was coming "into the height of his powers," a favorite phrase of Lowell's and one he rarely employed when speaking of the living. In fairness to Lowell, he was teetering on the brink of a massive nervous breakdown, which occurred shortly thereafter when he journeyed to Cincinnati to occupy the Elliston Chair of Poetry. It's possible that he was merely feeling the full effects of Cincinnati on his sensitive and intense nature. Rumors of his hospitalization drifted back to Iowa City, and many of us felt guilty for damning him as a total loss.

How long Berryman was in town before he broke his wrist I no longer recall, but I do remember that the first time I saw him he was dressed in his customary blue blazer, the arm encased in a black sling, the effect quite dramatic. As person and teacher, John was an extraordinary contrast to Lowell. To begin with, he did not play favorites: everyone who dared hand him a poem burdened with second-rate writing tasted his wrath, and that meant all of us. He never appeared bored in the writing class; to the contrary he seemed more nervous in our presence than we in his. Whereas Lowell always sprawled in a chair as though troubled by his height, John always stood and often paced as he delivered what sounded like memorized encomiums on the nature of poetry and life. Lowell's voice was never more than faintly audible and always encased in his curiously slothful accent, while Berryman articulated very precisely in what appeared to be an actor's notion of Hotspur's accent. His voice would rise in pitch with his growing excitement until it threatened at times to become one that only dogs could hear. John tipped slightly forward as though about to lose his balance, and conducted his performance with the forefinger of his right hand. The key word here is performance, for these were memorable meetings in which the class soon caught his excitement, for all of us seemed to sense that something significant was taking place.

Beyond the difference of personal preferences and presentation was a more significant one. Lowell had pushed us toward a specific poetry, one written in formal meters, rhymed, and hopefully involved with the griefs of great families, either current suburban ones or those out of the great storehouse of America or Europe's past. We got thundering dramatic monologues from Savanarola and John Brown that semester. For Berryman it was open house. He found exciting a poem about a particular drinking fountain in a bus station in Toledo, Ohio. Lowell certainly would have preferred a miraculous spring in that other Toledo, though now that he was no longer a practicing Catholic, sainthood seemed also to bore him. Berryman was delighted with our curious efforts in the direction of free verse and was eager to share with us his complex notions on the structure and prosody of same. He even had the boldness to suggest to us that contemporary voices could achieve themselves in so unfashionable and dated a form as a Petrarchan sonnet. To put it simply, he was all over the place and seemed delighted with the variety we represented.

Their contrasting styles became more evident during the second meeting of the class. Lowell had welcomed a contingent of hangers on, several of whom were wealthy townspeople dressed to the nines and hugging their copies of *Lord Weary's Castle*. Now and then one would submit a poem, and Lowell would say something innocuous about it and let the discussion hang in midair for a moment and move on to something else. Berryman immediately demanded a poem from one of this tribe and then began to eviscerate it. The poem, a rather conventional expression of distaste for the medical profession, dealt with the clichés of greed and indifference to suffering. (We later learned it was written by a doctor's wife.) John shook his head violently. "No, no," he said, "it's not that it's not poetry. I wasn't expecting poetry. It's that it's not true, absolutely untrue, unobserved, the cheapest twaddle." Then he began a long monologue in which he described the efforts of a team of doctors to save the life of a friend of his, how they had struggled through a long night working feverishly and having failed wept. "They did not work for money. There was no money in it. They worked to save a human life because it was a human life and thus precious. They did not know who the man was, that he was a remarkable spirit. They knew only that he was too young to die, and so they worked to save him, and failing, wept." (It turned out the man was Dylan Thomas, but Berryman did not mention this at the time.) A decent poet did not play fast and loose with the facts of this world, he or she did not take television's notion of reality. I had never before observed such enormous cannons fired upon such a tiny target. The writer left the room in shock, and those of us who had doubts about our work—I would guess all of us—left the room shaken.

We returned the next Monday to discover Berryman had moved the class to a far smaller and more intimate room containing one large seminar table around which we all sat. John was in an antic mood, bubbling with enthusiasm and delighted with our presence. He knew something we did not know: all but the hard core of masochists had dropped, leaving him with only the lucky thirteen. The "serious ones," he called us that day. "We are down to the serious ones," he announced. He seemed pleased with the situation and never again turned such powerful weapons on such tiny life rafts. In truth once we'd discovered what he'd accomplished, we too were pleased not to have to share his attention with writers we knew were only horsing around.

Now came the hard task on his part of determining what we knew and what we didn't know. At least half of us were trying to write in rhyme and meter, and a few of us were doing it with remarkable skill. It was at this meeting that he asked each of us to turn in a Petrarchan sonnet so that he might have some idea how far we'd come on the road to grace and mastery in the old forms. (The logistics were simple: we turned in our work on the Friday before our Monday meeting, and John selected the work to be dittoed and discussed in class.) He presented us with two models, both recited from memory.

The Sirens
by John Manifold

Odysseus heard the sirens; they were singing
Music by Wolf and Weinberger and Morley
About a region where the swans go winging,
Vines are in color, girls are growing surely

Into nubility, and pylons bringing
Leisure and power to farms that live securely
Without a landlord. Still, his eyes were stinging
With salt and seablink, and the ropes hurt sorely.

> Odysseus saw the sirens; they were charming,
> Blonde, with snub breasts and little neat posteriors,
> But could not take his mind off the alarming
>
> Weather report, his mutineers in irons,
> The radio failing; it was bloody serious.
> In twenty minutes he forgot the sirens.

Recited in his own breathless style it sounded like something he might have written; he had an uncanny knack of making a great deal of poetry sound like something he might have written. And who was John Manifold? we asked. An obscure Australian poet who fought in World War II, someone we should discover if we were serious, as he was about poetry. The second sonnet was Robinson's "Many Are Called," which you may recall begins "The Lord Apollo, who has never died . . . " After reciting it he went back to a passage in the octave:

> And though melodious multitudes have tried
> In ecstasy, in anguish, and in vain,
> With invocation sacred and profane
> To lure him, even the loudest are outside.

"Who are those multitudes?" he almost shouted. Petrie, a great lover of Robinson, answered, "The poets." "Exactly, Mr. Petrie, the poets. Certainly the poets in this room." It was perfectly clear he did not exclude himself.

Much to my horror my Petrarchan sonnet was selected for discussion on that third meeting. (I believe the poem no longer exists; I had the good luck never to have had it accepted for publication.) Actually it was not that bad: it was about food, which had become an obsession of mine for several months; I was running out of money and so ate very little and very badly. To be more precise the poem was about my mother's last Thanksgiving feast, which I had returned home to participate in; since my mother was a first-rate office manager and a tenth-rate cook, the event had been a disaster. John discussed four poems that day. The first was not a Petrarchan sonnet and as far as he could determine had no subject nor any phrasing worth remembering. The second had a subject. John went to the board and began to scan it. "This is NOT iambic," he said. After getting through four lines he turned and headed directly toward the cowering poet, suspended the page over his head, and finally let it fall. "This is metrical chaos. Pray you avoid it, sir." I was next. Much to my relief, John affirmed that, yes, this was a Petrarchan sonnet, it was iambic and it did possess a fine subject—the hideous nature of the American ritual meal became a farce. He paused, "But, Levine, it is not up to its most inspired moments, it has accepted three mediocre rhymes, it is padded where the imagination fails. If it is to become a poem the author must attack again and bring the entire poem up to the level of its few fine moments." In effect John was giving us a lesson in how poems are revised: one listened to one's own voice when it was "hot" (a word he liked) and let that "hot" writing redirect one toward a radical revision. "No hanging back," he once said, "one must be ruthless with one's own writing or someone else will be." (I did make the effort, but in truth I did not improve the poem, for as yet I had not learned even at age twenty-six to trust the imagination.)

It was clear that among those poems considered, mine had finished second best, and for this I was enormously relieved. What follows is the best, exactly in the form we saw it on that late February Monday in 1953.

Sonnet
by Donald Justice

The wall surrounding them they never saw;
The angels, often. Angels were as common
As birds or butterflies, but looked more human.
As long as the wings were furled, they felt no awe.
Beasts, too, were friendly. They could find no flaw
In all of Eden: this was the first omen.
The second was the dream which woke the woman:
She dreamed she saw the lion sharpen his claw.
As for the fruit, it had no taste at all.
They had been warned of what was bound to happen;
They had been told of something called the world;
They had been told and told about the wall.
They saw it now; the gate was standing open.
As they advanced, the giant wings unfurled.

After reading the poem aloud, John returned to one line: "As for the fruit, it had no taste at all." "Say that better in a thousand words," he said, "and you're a genius." He went on briefly. "One makes an assignment like this partly in jest, partly in utter seriousness, to bring out the metal in some of you and to demonstrate to others how much you still need to learn. No matter what one's motives are," he went on, "no teacher has the right to expect to receive something like this: a true poem." Class dismissed.

A week later a telling incident occurred. The class considered a sonnet by one of its more gifted members, a rather confused and confusing poem which Berryman thrashed even though one member of the class found it the equal of the Justice poem from the previous week. The tortured syntax suggested Berryman's own "Mad Songs," but he saw little virtue in the poem and felt it was more in the tradition of Swinburne than any contemporary poem should be, writing that tried to bully the reader with rhetoric rather than move him or her with the living language of the imagination. "Write good prose diction in a usual prose order," he said, "unless you've got a damn good reason for doing otherwise." (It was clear he must have felt he had a damn good reason for doing otherwise when he wrote "Bradstreet".) After class as we ambled back to the student union for coffee and more poetry talk, the same student who had defended the poem informed Berryman that the author had recently had a sheaf of poems accepted by *Botteghe Oscure,* then the best-paying and most prestigious literary magazine in the world. Berryman froze on the sidewalk and then turned angrily on the student and shouted, "Utterly irrelevant, old sport, utterly irrelevant!" He assured the man that absolute "shit" appeared in the "best" publications while much of the finest poetry being written went begging. (No doubt his own difficult early career had taught him that.) "You're stupid to have raised the subject, stupid or jejune." He paused a moment. "I'll give you the benefit of the doubt: jejune," and John smiled, and the incident passed. The man was incredibly serious about poetry, and one of us had learned that the hard way. In her gossipy *Poets in Their Youth,* Eileen Simpson would have us believe that all the poets in "the Berryman circle" ached to be the elected legislators of the world and suffered deeply because they were not among the famous and powerful. All that I saw during that semester contradicted that view: the reward for writing a true poem was the reward of writing a true poem, and there was none higher.

In spite of his extraordinary sense of humor, the key to Berryman's success as a teacher was his seriousness. This was the spring of the Army-McCarthy hearings, the greatest television soap opera before the discovery of Watergate. John, as addicted reader of the *New York Times,* once began a class by holding up the front page of the *Times* so the class might see the latest revelation in the ongoing drama. "These fools will rule for a while and be replaced by other fools and crooks. This," and he opened a volume of Keats to the "Ode to a Nightingale," "will be with us for as long as our language endures." These were among the darkest days of the Cold War, and yet John was able to convince us—merely because he believed it so deeply—that nothing could be more important for us, for the nation, for humankind, than our becoming the finest poets we could become. And there was no doubt as to how we must begin to accomplish the task; we must become familiar with the best that had been written, we must feel it on our pulse.

"Levine, you're a scholar," he once roared out at me in class, "tell us how you would go about assembling a bibliography on the poetry of Charles Churchill." A scholar I was not, and John knew that, but the point was that the know-nothing poet was a total fiction, a cousin to Hollywood's notion of the genius painter who boozes, chases girls, and eventually kills himself falling off a scaffold in the Sistine Chapel. "Friends," John was saying, "it's hard work, and the hard work will test the sincerity of your desire to be poets." He rarely mentioned inspiration, perhaps because he assumed that most of us had been writing long enough to have learned that it came to those who worked as best they could through the barren periods, and this was—he once told me—a barren period for him. So we knew how to begin the task of becoming a poet: study and work. And how did it end? Here John was just as clear: it never ended. Speaking of the final poems of Dylan Thomas, he made it clear they were merely imitations of the great work of his early and middle period. "You should always be trying to write a poem you are unable to write, a poem you lack the technique, the language, the courage to achieve, otherwise you're merely imitating yourself, going nowhere because that's always easiest." And suddenly he burst into a recitation of "A Refusal to Mourn the Death by Fire of a Child in London," ending:

Deep with the first dead lies London's daughter,
Robed in the long friends,
The Grains beyond age, the dark veins of her mother,
Secret by the unmourning water
Of the riding Thames.
After the first death, there is no other.

"Can you imagine possessing that power and then squandering it?" he said. "During our lifetime that man wrote a poem that will never be bettered."

No doubt his amazing gift for ribaldry allowed him to devastate our poems without crushing our spirits, that and the recognition on his part that he too could write very badly at times. He made it clear to us from the outset that he had often failed as a poet and for a variety of reasons: lack of talent, pure laziness ("Let's face it," he once said to me, "life is mainly wasted time"), and stupid choices. "There are so many ways to ruin a poem," he said, "it's quite amazing good ones ever get written." On certain days he loved playing the clown. One Monday he looked up from the class list sent to him by the registrar and asked Paul Petrie why he was getting twice as much credit for the course as anyone else. Paul said he wasn't sure. "Perhaps," said John, "you're getting the extra units in Physical Education and Home Economics. I'd like you to arrive twenty minutes early and do fifty laps around the room and then erase the blackboard. You might also do a few push ups or work on your technique of mixing drinks." He then discovered my name was not on the roll. (The truth was, lacking sufficient funds, I had not registered.) He asked me if I thought the registrar was anti-Semitic. No, I said, just sloppy. "You realize," he said, "that until your name appears on this list you do not exist. Tell me," he added, "does anyone else see this Levine fellow? Sometimes I have delusions." As the weeks passed my name continued not to appear on the roster, and John continued to make a joke out of it. "Levine, should I go see the registrar and remedy this hideous state of affairs." I assured him it was unnecessary, that it was just a meaningless slip up, and I wasn't taking it personally. "You're quite sure it's not anti-Semitism, Levine? These are dark times." Indeed they were for many Americans, but for the young poets in this workshop they were nothing if not glory days.

"Levine," he said on another day, "when was the last time you read your Shakespeare?" "Last week," I said. "And what?" "*Measure for Measure*." "Fine. I've noticed you consistently complain about the quantity of adjectives in the poems of your classmates." This was true. "Is it the number that matters or the quality?" I failed to answer. "Remember your Blake: 'Bring our number, weight, & measure in a year of dearth.'" I nodded. "'Thy turfy mountains where live nibbling sheep.' Two nouns, two adjectives. Any complaints, Levine?" I had none. "Who wrote the line?" "Shakespeare," I said. "What play?" Again I was silent. His long face darkened with sadness. La-Follette answered, "*The Tempest*." "Levine, do not return to this class until you have reread *The Tempest*. I assume you've read it at least once." I had. "'Fresher than May, sweeter / Than her gold buttons on the boughs . . .' Recognize it?" I did not. "There is great poetry hiding where you least suspect it, there for example buried in that hideous speech from *The Two Noble Kinsmen,* act 3, scene 1." Much scratching of pens as the class bowed to their notebooks. "We must find our touchstones where we can."

Knowing I had gone to Wayne University in Detroit where John had once taught, he asked me if I'd studied with the resident Shakespeare scholar, Leo Kirschbaum, whom I had found a brilliant teacher. "Amazing fellow, Dr. Kirschbaum, singlehandedly he set back Lear scholarship two decades." Little wonder I'd failed to recognize the line from *The Tempest*. While he was on the subject of Shakespeare, he required the entire class to reread *Macbeth* by the next meeting. "'And yet dark night strangles the travelling lamp.' Hear how the line first strangles and then releases itself. Read the play carefully, every line, let it heighten your awareness of the extraordinary possibilities for dense imagery. You should know that Shakespeare had less than two weeks to complete the play. Why was that, Mr. Justice?" Don, well on his way to his doctorate, explained that the ascendancy to the English throne of James VI of Scotland called for a play in praise of James's Scotch ancestry. Berryman nodded. "Took him no time at all to write it, and yet it would take half the computers in the world a year to trace the development of the imagery that a single human imagination created and displayed in a play of unrivaled power." So much for the School of Engineering. We were never to forget that men and women of the greatest intellect and imagination had for centuries turned toward poetry to fulfill their private and civic needs.

Certain classes were devoted to special subjects relating to poetic practices, prosody for example. For two hours John lectured on the development of this study and how amazingly fragmented and useless the literature was. People of great learning and sensitivity had come to preposterous conclusions, and nothing in print was reliable. It was our duty to master this literature and discover what was useful and what was nonsense. "A man as learned as George Saintsbury, a man who had read and absorbed so much that in old age he took to studying doctoral dissertations from American universities just to keep busy, a man of that breadth of knowledge, gave us a three-volume study of prosodic practices in British and American poetry, and on almost every significant point he is wrong." Still, he urged us to read the work, for if nothing else it was a brilliant anthology of the diversity and richness of poetry in English. We, the hungry students, demanded to know to whom he went for "the scoop," another of his expressions. He laughed and pointed to his ear. There was no such book, and as in everything else we were thrown on our own. We were all in the same boat, and John was with us. We would develop a prosody that would allow us to write the poetry we needed to write; or we wouldn't, and that poetry would never be written, for there was no one to write it for us. Nonetheless in order to do it right, we had to learn from the practices of those poets who'd done it, for as John made clear, those who best understood prosody—Shakespeare, Milton, Keats, Blake, Hopkins, Frost, Roethke—had better things to do than write handbooks for our guidance.

"Let us say you are appalled by the society in which you live—God knows it is appalling—and you want to create a poetry that speaks to the disgusting human conditions around you, you want to mount a powerful assault, you want to be the prophet Amos of the present age, to what poet would you turn for aid?" Silence from the class. "You want to evoke your rage, your righteous indignation in numbers that will express the depthless power of your convictions, to whom do you turn?" A voice from the class: "Robert Lowell." "Good choice, but there is a danger here, correct?" The voice: "Yes, I already sound too much like Lowell. I'm doing my best to avoid him." Berryman: "Indeed you are. When I first saw your poems I though you'd borrowed Cal's old portable Smith-Corona. Why not go to Cal's source, the poet upon whom he based the movement and the syntax of his own work? And who would that be?" Another voice from the class: "Pope." "No, no, you're blinded by his use of the couplet. Milton, our great Milton." Affirmative nods from the class; how could we not know something so obvious. John quoted "On the Late Massacre in Piedmont," using his forefinger to mark the ends of the lines so we heard how powerful the enjambment was. "Bring the diction 300 years toward this moment and you have one of Cal's early sonnets." More nodding of heads. "And the key to such rhythmic power is?" Silence. "Speed, achieved by means of a complex syntax and radical enjambment. Speed translates always into rhythmic power, and speed is unobtainable in a heavily end-stopped line."

Then he turned to me. "For the power you so dearly aspire to, Levine, you must turn to the master, Milton, the most powerful poet in the language, though you might do well to avoid the Latinate vocabulary. Have you studied Latin?" Levine: "No." "You might consider doing so; that way you'll know what to avoid when you're stealing from Milton. Do you have another favorite among your contemporaries?" Levine: "Dylan Thomas." Berryman: "It doesn't show, Levine, it doesn't show; you've done a superb job of masking that particular debt. How have you managed that?" Levine: "I didn't. I wrote through my Dylan Thomas phase and quit. It was impossible for me to write under his influence and not sound exactly like him except terrible." Berryman: "Levine, you've hit upon a truth. Certain poets are so much themselves they should not be imitated; they leave you no room to be yourself, and Thomas was surely one of them, as was Hart Crane, who probably ruined the careers of more young poets than anything except booze. Levine, you might go to the source of Dylan's own lyrical mysticism, and who would that be?" Silence. "Mr. Justice?" Justice: "Blake." "Exactly, you might go to Blake, who is so impossibly lyrical and inventive no one in the world has the talent to sound like him." In an unusually hushed voice he recited all of Blake's early "Mad Song," ending,

> I turn my back to the east,
> From whence comforts have increased;
> For light doth seize my brain
> With frantic pain.

"Better to learn from a poet who does not intoxicate you," said Berrryman, "better to immerse yourself in Hardy, whom no Ameri-

can wants now to sound like. A great poet seldom read." After class
Henri Coulette said to me that he'd passed over Blake's "Mad Song"
a dozen times and never heard it until John incanted it.

No one escaped unscathed. John advised Petrie to set aside his Shelley
and Elinor Wylie and leap into modernism. Coulette was told to
loosen up his strict iambics, to try to capture the quality of living
speech. Strangely, he underappreciated the formal elegance of
Dickey's work. Neither Petersen nor Jane Cooper were productive
that semester; Jane later said she was put off by John's sarcasm.
Shirley Eliason's work he found wonderfully dense and mysterious;
he wanted more. "Write everything that occurs to you," he told us
all, "you're young enough to still be searching for your voice, you
certainly don't want to find it before you find your subject. And
you're still young enough to accept failure." LaFollette seemed the
greatest enigma to him. "Yes, yes, you have a genuine lyrical gift,"
he said one day in class, "but who encouraged you never to make
sense, always to be opaque?" LaFollette eagerly revealed that he'd
just finished a year's work with Roethke. "Yes," said John, "I can see
the influence of Roethke, but Ted's best early work is remarkably
straightforward on one level. Of course there is always the shadow
of something more formidable, darker. Did Cal encourage this sort
of obscurity?" LaFollette revealed he had also studied with Richard
Eberhardt. John's mouth fell open as he stood speechless for several
seconds. "You let Dick Eberhardt read your poems, and you are here
to tell the tale. Amazing!"

He always wanted more work from Robert Dana, though when
Dana finally gave him a poem of ninety-eight lines, he mused over it
for a time and finally noted two good images. His parting words
were, "If you're going to write something this long why don't you
try making it poetry?" Meeting after meeting produced the same
advice: "Write everything that occurs to you; it's the only way to
discover where your voice will come from. And never be in a hurry.
Writing poetry is not like running the 400 meters. Coulette, do you
remember what Archie Williams said his strategy was for running the
400 meters?" (Coulette, the resident sports maven, did not know.
Williams had won the gold at the '36 Berlin Olympics.) John went
on: "Archie said, 'My strategy is simple; I run the first 200 meters as
fast as I can to get ahead of everyone, and I run the second 200 meters

as fast as I can to stay there.' Now that is NOT the way we write poetry, we are not in a race with anyone, but all of us are getting on in years and we'd better get moving." In other words, go as fast as you can but don't be in a hurry; we had a lifetime to master this thing, and with our gifts it would take a lifetime.

Even Justice got mauled. John found his "Beyond the Hunting Woods" a bit too refined, a bit too professionally Southern. Those dogs at the end of the poem, Belle and Ginger, all they needed were a few mint juleps. And Levine? Levine got his. According to John, Levine's best poem that semester was "Friday Night in the Delicatessen." (I'm sorry to say if you knew the craft of bibliography you could locate it in print in almost the same form in which John both praised and admonished it.) In it a Jewish mother laments the fact her sons are growing away from her, becoming Americans, becoming— you should forgive the expression—goyim. At one point she describes them with "hands for fights and alcohol." "Hands for fights, yes," said John, "but hands for alcohol? No. We drink alcohol, Levine, as I know you've learned, we absorb it through the digestive system. The fact we hold a glass of whiskey in our hands is not enough. The parallel structure is false, but this is an amazingly ambitious poem." (I lived on that word, *ambitious,* for weeks, even after a friend said, "He forgot to add, 'Ambition should be made of sterner stuff.'") Again I had finished second best, for this poem was written to fulfill John's assignment for an ode. The clear winner was "A Flat One," by De Snodgrass, a poem of enormous power; it depicted the slow and agonizing death of a World War I veteran, and the vet's relationship with a hospital orderly who must kill to keep him alive. Even in this earlier "static semi-Symboliste version" (Snodgrass's description), it was a startling poem. (Although Lowell is generally credited for being the mentor behind the poems of *Heart's Needle* ["A Flat One" actually appears in De's second book, *After Experience*], De now claims that Lowell discouraged the writing of those poems and quite forcefully. "Snodgrass, you have a mind," he'd said to him, "you mustn't write this kind of tear-jerking stuff." Berryman never found them sentimental; he tried to move De's writing further from traditional metrics, as De put it, "more like his own experiments at the time . . . more like regular speech . . . less like the poetry being written at the time.")

A later class also began with a demonstration from the front page of the *New York Times*. "Allow me to demonstrate a fundamental principle of the use of language, which is simply this: if you do not master it, it will master you. Allow me to quote Senator McCarthy speaking of his two cronies, Cohen and Shine." (Roy Cohen and David Shine were two assistants—investigators, he called them—of the senator's for whom he had gained extraordinary privileges, which allowed Shine, for example, an ordinary enlisted man in the army, to avoid any of the more onerous or dangerous work of a soldier.) "The senator said the following: 'I stand behind them to the hilt.' We now know what Mr. McCarthy thinks we do not know, that he is about to stab them in the back, abandon them both as political liabilities." [John was of course correct; within a few days the deed was done.] "Because he is an habitual liar, Mr. McCarthy has blinded himself to the ability of language to reveal us even when we're taking pains not to be revealed. Exactly the same thing holds true with poetic form; if we do not control it, it will control us." He went on: "I do not mean to suggest that each time we enter the arena of the poem we must know exactly where we're headed. We have all learned that that is preposterous, for the imagination leads us where it will, and we must be prepared to follow, but—and this is the crucial point— should we lack the ability to command the poetic form, even if that form is formlessness, toward which our writing travels, we shall be mastered by that form and what we shall reveal is our ineptitude." He then turned to a student poem in formal meters and rhymed couplets. He painstakingly analyzed it from the point of view of how the need to rhyme and to keep the meter had produced odd and unconvincing movements in the poem's narrative as well as needless prepositional phrases and awkward enjambments. "A poem of real fiber, a rhymed poem, will find its rhymes on subjects, objects, and especially verbs, the key words of its content." He then quoted a poem of Hardy's that ended:

So, they are not underground,
But as nerves and veins abound
In the growths of upper air,
And they feel the sun and rain,
And the energy again
That made them what they were!

Again with his forefinger he scored the key words, and finally repeated that final line, "'That made them what they were'—my friends, what they were! That is the artist in command, that is triumph!"

Once again he seemed like what he was, a walking anthology of poetic jewels, and once again we learned how exacting this thing with the poetry was. Later in Kenny's tavern, where many of us assembled after class, one poet recalled that Ignacio Sánchez Mejías, the matador elegized in Garcia Lorca's great poem had once remarked, "This thing with the bulls is serious," and thus we produced a catch phrase for John's class, "This thing with the poems is serious."

What became increasingly clear as the weeks passed was that while John was willing on occasion to socialize with us, he was not one of us; he was the teacher, and we were the students. He had not the least doubt about his identity, and he was always willing to take the heat, to be disliked if need be. In private he once remarked to me that teaching something as difficult as poetry writing was not a popularity contest. "Even a class as remarkable as this one," he said, "will produce terrible poems, and I am the one who is obliged to say so." He sensed that the students had themselves developed a wonderful fellowship and took joy when any one of them produced something fine. Whether or not he took credit for any of this I do not know. To this day I can recall Bill Dickey studying a Justice poem almost with awe. "Do you see those rhymes," he said to me, "My God, what rhymes. I'll bet this is the first time they've been used in all our poetry!" I shall never forget Don Petersen's welcoming me up the mountain of poetry—at that time Don seemed to believe he was the guardian of the mountain. He told me in his curious gruff and tender voice that a particular poem of mine was in fact a poem, and though the class—including John—had not taken to it, it was evidence that I had become a poet. His words were welcomed and genuine. I can recall my own thrill on seeing a particular poem by Jane Cooper in which her portrayal of a nocturnal hedgehog came so vividly to life I shuddered. I expressed my wonder openly and knew she heard it. One day both Henri Coulette and Robert Dana took me aside to tell me they could scarcely believe how far I'd come in a single year. We were all taking pride and joy in each other's accomplishments.

This fellowship was a delicate and lovely thing, a quality that always distinguishes the best creative-writing classes. We were learning how much farther we could go together than we could singly, alone, unknown, unread in an America that never much cared for poetry. I don't honestly know how large a role John played in the creation of this atmosphere, but I do know it had not existed during Lowell's tenure; his favoritism, his intimacy with some students and visible boredom with others, tended to divide us into two hostile factions, the ins and outs. In John's class we were all in and we were all out, we were equals, and instead of sinking we swam together. In spite of John's willingness to be disliked, he clearly was not disliked. Of course he was a marvelous companion, and on those evenings he sought company we were all eager to supply it, but we never forgot that come Monday afternoon the camaraderie would be forgotten and he would get to the serious business of evaluating and if need be decimating poems.

Sometimes his seriousness could be more than a little intimidating. On one occasion over drinks before going to dinner with a group of student writers and faculty, John began to muse over a remarkable poem by the Welshman Alun Lewis, "Song: On seeing dead bodies floating off the Cape." Berryman believed that Lewis was one of the great undiscovered talents of the era. He quoted a portion of the poem, an interior monologue by a woman who has had a vision of her lover's death at sea; then his memory failed him, and he apologized to the group. It so happened one of the poets present knew the poem and took up the recitation:

> The flying fish like kingfishers
> Skim the sea's bewildered crests,
> The whales blow steaming fountains,
> The seagulls have no nests
> Where my lover sways and rests.

His memory primed, John completed the poem, which ends with the woman lamenting the "nearness that is waiting" in her bed, "the gradual self-effacement of the dead." After a moment's silence John remarked, "The dead do not efface themselves; we, the living, betray their memories." John seemed lost in his reverie on the life and early death in war of the poet when another poet present, an enormous man who worked in town as a bartender and bouncer began to praise one of John's own war poems that had appeared in *The Dispossessed*.

Suddenly awakened, John shouted in the man's face, "We are talking about great poetry, do you get it, old sport, great poetry, and not the twaddle you have in mind. I do not appreciate bootlicking." A silence followed, and the moment passed. This thing with the poetry was indeed serious.

That semester Berryman conducted the most extraordinary seminar I've ever been a part of; again, for lack of funds, I was not registered, but I missed only a single class and that when the obligation to make some money took me elsewhere. The students were assigned a single long paper of considerable scope, the subject agreed upon by teacher and poet, for all the registered students were from the workshop. The papers themselves were never presented in class, and this was not because Berryman found them inadequate. Indeed he raved about the quality of many of them. The reason was simply that John felt he had news to bring us on the subject of poetry in English from Whitman to the present. The highlight of the semester was John's presentation of the whole of "Song of Myself," which included the most memorable and impassioned reading of a poem I have ever in my life heard, along with the most complex and rewarding analysis of Whitman's design, prosody, and imagery ever presented. When he'd finished the reading he stood in silence a moment and then from memory presented the final section again, concluding:

> I bequeath myself to the dirt to grow from the grass I love,
> If you want me again look for me under your boot-soles.
>
> You will hardly know who I am or what I mean,
> But I shall be good health to you nevertheless,
> And filter and fibre your blood.
>
> Failing to fetch me at first keep encouraged,
> Missing me one place search another,
> I stop somewhere waiting for you.

He stood for a moment in silence, the book trembling in his hand, and then in a quiet voice said, "Do you know what that proves? That proves that most people can't write poetry!"

When the semester began I was the only nonenrolled student

attending, but so extraordinary were his performances that the news spread, and by the time he gave his final Whitman lecture the room was jammed to the bursting point. Crane, Stevens, Elizabeth Bishop, Roethke, Eliot, Auden, Dylan Thomas, and Hardy were also subjects of his lectures. These were not talks he gave off the top of his head. Far from it. He entered the room each night shaking with anticipation and always armed with a pack of note cards, which he rarely consulted. In private he confessed to me that he prepared for days for these sessions. He went away from them in a state bordering on total collapse. It would be impossible to overestimate the effect on us of these lectures, for this was an era during which Whitman was out, removed adroitly by Eliot and Pound, and kept there by the Ironists and the New Critics who were then the makers of poetic tastes. In 1954 in Iowa no one dreamed that within a few years Williams would be rescued from hell, the Beats would surface, and Whitman would become the good gray father of us all. (John himself later claimed the Beats didn't know how to read Whitman and mistook his brilliant rhythmic effects for prose. "They don't write poems," is the way he put it.) I cannot speak for the entire class, but I know that Petrie, Jane Cooper, Dana, Coulette, Justice, Snodgrass, and I were totally convinced that "Song of Myself" was the most powerful and visionary poetic statement ever made on the continent. Those lectures not only changed our poetry, they changed our entire vision of what it meant to write poetry in America, what it meant to be American, to be human. "There is that lot of me and all so luscious," I suddenly sang to myself, and I believed it, and thanks to John and father Walt, I still believe it. Whitman had laid out the plan for what our poetry would do, and so large was the plan there was room for all of us to take our part, as for example, Roethke was doing, that poet who according to John "thought like a flower."

Unlikely it seems now that Berryman would have performed that task, for was he not an Eastern intellectual poet and part-time New Critic himself, a protégé of Mark Van Doren and R. P. Blackmur? Like so much that concerns Berryman the answer is ambiguous. His reviews often sounded very much like what the New Critics were turning out, except they were far wittier and often more savage: in savagery only Yvor Winters could measure up to him. Who else would be bold enough to invent a poem that a poet might have written, nay should have written, as John did in a review of Patchen, and then define Patchen's weaknesses on the basis of the poem Berryman and not Patchen had written? But unlike Winters and the rest of the New Critics, he was unashamedly Romantic at the same time as he was distrustful of the "cult of sincerity." He was, as in so many things, his own man and in a very real sense a loner.

Before we parted that semester he performed two more services for me. The day before he left for New York City—he was going East to teach at Harvard that summer—we had a long conversation on what a poet should look like. The Oscar Williams anthology, one of the most popular of that day, included photographs of most of the poets at the back of the book; John and A. E. Houseman were the only exceptions—they were represented by drawings. John's was very amateurish and looked nothing like him. I asked him why he'd used it instead of a photograph. He claimed he wanted neither but Oscar had insisted, and he'd taken the lesser of the two evils. He thought either was a distraction, though the drawing did make it clear he was ugly enough to be a poet. I didn't catch his meaning and asked him to explain. "No poet worth his salt is going to be handsome; if he or she is beautiful there's no need to create the beautiful. Beautiful people are special; they don't experience life like the rest of us." He was obviously dead serious, and then he added, "Don't worry about it, Levine, you're ugly enough to be a great poet."

The next day at the airport he was in an unusually manic mood. "Think of it, Levine, in a few hours I shall be mine own John Poins." Not knowing Wyatt's poem written from exile in rural England to Poins in London, I asked John what he meant.

> I am not he, such eloquence to boast
> To make the crow in singing as the swan,
> Nor call the lion of coward beasts the most,
> That cannot take a mouse as the cat can.

He quoted from memory. "Wyatt, Levine, Wyatt, his rough numbers would be perfect for your verse, you crude bastard." ("Crude bastard" was his highest form of compliment.) Before he boarded he extended an invitation to send him four or five poems in a year or so, and he'd be sure to get back to me to tell me how I was doing. Having

seen an enormous carton of unopened mail in his apartment, I
doubted he'd ever answer, but nonetheless a year and a half later I
sent him four poems. His response was prompt and to the point; with
*X*s to mark the lines and passages he thought a disaster and checks
where he found me "hot," along with specific suggestions for revi-
sion; there was not a single line unremarked upon. There was also a
brief letter telling me things were going well in Minneapolis and that
he was delighted to know I was fooling editors with my "lousy
poems." He looked forward to seeing me one day. There was not the
least doubt about what he was in fact saying: our days as student and
teacher had come to an end. We could not exchange poems as equals
in poetry because we were not equals and might never be, and yet I
had come too far to require a teacher. I felt the same way. I'd had one
great poetry-writing teacher, I had studied with him diligently for
fifteen weeks. From now on I had to travel the road to poetry alone
or with my peers. This was his final lesson, and it may have been the
most important in my development.

As the years pass his voice remains with me, its haunting and
unique cadences sounding in my ear, most often when I reread my
own work. I can still hear him saying, "Levine, this will never do,"
and he rouses me again and again from my self-satisfaction and leth-
argy to attack a poem and attack again until I make it the best poem
I am capable of. His voice is there too when I teach, urging me to say
the truth no matter how painful a situation I may create, to say it
with precision and in good spirits, never in rancor and always to
remember Blake's words (a couplet John loved to quote): "A truth
that's told with bad intent / Beats all the Lies you can invent." For all
my teaching years, now over thirty, he has been a model for me.
No matter what you hear or read about his drinking, his madness,
his unreliability as a person, I am here to tell you that in the winter
and spring of 1954, living in isolation and loneliness in one of the
bleakest towns of our difficult Midwest, John Berryman never failed
his obligations as a teacher. I don't mean merely that he met every
class and stayed awake, I mean that he brought to our writing and
the writing of the past such a sense of dedication and wonder that he
wakened a dozen rising poets from their winter slumbers so that they
might themselves dedicate their lives to poetry. The most brilliant,
intense, articulate man I've ever met, at times even the kindest and

most gentle, who for some reason brought to our writing a depth of insight and care we did not know existed. At a time when he was struggling with his own self-doubts and failings, he awakened us to our singular gifts as people and writers. He gave all he had to us and asked no special thanks. He did it for the love of poetry.

Peter Stitt

John Berryman: His Teaching, His Scholarship, His Poetry

As a senior at the University of Minnesota in the fall of 1961, I enrolled in a course called The European Heritage. The other courses I had taken in the humanities program had been interesting, and Humanities 61—the first course in a full-year (three quarters) sequence covering Western culture from Hesiod's *Theogony* through the poems of St. John of the Cross—promised me a strengthened foundation for the graduate study in English and American literature that I hoped to begin the next year. In other words, I signed up for this course strictly on the basis of the subject matter studied in it. All I knew about the teacher at the time of registration was his name. To this day, however, his brilliance remains unsurpassed in my experience; though I have been lucky enough to study under and work as a colleague with some truly outstanding teachers, none of them was better than John Berryman.

Certainly he was a talented performer, well skilled in the use of histrionic pronouncements calculated to capture the attention of undergraduate students. He made the literature come alive, forced us to identify with the characters and somehow live through the situations in which they found themselves. For example, when we came to the point in *Oedipus Rex* where the young Oedipus, fully aware of the prophecy that he would murder his father and marry his mother, kills a noble, old man and then marries a recently widowed woman twice his own age, Berryman said—with drama, conviction, and a sense of irony: "This is RASH!" I can still hear that and a hundred other similar statements, given in his absolutely authoritative voice. He would almost hiss at such times, would even put a kind of muted screeching into the emphasized word. I am not being entirely accurate, however, in using the words *performer* and *histrionic.* Berryman was certainly a dramatic teacher, but he was not merely putting on an act. What was most convincing about his teaching was his total commitment to the material; literature mattered to him, desperately. Literature *and* learning.

There was no fooling around in his classes; no jokes were delivered just for their own sakes. He was not interested in himself in the classroom. His insights were presented not as his but as belonging to the world of knowledge, the realm of truth. He seemed to have read everything related to the materials of the course, and he wanted us to read it as well. Thus his syllabi were loaded down with such recommendations as this one, given after the assignment in Savonarola:

> Recommended as additional: J. A. Symonds, THE REVIVAL OF LEARNING (Capricorn), and R. Roeder's THE MAN OF THE RENAISSANCE, on Savonarola, Aretino, etc., is in pb. THE PIRENNE THESIS, ed. A. F. Havighurst (Heath pb) is a good intro. to a different way of looking at these grand divisions of Western history, and two of Pirenne's main works are in pb, or rather three.

He also recommended additional reading on a daily basis, at the beginnings of class periods. When we started *Don Quixote,* for example, he suggested Americo Castro's *The Structure of Spanish History,* V. S. Pritchett's *The Spanish Temper,* and Harry Levin's *The Over-Reacher;* when we started Dante he recommended Vossler's *Medieval Culture,* Witte's *Essays on Dante* (especially one called "How Not to Read Dante"), Francis Ferguson's *On the Purgatorio,* and books by Singleton and Barbi ("the best to start with"), the titles of which I missed.

In addition to the insights that so impressed me, Berryman was always attentive to the basic elements. My notes are filled with lists of points and characteristics—for example this analysis of "The Greek Mind (Homer especially)":

1. Lucid.
2. Orderly, proportioned (abstract), mathematical.

3. Concise (non-Asiatic).
4. Flexible (tragedy *and* comedy).
5. Profoundly ironic (ambiguous treatment of supernatural).
6. Realistic (non-romantic and non-superstitious), consistent with highest degree of abstract art.
7. Non-sentimental (about human nature *and* fate).
8. Sense of inevitability and freedom (there is no word for *choice* or *decision* in Greek).
9. Complete (knew all the world there was).

All of these characteristics, Berryman went on to say, are embodied in "the 'Shield' of Achilles"—which, he began, "is not a shield at all, for it cannot help Achilles in any way—he is invulnerable except for his heel. Hephaestus and Thetis knew this." There follow two pages of notes on every aspect of the shield.

Even though Berryman took care not to feature himself in his classes, it was his powerful personality that drew most students to him; during office hours he would generally be attended by several adoring acolytes, whom he would alternately browbeat and entertain. He dressed impeccably, always in a jacket, a white shirt, and a bow tie. And he would sweat—partly because of nervousness, I am certain, and partly because of his drinking. But who knows anything about drinking at the age of twenty? The most common rumor one heard about him was that he suffered from Hodgkin's disease. I remember the enigmatic smile my academic adviser gave me when I asked him about that. Perhaps the hardest thing to believe now is that Berryman was not known among the students as a poet, even though his *Homage to Mistress Bradstreet* had been published several years earlier. My own introduction to his work began one day when the woman who sat beside me in class said, "He writes poems about someone named Henry. Very strange poems." She had seen some of the early Dream Songs in a magazine.

What chiefly stands out in my mind about him as a teacher is that he took us seriously. He was interested in our minds, and if he came across someone he thought was smart, he would lavish praise upon that person—for example, Kent Nichols. On the day he was ready to return our papers one quarter, Berryman began the class by saying something like this: "Ladies and gentlemen, there is a genius in this class, someone I am ashamed to say I have overlooked. His name is Kent Nichols." I did not know Kent Nichols before then, and I do not know him now; but I will never forget his name. My own moment of glory came early in that first quarter, when Berryman for some reason was talking about how people will coddle up to persons of position and influence. He said something like this: "We have such a person in this class, ladies and gentlemen, the poetry editor of the *Ivory Tower,* Mr. Peter Stitt, whom I am sure is besieged day and night by aspiring writers." My astonishment at being thus singled out was only partly in response to the absurdity of what he was saying (so little a person of position and influence was I that, in my three full years as an editor of the student magazine, I received no more than two or three calls from young writers, all of them more interested in calling me names than in buying my influence with the drinks that Berryman imagined me receiving). More striking to me then was that Berryman had noticed me at all: I had had no individual contact with him and could not understand how he had singled me out in a class of sixty students. Later, of course, it became obvious that he read things, including both the *Ivory Tower* and the rosters for his own classes.

The same qualities that made Berryman a brilliant teacher—attention to detail, an authoritative voice, the willingness to do his homework—also made him an outstanding literary critic, as can be seen in the posthumously published collection, *The Freedom of the Poet* (1976), which gathers essays, lectures, reviews, and even short stories originally written over a thirty-year period. The earliest piece, on Yeats's plays, first appeared in the *Columbia Review* in 1936, when Berryman was still an undergraduate. The latest pieces, on poems by Thomas Hardy and John Crowe Ransom, appeared in the Oscar Williams anthology *Master Poems of the English Language* in 1966.

That Berryman was deeply serious about literature is proven on every page of this book. He has as much contempt for nonserious writing, for "the popular boys," as he has admiration for the real thing—and the real thing is, by its nature, intellectual: "All the artists who have ever survived were intellectuals—sometimes intellectuals *also,* but intellectuals" (215; here, as in my other quotations from *The Freedom of the Poet,* the italics are Berrryman's). Berryman makes this heavy demand of all the writers that he considers; either they have something important to say or they are nothing, either they appeal to the intellect or they are nowhere. Several writers come up wanting in this regard—Thomas Nashe, Monk Lewis, and Theodore Dreiser, among others—but only one fails the test completely. Ring Lardner "never studied anybody," writes Berryman: "scorn and hatred for everything 'highbrow' is one of his chief marks" (FP, 215).

Clearly Berryman himself was an intellectual; one of the most impressive characteristics of his critical writing is how well and how completely he did his homework. In areas that I am able to judge, the record is striking. For example, in a piece first published in the *Sewanee Review* in 1945, Berryman takes time to instruct the uninitiated in how to read Henry James's works, suggesting even the order in which they should be read:

> The indispensable Henry James is in *The American* and *The Portrait of a Lady*, of the early period: "The Liar," "The Aspen Papers," "The Pupil," some of the stories of the Artist, and *The Spoils of Poynton*, of the middle period; *The Ambassadors*, *The Wings of the Dove*, and all five stories in *The Finer Grain*, of the last period. There is a good deal of invaluable criticism in the *Hawthorne* and in essays . . . scattered through four other books; his critical prefaces to his selected works (collected ten years ago in *The Art of the Novel*) are best taken singly, with strict attention, with salt, each after the work to which it refers. The finest of the half dozen descriptive books is *The American Scene;* of the volumes of reminiscence, *Notes of a Son and Brother*. These are the works, therefore, which should be read first. (FP, 161)

The authority with which Berryman presents this reading list is impressive; when he says that these are not the only works by James that we should read but just the "first" things we should read, we understand that he himself has read much more. The only soft spot I can find in the list is the vague reference to "some of the stories of the Artist"—but even this small doubt is put to rest a few pages later when Berryman gives a detailed discussion of these very stories. Moreover, to support his judgment that James improved his novels when he revised them for the New York Edition, Berryman compares several passages from both versions of several different works. An impressive bit of homework indeed.

Similar examples that could be drawn from many other pieces

in the book would demonstrate a breadth of reading as impressive as the depth just shown. Berryman shows a command of the criticism on Thomas Nashe, on Christopher Marlowe, on Ezra Pound, on Theodore Dreiser; he gives brief bibliographies for the study of Spanish history, the Spanish mind, the development of popular American culture. There is even a brief stylistic analysis of the obituary for John McTaggart Ellis McTaggart that C. D. Broad delivered before the British Academy. All of this, we must remember, comes from a man whose first commitment was not to learning and scholarship but to his own development as a poet.

Despite his devotion to the impersonal art of scholarship, Berryman never forgot that books are written by people. The most common complaint he makes in *The Freedom of the Poet,* in fact, is against what he calls "T. S. Eliot's intolerable and perverse theory of the impersonality of the artist" (12). Just as he chose to give the question of personality, usually of his own personality, a central position in his own poems, Berryman was always willing in his criticism to refer matters of interpretation and emphasis back through the authors' writings to their lives. His general position is explained by this statement, made in reference to Robert Lowell: "One thing critics not themselves writers of poetry occasionally forget is that poetry is composed by actual human beings, and tracts of it are very closely about them" (*FP,* 316).

Berryman's reliance upon the life and personality of the author is evident in small issues as well as in large ones. His response to some lines from *Hamlet* is typical: "Nobody, I suppose, who had not himself *been* passion's slave could have made the longing envy in these lines so central in his most personal play" (*FP,* 82). On a larger scale, F. Scott Fitzgerald's failure to develop is explained on the basis of his inability to follow his own advice—to forget about money and fame and concentrate upon his craft. The approach is sometimes revealing about Berryman's own poems—as when he points out the semiautobiographical basis of the *Cantos* (in *The Dream Songs,* Berryman took Pound's method a step further)—and sometimes the approach is poignant. The brilliant essay "Shakespeare at Thirty" gains much of its power from Berryman's implicit identification with his subject, whom Berryman imagines in 1594, forced out of London by the closing of the theaters because of the plague, as frustrated and stalled, aware of his powers but uncertain of his future. In 1953, when the essay first appeared, Berryman (always confident of *his* powers) was nearing the age of forty but still had not published his first important poem, *Homage to Mistress Bradstreet.*

Berryman does not always handle his version of the biographical fallacy with such skill. "Conrad's Journey" is a psychoanalytical reading of *Heart of Darkness* that gets a little better, but not much better, than this sample passage: "There is a *penetration* of the Dark Continent (the mother's body; it is also called Hell... and contains... a chief devil, the father-figure Kurtz) by Marlow (the son, the author's unconscious)" (*FP,* 110). Berryman's knowledge of Freud serves him well in the Dream Songs, but turns this essay (along with parts of his critical biography, *Stephen Crane*) into something verging on parody of psychoanalytic theory. It is typical of Berryman, however, to proceed authoritatively and with élan, even when he is marching into a swamp. Like everything that he wrote, this book is dominated by his voice and personality, and generally the effect is entirely positive.

For one thing, the essays are witty. In his discussion of Anne Frank's *Diary,* there is a passage, consisting of quotation and analysis, that reveals the basis of much of Berryman's own wittiness: "'Margot... She's a darling, she's good and pretty, but she lacks the nonchalance for conducting deep discussions.' The criticism is given as decisive," Berryman comments, "and I think it may puzzle the reader until we recall that Socrates's interlocutors were frequently baffled to decide whether he was in earnest or not. She objects, let's say, to an *absence of play of mind*" (*FP,* 104–5). Intellectual playfulness is present everywhere in Berryman's writings, poetry and prose; it is what allows him, for example, to analyze the style of Broad's eulogy for McTaggart, and it is what allows him, in a footnote, to give this capsule portrait of R. B. McKerrow: "Few men more conservative can ever have lived. Sir Walter Greg, a life-long friend, tells one extraordinary story in the memoir of McKerrow he did for the British Academy. McKerrow was interested in science and was heard, years after the Michelson-Morley experiment, when it was mentioned in his presence, to murmur regretfully to himself, 'Yes, I suppose it is true'" (*FP,* 19).

Other examples are more self-indulgent, but add their measure of amusement and charm nevertheless. For example, writing on Dreiser's descriptions of Chicago in *The Titan,* Berryman editorializes: "How flatulent it seems beside the invocation of Saul Bellow at

the beginning of a novel about Chicago that better evokes it: 'Chi-
cago, that somber city.' (Chicagoans are so touchy that perhaps the
present writer should explain that he has four or five reasons for being
grateful to Chicago and nothing much in particular against it)" (*FP*,
195). More striking, more personal, even more confessional are the
opening sentences of the essay on Anne Frank: "When the first install-
ment of the translated text of *The Diary of Anne Frank* appeared in the
spring of 1952, in *Commentary*, I read it with amazement. The next
day, when I went into town to see my analyst, I stopped in the
magazine's offices—I often did, to argue with Clem Greenberg" (*FP*,
91). Berryman was a master at the use of this kind of intimate, at
times irritating detail.

I would like now to turn from this consideration of the content and
techniques of *The Freedom of the Poet* to a brief attempt to relate
Berryman's criticism to his poetry. I see four general areas. First,
there is the question of modernism as seen by a latter-day poet who
intended his work to exist in rebellion against it. Second, I want to
consider what Berryman says about style and how this is reflected in
his own writing. Third, I am additionally interested in what he has
to say about the topic of the poet's manipulation of his own personal-
ity in his works. Fourth, there is the problem of fame or, more
generally, the poet's relationship with his readers.

John Berryman was a member of the first generation of "con-
temporary" poets, those who began to write immediately after the
modernist period (1912–1945). The modernist poets tried to be ob-
jective, detached, impersonal, almost scientific in their attitude; they
fulminate at length against the subjectivism of the Romantic poets.
Their verse is experimental—traditional forms are rejected or
modified almost beyond recognition. Their poems are allusive and
often have an almost clinical intellectuality about them. They tend to
be pessimistic about humanity's chances (a result of the death of God
and the carnage of World War I), contemptuous of modern civiliza-
tion, and rebellious against modern society. Obviously these traits
apply very well to some poets (Eliot, Pound, and Auden especially),
moderately well to others (Williams, Yeats, Stevens), and almost not
at all to others (Frost in particular).

Much of the poetry that follows modernism enacts a reaction

against it, especially against its impersonality and coldness. The most obvious characteristic of contemporary poetry may be its emphasis upon the question of identity or personality, usually that of the poets themselves; objectivism is largely rejected in favor of a more subjective and humanistic attitude. Traditional forms seem to make a comeback (Roethke, Lowell, some Berryman), but are superseded later by an even more relaxed informality (the free-verse style so much in vogue today). Contemporary poets may recently have become more optimistic than the modernists, but it is hard to be sure; after all, this is still the twentieth century—not an optimistic time—and we've had a second war to top the first. Likewise, the recent poets may be friendlier to society, but I suspect the truth is that they've given up altogether on society at large and formed a self-sustaining group of their own. Again, these traits must be applied loosely and in various ways to contemporary poets.

As a member of the first generation, Berryman might be said to occupy a middle ground between the truly modernist and the truly contemporary. His own definition of modernism, formulated as early as 1948, is only partial: "By 1935—referring only, for the moment, to this country—the Auden climate had set in strongly. Poetry became ominous, flat, and social, elliptical and indistinctly allusive; casual in tone and form, frightening in import" (FP, 297). This is as accurate a description of Berryman's own early poems (The Dispossessed was also published in 1948) as we are likely to find; clearly Berryman was laboring under what he elsewhere calls "the influence (Auden) that has strait-jacketed much talent among men just older than [Lowell]" (FP, 287). Berryman's tone makes it obvious that he was not happy writing in the shadow of Auden.

We now know, of course, that even before these comments were written Berryman had very effectively thrown off the Auden strait-jacket. In his Sonnets, written in 1947, Berryman adopted his own voice and style and was mostly his own person from that time forward. In his prose, Berryman has indirectly described this stylistic transformation. In the review, "Robert Lowell and Others" (also first published in 1948), he puts it this way: "Lowell's poetry is the most decisive testimony we have had, I think, of a new period, returning to the deliberate and the formal. In other respects, it is true, the break is incomplete. Our best work is still difficult, allusive, and more or less didactic in intention" (*FP*, 291). The passage—for me at least—perfectly describes many of the ways in which Berryman straddles the border between the modernist and the contemporary.

It was not until his last two books of poems—*Love & Fame* (1970) and *Delusions, Etc.* (1972)—that Berryman made any real attempt to loosen his dense, turgid style. Even then, his revolution stopped far short of what we had seen happening in the later work of Lowell, Kunitz, and so many others. Berryman never wanted to sound like anyone else; his ultimate stylistic goal seems to have been distinctiveness, individuality. What he has to say about style in general can be applied to his own practice: "The notion 'style' points in two contrary directions: toward individuality, the characteristic, and toward inconspicuous expression of its material. The latter is the more recent direction (George Orwell a superb practitioner); we may range it with T. S. Eliot's intolerable and perverse theory of the impersonality of the artist; it may have something wrong with it" (*FP*, 12). Clearly, Berryman wanted his own style to have "individuality" and to be "characteristic" of his voice, and of no one else's.

I have always thought that Berryman's style is based more upon the writers of the British Renaissance than upon his immediate predecessors. In his discussion of Thomas Nashe's prose style, it seems to me that Berryman is also describing the effects he himself hoped to achieve—in both prose and poetry. Here are the characteristics he finds in Nashe: "Inversion or rearrangement for rhythm, emphasis, and simulation of the (improved) colloquial. . . . Rapid, offhand, natural, the order is still highly periodic . . . how physical it is . . . a self-conscious style, but *alert,* not laboured. 'Extemporal'. . . . Anti-pedantic, spontaneous (apparently), but showmanlike . . . " (*FP*, 13). Examples of these traits are abundant in Berryman's mature verse.

The most distinctive quality of Berryman's style lies in his manipulation of syntax, a characteristic that accounts, perhaps paradoxically, both for much of his stylistic brilliance and for much of the difficulty many readers have with his poems. In an early essay, he points out the blandness of most contemporary syntax: "It is hard to measure what has been lost in our prose by the uniform adoption of a straight-on, mechanical word order (reflecting our *thoughtless* speech)" (*FP*, 14). Berryman's recognition of the power inherent in syntactical variety is obvious in his later comment on Ezra Pound's unfaltering, encyclopedic mastery of tone—a mastery that compensates for a comparative weakness of syntax. (By instinct, I parenthesize, Pound has always minimized the importance of syntax, and this instinct perhaps accounts for his inveterate dislike of Milton . . . ; not only did Milton seem to him, perhaps, anti-romantic *and* anti-realistic, undetailed, and anti-conversational, but Milton is the supreme English master of syntax. (*FP*, 264)

This regard for syntactical complexity shows up everywhere and takes many forms in Berryman's mature poetry. Most often and most obviously it can be seen in a word order that is simply inverted from the normal pattern. Thus we are not surprised when, after quoting this line of poetry in a critical essay—"They are kicking a man in the head to death"—Berryman comments" "I see no loss, some gain, in an order altered to 'kicking in the head a man' . . . " (*FP*, 304). Nor are we surprised to find Berryman penning this prose sentence: "Or had he it all in mind at first?" (*FP*, 11). Such a style, when taken to an extreme, can be counterproductive. It isn't just the minor irritation we feel when reading a sentence such as this; there is also the possibility that density will cause obscurity. Berryman described the problem in his review of Lowell, whose sonnets, he says, "tend to be inferior to other forms. The chief danger for a writer so dense is obviously turgidity, and in the sonnets it is least successfully avoided" (*FP*, 291–92). Needless to say, Berryman's own use of tight stanzaic patterns leads to the same trouble sometimes.

As contemporary poetry has developed, it has become steadily more personal. The modernists in general accepted Eliot's "theory of the impersonality of the artist," and early in the history of the contemporary we can find a similar de-emphasis of personality. In 1947, for example, Berryman pointed out: "It is to be noted that Lowell is an *objective* poet; except as a Christian or a descendant he scarcely appears in his poems" (*FP*, 288–89). For Lowell, the point of change came in 1957 when he started writing the highly personal poems later collected in *Life Studies* (Monroe Spears dates the beginning of postmodernism at 1957 for this reason). Berryman commented on the change in 1964: "Lowell's recent poems, many of them, are as personal, autobiographical, as his earliest poems were hieratic" (*FP*, 316).

Modernist poetry, of course, is by no means uniformly impersonal; there are those, in fact—Stephen Spender prominent among them—who argue that even Eliot's poetry is largely (if indirectly) autobiographical. Perhaps the most personal of the modernists, however, is the Pound we see in the *Cantos*. In his brilliant essay on Pound, to my mind, the best piece of criticism he ever wrote, Berryman points out that the subject of the *Cantos* is almost but "not quite Ezra Pound himself. . . . Pound is his own subject *qua* modern poet" (*FP*, 263). Pound, that is, depersonalizes himself for the purpose of his poem and becomes a kind of representative man. Thus, because of "the peculiar detachment of interest with which Pound seems to regard himself," the work "is personal, but it is not very personal" (*FP*, 264). All this is relevant to the Dream Songs, where Henry bears a strong (if selective) resemblance to Berryman, and is another representative figure for the modern artist. The difference, of course, is that Berryman regarded himself with a passionate interest; thus *The Dream Songs* is a very personal work.

Also relevant to *The Dream Songs* is Berryman's comment on the structure of the *Cantos:* "I have the impression that Pound allowed, in whatever his plan exactly is (if it exactly is, and if it is one plan), for the drift-of-life, the interference of fate" (*FP*, 269). When asked by an interviewer about the structural plan of *The Dream Songs,* Berryman replied that it all depended on what happened to Henry—in other words, the drift-of-life. In a similar vein is Berryman's analysis of Whitman's "*personal* intention" in "Song of Myself" (*FP*, 230). He quotes Whitman's expression of his desire "to put *a Person,* a human being (myself, in the latter part of the Nineteenth Century, in America,) freely, fully and truly on record." This corresponds very closely to Berryman's statement that the structural basis of *The Dream Songs* is "Henry, the personality of Henry." Finally, there is the question of whether Henry really is John Berryman in slight disguise. The answer, which Berryman gave so many times, is that he both is and isn't. In *The Freedom of the Poet,* he expressed his point in general terms: "The necessity for the artist of selection opens inevitably an abyss between his person and his persona. I only said that much poetry is 'very closely about' the person. The persona looks across at the person and then sets about its own work" (321). *The Dream Songs,* then, is "very closely about" Berryman, and Henry is based upon the poet—but inevitably, they are not identical.

The problem of the artist's relationship to his audience is, for Berryman, an especially tricky one in America. It may well be that serious art is an elite, rather than a popular, preoccupation—elite in the sense that one must have both intelligence and education to understand and appreciate serious works of art. Berryman makes it very clear that this is his perspective in his essay on Ring Lardner: "everything good in the end is highbrow. . . . When Shakespeare mocked Chapman and Raleigh and their school of intellectual art, he did it with a higher brow than theirs" (FP, 215). Of course America is a democratic country, and this notion of artistic excellence is essentially antidemocratic—artistic quality cannot be determined by a popular referendum. This is the source of the artist's problem in America. As Berryman says, "It is a disconcerting feature of much American literary art that either it's so closely bound up with the world of popular entertainment that the boundaries are not easy to fix, or else . . . it has no relation to the world at all" (FP, 204). Either an American writer is a celebrity—Jacqueline Susann, Eric Segal—or virtually unknown. And, unfortunately, almost all of our most serious and best writers fall into the second category.

The rewards being what they are, and human beings what we are, is it any wonder that many of our serious writers have longed to be, tried to be, popular? Berryman comments on the dangers: "popularity in the modern American culture [has] proved for . . . authors not yet physically dead a blessing decidedly sinister. . . . The secular dangers are to candour and development, perhaps to fellow feeling, considering the kind of honour a comics culture can confer; self-consciousness is the general reef" (FP, 290). Berryman touches on several popular writers in his book but the most significant example of the dangers inherent in popularity is F. Scott Fitzgerald, who "accepted its standards, made his friends in it, castrated his work for it, and took its rewards. When halfwits in editorial offices cracked the whip, Fitzgerald danced" (FP, 203).

It may well be that John Berryman himself succumbed to some of these dangers late in his own career. He loved to be treated as a celebrity, gave indiscreet interviews to large-circulation magazines, and even wrote a series of poems (in Love & Fame) that seem more nearly addressed to a popular than a serious audience. The response that he made to American culture earlier in his career may have been more in accord with his own high standard: "One feels . . . a certain hostility on the part of the poet. The modern poet, characteristically, has *lost confidence* in his readers (this is not altogether surprising, considering the quality of most contemporary education); but so far from causing him to reduce his demands therefore, this loss of confidence has led to an *increase* in his demands. Good poetry has never been easy to read with any advanced understanding, but it has seldom been made so deliberately difficult" (*FP*, 271–72). Obviously, Berryman's own relation to his audience was shifting and uncertain. Though his instinct as an intellectual was to adopt the high-minded, obscurantist standards of the modernists, his instinct as a person was to seek adoration. Thus he seems, in his late work, to have given up his monastic pursuit of pure excellence in favor of courting popularity.

Viewed from the perspective of time, that late impulse looks more and more like an unimportant blip on the graph of this poet's life. The real John Berryman is the teacher I knew at the University of Minnesota, the critic of most of the essays in *The Freedom of the Poet*, and the poet of the *Sonnets, Homage to Mistress Bradstreet,* and *The Dream Songs.* The real John Berryman is the man who defined his life's vocation, and avocation, in this way:

The motives for making poetry have regularly been complex beyond analysis: love of the stuff and of rhythm, the need to invent, a passion for getting things right, the wish to leave one's language in better shape than one found it, a jealousy for the national honour, love for a person or for God, attachment to human possibility, pity, outletting agony or disappointment, exasperation, malice, hatred. Desire for fame and entertaining an audience are only two other motives, forgoable, particularly in the consciousness of a final two, which may be more central than any yet mentioned. Poetry is a terminal activity, taking place out near the end of things, where the poet's soul addresses one other soul only, never mind when. And it aims—never mind *either* communication or expression—at the reformation of the poet, as prayer does. In the grand cases—as in our century, Yeats and Eliot—it enables the poet gradually, again and again, to become almost another man. (*FP,* 312)

Paul Mariani

Lowell on Berryman
on Lowell

Five A.M. 11 May 1964. Another night of insomnia, and John Berryman still reeling from Lowell's maddening review of his *77 Dream Songs* in The *New York Review of Books*. But now, having ingested that bitter aspic, he sits down at a table in his Washington, D.C. apartment to compose himself by composing another Dream Song. He feels despondent, angry, betrayed. He has waited twenty years to hear what Lowell will say in print about him, and surely he expects something closer to the praise he—like Randall Jarrell—had lavished on a younger Lowell. Well, Berryman has his answer now, misprintings and misreadings there on the page in black and white before him.[1]

Had he not just returned from five weeks of convalescence at Abbott Hospital in Minneapolis, still exhausted, his body toxic with alcohol, the result—he believed—of working so hard on his *Dream Songs?* It was while recovering in the hospital that the first copies of *77 Dream Songs* had reached him, along with a few welcome but scattered letters from poets amid what at first seemed a thundering silence. Then Berryman had heard from his publisher that Lowell was planning to review the book, though why, he pondered ingenuously, someone of Lowell's giant stature should take on the chore of reviewing *his* book was beyond him. In truth, remembering how Jarrell, Lowell's old friend as far back as Kenyon College, had run a rapier through Berryman's first book of poems sixteen years before, Berryman grew afraid now, anxious, indifferent, huffy, imperious.

When he received an advance copy of Lowell's review, Berryman's heart sank, for after briefly surveying his friend's checkered career as a poet up to the present, Lowell had concluded that *77 Dream Songs* had turned out to be "larger and sloppier" than any of Berryman's previous work. "At first," Lowell admitted, "the brain aches and freezes at so much darkness, disorder, and oddness." And though "the repeated situations" (the book's plot) and their racy jabber (the book's multileveled styles) had with rereading "become more and more enjoyable," even now he didn't think he could "paraphrase accurately" even half of what he'd read.

Lowell did manage to praise certain passages and singled out— not surprisingly—Dream Song 29 as "one of the best and most unified" in the book. Finally, however, he had had to put the book down as "hazardous" and "imperfect," its "main faults" being its mannerisms and, "worse—disintegration." For a long time now he had felt that disintegration was the chief mark of Berryman's life, but now he was applying the term to include Berryman's poems as well. How often, he complained, "one chafes at the relentless indulgence, and cannot tell the what or why of a passage." So here it was again: the same old bugbear of anacoloutha—radical disjuncture of syntax and narrative—that Lowell had been warning Berryman against since the late 1940s. There never had been enough logical sequencing in Berryman's lyrics, and now he watched appalled as the individual Songs exploded again and again "into three or four separate parts."

In noting the lack of sequence in the Dream Songs, Lowell meant to draw attention to the difficulty he as reader had in following almost any of the poems from start to finish. His own work was—at the time of the review—far more linear and unified than Berryman's in terms of plot and consistency of metaphor, each part careful to connect with every other part. Moreover, the individual poems in his own work, especially since 1957, were clearly intended to form parts of a larger thematic unity. *Life Studies* demonstrates this, for there—as in *For the Union Dead,* the new book he had recently completed— Lowell had followed a thematic norm for which his predecessors were Flaubert and Joyce, as well as those earlier Henrys: Henry Adams and Henry James.

But when he first read the review in his hospital room, Berryman took Lowell's strictures to mean that the book as a whole lacked sequential order. The outcome was that Berryman spent the better part of a day and night reviewing the complex ways in which the Songs advanced upon each other, opening up theme by theme one song into the next. At last, exhausted, he reassured himself that the various orders he had worked so assiduously to create were indeed there, that the problem lay with Lowell and not with himself. Still, there it was: Lowell's first public—and negative, friends, negative—assessment of Berryman in print.

And *this* by an old friend. Could Jarrell himself have done worse, he must have wondered. No doubt about it: Lowell, the man Berryman still thought of as America's chief poet—now that Frost and Williams were gone—and, moreover, the recognized public arbiter of poetic taste, had not only betrayed him but was intent on keeping him out of the spotlight he believed he had a right to share now with Lowell. Had not others, especially in England, already named Berryman as Lowell's chief competitor for the number one place among American poets? Hadn't the British critic, Tony Alvarez, already implied as much by allowing only these two Americans into the first edition of his anthology, *The New Poetry?*[2]

So now, on this May morning in the nation's capitol, Berryman sat down to compose what was to become Dream Song 177. In the poem, Lowell figures as Addison. Why Addison? Perhaps because Addison had been for the early eighteenth century what Lowell surely was on his way to becoming for the 1960s: the apotheosis of the public poet. Perhaps too because Steele is remembered as the drunken buffoon in the Addison-Steele equation. Perhaps, considering the way Berryman's mind seems to have worked, Addison also suggested both the offspring of a poisonous snake—adder's son—as well as Yeats's famous incubus, Robert Artison, who appears in that apocalyptic sequence, *Nineteen Hundred and Nineteen*.

"Am tame now," Berryman began, composing himself on the page:

> You may touch me, who had thrilled
> (before) your tips, twitcht from your breast your heart,
> & burnt your willing brain.
> I am tame now. Undead, I was not killed
> by Henry's viewers but maimed. It is my art
> to buzz the spotlight in vain,

flighting "at random" while Addison wins.
I would not war with Addison. I love him
and Addison so loves me back
me backsides, I may perish in his grins
& grip. I would he liked me less, less grim.
But he has helpt me, slack

& sick & hopeful, anew to know what man—
scrubbing the multiverse with dazzled thought—
still has in store for man:
a doghouse or a cave, is all we could,
according to my dreams. I stand in doubt,
surrounded by holy wood. (*DS*, 177)

No one—including Lowell himself—seems to have suspected
that this Song, buried among hundreds of others, was aimed at Low-
ell. After all, as Berryman warned his readers in the very first of his
Songs, Henry had long been a master at hiding the day. Still, there it
is: Berryman's anguished, comic, and veiled perception of Lowell's
betrayal, leaving Henry in doubt as to the worth of his long poem.
No, Berryman knows, Henry has not been killed by the (re) viewers,
anymore than Keats had been. But he has been maimed, accused of
"flighting" (i.e., composing) his Songs "at random." And *this* by the
very man who would most benefit from keeping his friend under, in
a "doghouse or a cave."

Those "dreams" in the penultimate line are of course Berryman's
Dream Songs. And the reference in the last line to "holy wood"
evokes not only the legend of the one priest who may sing at any one
time in the Sacred Wood (an image Eliot had evoked forty-five years
before in his first volume of essays), but suggests as well that Lowell
(the man Berryman used to quip had such Hollywood good looks)
still wanted to hog the spotlight, while poor Henry, true priest of the
imagination, must stay lost in the woods. So much for Berryman's
myopic perspective.

As for Lowell, he really does seem to have been puzzled and upset
by the Dream Songs. Ironically, the same day Berryman composed
his attack on Lowell, Lowell was writing Jarrell himself that he'd just
finished a review of Berryman that he was sure Jarrell would find too
positive. "I've always felt he threw all he had into writing," Lowell

defended himself, "and more and more as time went on," so that writing the review Lowell found himself throwing in "all my larger, more enthusiastic impressions." True, the Dream Songs didn't quite come up to the Bradstreet poem, and Berryman would probably read the review and feel Lowell had "hemmed him in with barbs."[3]

Three weeks later, reading Adrienne Rich's very positive assessment of the Dream Songs in the *Nation*, Lowell wrote her to say that he'd been harsher on Berryman than she'd been because the poems had affected him so much. Such "smash and vehemence," such "unleashed power," had been too much for Lowell. Besides, there was something in Berryman's character so close to his own that for Lowell to look on Berryman "even in the imagination" was to feel as if he were drowning. Encountering him was rather like a blast of "oxygen coming into one's lungs and then failing."[4]

Months later Lowell was still trying to analyze the weird effect the Songs were having on him. Writing to William Meredith in October, he summed up what he had tried to accomplish in his review. Perhaps, he said, it had "some value as a record of a man's struggle"— he meant his own—"with the text, a climbing of barriers." He could see now more clearly that with the Dream Songs Berryman had actually made himself into "a new poet, one whose humor and wildness make other new poets seem tame." But he was still reading him "with uncertainty and distress and quite likely envy," though to read with envy was itself a "tribute." And yet, if he still read Berryman "only here and there . . . with the all-out enjoying amazement" he reserved for Bishop, Plath, Larkin, and Roethke, there was still that handful of Songs to contend with that *no* one else had equaled.[5]

By the time Lowell wrote his review, he and Berryman had known each other for nearly twenty years. In the summer of 1946, the two had spent two heady weeks together—they and their first wives, Lowell's Jean Stafford and Berryman's Eileen—at the Lowell's summer place in Damariscotta Mills, thirty miles north of Bath, in Maine. There, in a spacious, newly redecorated early nineteenth-century clapboard farmhouse, the men wrote and discussed Browning and Spenser and Leontes's choppy, disjunctive syntax in *The Winter's Tale*. Those two weeks would remain for Lowell—even after Berryman's death—a pastoral philosopher's circle where he and his Scholar Gypsy friend had talked poetry until time itself had seemed to stop.[6]

Then, at the end of that September, Lowell—separated now from Stafford and living in a run-down apartment in lower Manhattan—went with Randall Jarrell down to Princeton to see his Scholar Gypsy friend once again. It proved to be an ill-fated visit, for Jarrell, suffering miserably from a poisoned canape, lay on the Berryman's couch, on the one hand making up cruel parodies of Lowell's poems and, on the other, contradicting almost everything Berryman had to say.

A year and a half later, when Berryman came down to Washington at Lowell's invitation to record his poems for the Library of Congress, the two went to visit Ezra Pound at St. Elizabeth's Hospital. Berryman kept good notes of this visit, but one incident he did not see fit to record Lowell described in a letter to Peter Taylor. At one point during the visit, Lowell noted with barely suppressed glee, Berryman had wondered out loud if piety, taken to an extreme, might not itself become a vice. "That," Pound roared, "sounds like a survival from the time when you believed in saying things that were clever."[7]

In 1954, when Berryman was separated from *his* wife and in desperate need of a job, Lowell made room for him at the University of Iowa when he went to the University of Cincinnati for a term as Elliston Professor of Poetry—a position Berryman had held the year before. When one or the other was down, as often they were because of alcohol or depression, they wrote or phoned to offer the other a shoulder. Yet somehow, for nearly ten years—from late 1953 until the spring of 1962—the two did not see each other, though Lowell especially kept hoping he and Berryman might find a way to replicate their Maine talks.

During those years, of course, both poets continued to develop. Lowell had gone from the Catholic visionary phase of *Lord Weary's Castle*—which had won him a Pulitzer at the age of twenty-nine—through the difficult symbolist phase of *The Mills of the Kavanaughs,* and on to the ground-breaking, prizewinning personal phase of *Life Studies*. Berryman's development, though less spectacular, was every bit as significant as Lowell's. After publishing his first full-length book of poems, *The Dispossessed,* to faint and scattered praise in 1948, Berryman turned briefly to prose with a critical biography of Stephen Crane and several brilliant essays on Shakespeare. In 1953 he wrote his powerful and gnarled *Homage to Mistress Bradstreet*. Then—for five years—he published almost nothing. In 1958 he did manage to produce a thin small-press pamphlet of new poems called *His Thought Made Pockets & the Plane Buckt,* containing all the verse he'd thought worth publishing since *The Dispossessed.* But by then Berryman had given himself completely over to writing Dream Songs.

He was also teaching full time, writing additional essays and introductions, and putting together a literature anthology for undergraduates. In the summer of 1955 he had begun writing the Dream Songs, but only after spending most of the previous year analyzing on paper the complex levels of nearly two hundred of his dreams. (He had uncovered seventeen distinct levels, he crowed, for one of his dreams alone.) Four years later he began publishing the Songs, beginning with several of them printed together in a single spread in the London *Times Literary Supplement.* Soon others were appearing in the American quarterlies and magazines. Some of these Lowell saw in print, others he saw in manuscript, others Berryman read to him over the phone at four in the morning. Like many readers, Lowell seems initially to have been bemused and ambivalent about them.

So the two poets continued to have some contact through Berryman's famous late-night phone calls, one of which came on the night of 18 September 1959. Suicidal with insomnia and despondency and living a seedy bachelor's existence in a run-down Minneapolis apartment in the notorious Seven Corners section of the city, Berryman phoned Lowell at his brownstone on Boston's "hardly Passionate Marlboro street." Lowell had just finished writing *Life Studies* and, fearing a breakdown, had had himself committed once more for psychiatric treatment. As it turned out, when Berryman called, Lowell had only just been released from the hospital.

Well, he too had just been through hell, Lowell wrote Berryman the day after Berryman's call, but he'd managed to make it back. In time things had even lightened up again. The "dark moment comes," he explained. "It comes and goes." He congratulated Berryman on the new Songs, this time getting even Henry's name wrong. "The new poem about Harry in its sixty parts must be a deluge of power," he wrote. "It will be exciting to see the parts you are about to publish. . . . You must believe that it will reach its finished form."[8]

Though he sounded positive in his letter, Lowell still had serious reservations about Berryman's opaque and difficult style. Some of these reservations he had already mentioned to Berryman over the years. Back in the fall of 1947, for example, after the two men spent what Lowell thirty years later would remember as "a very companionable weekend" together in Washington, they had exchanged poems. But while Berryman was enthusiastic about Lowell's work (the poems that would eventually appear in *The Mills of the Kavanaughs*), Lowell was uncertain about the poems that were about to appear in *The Dispossessed*. "I guess I must get used to reading my friends' poems, and not having them read mine," Lowell would remember Berryman writing him at this time. The tone of Berryman's letter, Lowell would recall in a letter to William Meredith four years after Berryman's death, still uneasy with the memory, had been "too lighthearted to be a whiplash." And yet Lowell had "felt rebuked particularly as I had done my best."

In truth, Lowell added, Berryman's "jumpy style (later to soar) made me stumble, and reveal my reserve." Lowell wrote these words in the summer of 1976 only a year before his own death, and they seem to express his mature opinion of Berryman's earlier work. Thinking back to their beginning as poets—his and Jarrell's and Berryman's beginnings—Lowell felt that Berryman had been, "compared to other poets," "a prodigy." But, compared with Jarrell (and by extension Lowell himself) John had been "a slow starter."[9]

When *The Dispossessed* appeared in the spring of 1948, Berryman naturally sent Lowell a copy, then waited to hear what Lowell would say. When, after four months, he had not heard so much as a whisper, he wrote to ask Lowell if he'd received the book. Sheepishly, Lowell wrote back. It could not have helped oil Berryman's ragged nerves that Lowell should now misremember even the book's title. "Many apologies for not thanking you for *The Possessed*," he wrote, before praising what little in the book he could. Well, "the new difficult poems" were "the most wonderful advance anyone has made," he noted, repeating verbatim what Jarrell had already written in his guarded review of Berryman for the *Nation*.

Lowell also had to agree with Randall's assessment that the poems existed rather as "bits and passages—so many breaks, anacoloutha etc. that the whole poem usually escapes me." No doubt Berryman had the ability and the "equipment to do almost anything." But the clear implication remained that he hadn't yet done so, though—Lowell added—all that was needed was for Berryman to "dock" himself "in some overwhelming and unifying object." In short, all Berryman needed was a large-enough subject into which he could pour his energies.[10]

And yet more than a decade later Lowell was still wondering when Berryman would find his subject. Going through Berryman's new poems in *His Thought Made Pockets . . .* in the spring of 1959, Lowell asked Berryman if he really did need "so much twisting, obscurity, archaisms, strange word orders," ampersands, and the rest of it. Well, perhaps he did. At least, he added, "here as in the Bradstreet," Berryman had found, if not a subject, then at least a style and a voice. And that voice "vibrates and makes the heart ache."[11]

Three years later, in April 1962, Lowell visited his—and Berryman's—old mentor, Allen Tate, in Minneapolis, where he gave a reading at the Walker Art Center and managed to spend some time with Berryman. It was the first time Berryman and Lowell had seen each other since December 1953, and they had much to talk about. By then Berryman (47) was married for a third time, this time to a "girl of twenty-one" named Kate, whom Lowell described as possessed of a parochial Catholic background, "innocent beyond belief," and pregnant.

The Berrymans were at the moment living in a dull, two-room cinder-block apartment on Erie Place (Berryman had taken to spelling Erie as Eerie) near the university, where he had been teaching since the beginning of 1955. When Lowell visited Berryman there, he remembered Kate asleep in the next room, "getting through the first child pains," while Berryman and he talked in the other room among Berryman's thousand books. Berryman, he wrote Elizabeth Bishop afterwards, was now in "the 7th year" of a "long poem that fills a suitcase," the pieces of which, he confessed, had refused to yield themselves to his scrutiny.

Confused by Berryman's "Berryisms" and twisted baby talk, Lowell was convinced that the Dream Songs were all written in the voice of Berryman's five-year-old son, Paul, from his second marriage. The effect was, he summed up, a "spooky . . . maddening tortured work of genius, or half genius, in John's later obscure, tortured, wandering style, full of parentheses, slang no one ever spoke, jagged haunting lyrical moments etc." One shuddered, Lowell added, "to think of the child's birth."[12]

But it was Lowell too who in 1959 had suggested to Berryman that he publish a group of seventy-five or so of the Songs as a sort of dry run. That, he explained, would whet the appetite of Berryman's audience until he was ready to publish all of the Dream Songs together. But it was to take Berryman five more agonizing years, with much Hamletizing and interminable revising, before he could allow himself to publish even a selection. And it was the publication of the first seventy-seven, ironically, that was followed by Lowell's rejection of the ugly child he himself had asked Berryman to deliver.

So deep was Berryman's hurt when he read Lowell's review, in fact, that he nearly begged off from accepting the Russell Loines Award from Lowell at the American Academy of Arts in New York three weeks after the appearance of the review. But accept the award Berryman did, grasping Lowell's too-huge hand in both of his, before retiring back to Washington, unable to do much of anything for several weeks after except hide in his cave, drinking and commiserating with himself.

At the end of February 1966, Lowell and Berryman met again, this time at Yale at a memorial service for Jarrell, who, four months earlier, had plunged into the side of a moving car. Those present at the memorial included Jarrell's widow, Mary, Peter Taylor, Adrienne Rich, Richard Wilbur, Stanley Kunitz, Richard Eberhart, John Hollander, William Meredith, and Robert Penn Warren. Berryman, the great elegist for his generation, responded brilliantly to Jarrell's loss with several new Songs, eulogies as much as elegies, for the man he had both feared and admired for the past twenty years. In a drunken, inspired voice he read several of the new Songs that night at Yale, to the astonishment of those present. Yet, inspired though he was, Berryman was also in terrible physical shape, so much so that Rich and Lowell both wrote him afterwards, pleading with him to take better care of himself.

"This is really just to say that I love you," Lowell wrote Berryman two weeks later. "And wonder at you, and want you to take care. Your reminiscences of Randall were the height of the evening, and seemed for a moment to lift away all the glaze and constraints that dog us, and yet it was all in order." Then he added, without equivocation, that he, like so many others, was pleased by what Berryman was doing in the new (post-77) Dream Songs. In fact he had shown Lowell—and all poets, really—brand new resources for poetry if only "we had the nerve."[13]

When, six months later, Lowell read Berryman's *Opus Posthu-*

mous sequence, he wired him at once in Dublin that the new se-
quence constituted nothing less than "a tremendous and living tri-
umph." A month later Lowell followed this up by writing Berryman
that the sequence, which included a Song in which Berryman meets
Randall in hell, was in fact "the crown of your wonderful work,
witty, heart-breaking, all of a piece." "Somehow," he added, "one
believes you on this huge matter of looking at death."[14]

At the same time that he was congratulating Berryman, how-
ever, Lowell was writing Philip Booth to say that the new poems
were the product of a man living on the thin edge between life and
death. They were, in fact, Berryman's "own elegy and written from
the dirt of the grave." Because, he added, Berryman was "very sick,
spiritually and physically," it was no wonder the poems revealed
"personal anguish everywhere" in them. Well, he ended, we poets
"can't dodge it, and shouldn't worry that we are uniquely marked
and fretted and must somehow keep even-tempered, amused, and in
control. John B. in his mad way keeps talking about something evil
stalking us poets. That's a bad way to talk, but there's truth in it."[15]

Still, Lowell's enthusiasm for the *Opus Posthumous* sequence re-
mained bright. Writing to Bishop months later, he was still speaking
of these "marvellous" poems as somehow having been written "ex
humo, from beyond the tomb." By then he could add, with a sigh
of audible relief, that though he was sure Berryman had gone over
the edge, the imaginative descent into hell with its comically gro-
tesque return Lazarus-like to life, surrounded by the inevitable televi-
sion reporters and tax collectors, had in fact "resurrected" Berryman
once again.[16]

That was in February 1967, by which time Berryman had re-
turned to his drinking with a suicidal vengeance. In May the wildly
drunk, Irish-bearded poet flew into New York to receive an award
from the Academy of American Poets. But right after the ceremo-
nies, he was admitted to the French Hospital on Manhattan's West
Side, suffering from alcoholic toxicity. It was there that he was vis-
ited by Lowell and Meredith. What "a chaos and a ruin and a trial"
Berryman seemed, Lowell wrote Meredith afterwards. And yet un-
derneath it all the man was "in much better shape than anyone
dreamed, so that after three days in the hospital, all the shouting and
eccentricity had gone."

But, then, he'd seen Berryman like this before—on his visit to

Minneapolis in 1962, when Berryman had staggered through the halls of the University to teach, before collapsing and taking a cab back to Abbott Hospital. Somehow he had found the strength to resurrect himself once more, like some bright, disheveled phoenix. And so again at the French Hospital. "He's quite an actor," Lowell continued. "As soon as he has an unfamiliar audience he becomes three times as odd, then alone with him or with two or three friends, he becomes delightful." How did one deal with such behavior, he wondered. But then, he added, wasn't everyone—himself included—"waiting for a reckoning?"[17]

A month after visiting Berryman in the hospital, Lowell was in Castine, Maine, furiously writing the blank-verse sonnets that would make up *Notebook 1967–68*, followed by *Notebook*, followed in turn by *History* and *For Lizzie and Harriet*, each book rising from the dismembered remains of the earlier texts. Like Berryman's *Dream Songs*, the notebooks are extended, open-ended sequences whose distant precursors are the Elizabethan sonnet sequence once again—as with Berryman's Songs—modified and made contemporary. Like Pound's *Cantos* and Williams's *Paterson*, each has a fluid protagonist and incorporates both autobiography and the history of the tribe from its beginnings to the present. Obviously, the reservations Lowell had felt on reading the early Dream Songs had altogether disappeared by 1966, and he read Berryman's lengthy sequel—*His Toy, His Dream, His Rest*—on its publication in September 1968 with unmixed astonishment and admiration. At once he wrote Berryman to compare his own just-finished *Notebook 1967–68* with Berryman's now-completed epic, remarking especially how Berryman had incorporated so many different elements into the Songs: history, "learning, thought, personality."[18]

But even after publication, both Berryman and Lowell were still working on the long poems each had thought he'd finished, and they wrote each other in undisguised triumph and glee about their respective obsessions. Berryman was still writing new Songs and thinking of adding them to the published volume as an appendix and Lowell was adding new sonnets by the hundreds and revising nearly all his old ones. In 1969 Lowell published a new and much-expanded edition called, simply, *Notebook*, and then revised his revisions—often massively—over the next four years. When he wrote Berryman in September 1969 to congratulate him on the Dream Songs at last appearing under one cover, it was to emphasize their kinship: "I think anyone who cared for your book would for mine. Anyway, we're accomplished beyond jealousy. Without your book," he wrote, then enlarged what he meant by changing that to read, "without *you,* I would find writing more puzzling."[19]

The two men saw each other for the last time in mid-December of 1970, a year before Berryman's death. By then Lowell was separated from Hardwick and living with Caroline Blackwood in London and had returned to New York to see Hardwick and their daughter, Harriet, for the first time in nine months. For his part, Berryman had just completed a drunken reading tour of the Northeast, and the two men met at the Chelsea Hotel, where Berryman usually stayed when he was in New York. Between them, Lowell could not help feeling, lay the shadow of that other roaring boy, Dylan Thomas, who seventeen years before, in one of the rooms of the Chelsea, had lapsed into the coma from which he had never regained consciousness.

Lowell and Berryman sat over lunch at an empty cafeteria-bar near the hotel drinking, Lowell would later recall, until both were feeling "high without assurance." Towards the end of lunch, Lowell offhandedly asked Berryman when he would see him again, "meaning," Lowell explained, "in the next few days before I flew to England. John said, 'Cal, I was thinking through lunch that I'll never see you again.' I wondered how in the murk of our conversation I had hurt him, but he explained that his doctor had told him one more drunken binge would kill him."[20]

Two days after Christmas, Lowell wrote Berryman for what turned out to be the last time. He had just read Berryman's post-Dream Song volume, *Love & Fame,* and was stunned by the beauty and power of the "Eleven Addresses to the Lord." Thinking back to his own early, Catholic poems, Lowell could sense the "cunning" of Berryman's sequence, how it embodied the Corbière-like skeptic's point of view, while still sounding "like a Catholic prayer to a personal God." "It's one of the great poems of the age," he added, "a puzzle and triumph to anyone who wants to write a personal devotional poem." True, the first three sections of the book did seem "a little casual and shaggy," but what a closure. Then he added: "You write close to death—I mean in your imagination. Don't take it from your heart into life. Don't say we won't meet again."[21]

In early January, 1972, Berryman jumped from the Washington Avenue Bridge in Minneapolis to his death. By then Lowell was living in an eighteenth-century country house in Kent, England, with a new wife and a new son. There's a story—apocryphal, as it turns out—that Berryman left a suicide note for Lowell. It is supposed to have read, simply, "Your move, Cal." No one seems to know for sure how that story got started, though the finger is often pointed at Auden. But the truth is that Lowell was deeply affected by the news of his friend's death, more even than he let on.

A month after Berryman's death, Lowell wrote Frank Bidart that Marianne Moore had just died at the age of eighty-five. And yet, he noted, her death had made "little stir, unlike Berryman's—on whom each English week[ly] or arts page has a bad elegy." Berryman had been doomed, he understood now, at least since the time they'd taken that last meal together in New York. "Then it was drink, later he must have died from not drinking." Moore of course had been the more "inspired of the two" poets, he believed, but Berryman had done what few poets ever achieved in taking such enormous risks with himself. After so many years of agonizing apprenticeship, he added, Berryman had leapt "into himself in his last years bravely."[22]

In his memoir of Berryman, printed in the *New York Review of Books*—the same publication that had carried his assessment of the early Dream Songs—Lowell corrected what he had said eight years before. He knew that his own late style, with its unexpected turns, its fits and starts and anacoloutha, owed too much to Berryman to let his early assessment stand, for by 1972 Berryman had forever altered the poetic landscape. A style takes a lifetime to develop, and now that Berryman's arc was complete, Lowell could see where even the earlier jumps and fits had been tending, even if at times they seemed jammed and crowded to the point of confusion.

"Rattled by their mannerisms," Lowell could say now, he had misjudged Berryman's first seventy-seven Dream Songs. Later the Songs had become clearer and clearer until, finally, they had seemed "as direct as a prose journal, as readable as poetry can be." And yet, and yet. In the long run those first seventy-seven probably revealed the "clearest" Berryman, "almost John's whole truth." Once Lowell had taken Berryman's style "for forcing." But, he conceded, "no voice . . . or persona sticks in my ear as his. It is poignant, abrasive, anguished, humorous. A voice on the page, identified as my friend's on the telephone, though lost now to mimicry. We should hear him read aloud. It is we who are labored and private, when he is smiling."[23]

In the last year of his own life, Lowell came across Berryman's real suicide note, printed now in *Henry's Fate*. The note, Lowell could see, was also Berryman's last Dream Song. Weirdly, it was also Berryman's last comic leap, even at the end mocking itself with its final "catlike flight / from home and classes— / to leap from the bridge." And yet, in spite of the crushing impact of that death, Lowell could still take comfort from his friend's spirit, catching himself praying "*to not for*" his friend, thinking of Berryman and smiling as he himself drifted off to sleep.[24]

Smiling. It was what Lowell had noticed about himself as well in his obituary piece for Berryman. "I somehow smile," he wrote there, "though a bit crookedly, when I think of John's whole life, and even of the icy leap from the bridge to the hard ground. He was springy to the end, and on his feet."[25]

Springy even at the end, though it is usually beginnings one thinks of with spring. In the weeks following Berryman's death, Lowell was invited to come up to London for a BBC program remembering his friend. The focus of the evening was the BBC interview between a very drunken Berryman and the critic, A. Alvarez. It had been shot five years earlier in Dublin, when the Berrymans were living in Ballsbridge, and filmed half in Berryman's rented house, and half in Berryman's study, which also served as the local pub.

"John, close-up, just off drunkenness," Lowell wrote Elizabeth Hardwick in March 1972, misreading Berryman's drunken brilliance for a kind of manic sobriety. There was Berryman, larger than life, in dramatic white and black, mad beard wagging. Like Henry, Berryman was "mannered, booming, like an old fashioned star professor. His worst." And then once again he was thinking back twenty-five years to those impossibly innocent days along the Damariscotta River in high summer, when he and Berryman had discoursed happily on the stark, crabbed syntax of *A Winter's Tale,* when Berryman was still his own Scholar Gypsy, a brilliant presence amid the whispering trees and lakes. "I think of the young, beardless man," he wrote now, "simple, brilliant, the enthusiast . . . buried somewhere with the older."[26]

NOTES

1. Berryman frequently dates his poetry manuscripts down to the hour. The original manuscript for Dream Song 177 is one of those so dated, as if Berryman had left a clue as to the poem's personal significance (JB Papers). See also PM, 404–9. As for the unfortunate misprints in Lowell's review, including turning Dream Song 29 into prose, the *New York Review of Books* printed a "correction" in the following issue. Lowell's review, called "The Poetry of John Berryman," appeared in the *New York Review of Books* for 28 May 1964, 2–3. The correction appeared in the issue for 11 June. See "John Berryman," in Robert Lowell, *Collected Prose,* ed. Robert Giroux (New York: Farrar, Straus and Giroux, 1987), 104–18.

2. A. Alvarez, *The New Poetry* (London: Penguin Books, 1962). When, three years later, he expanded his anthology. Alvarez included two more American poets: Sylvia Plath and Anne Sexton.

3. Robert Lowell to Randall Jarrell, 11 May 1964, Henry W. and Albert A. Berg Collection, New York Public Library.

4. Lowell to Adrienne Rich, 3 June 1964, in the Schlesinger Library at Radcliffe College. Cf. also Berryman's letter to Rich, quoted in PM, 408, thanking her "for such insight, sensitivity & generosity that you make me wonder." The review, he noted pointedly, was in fact "the most remarkable American verse-review . . . since Jarrell's study of *Lord Weary's Castle.*" The implication here seems to have been that Lowell had missed the chance to do for him what Jarrell had effected for Lowell nearly twenty years before.

5. Lowell to William Meredith, October 1964, Berg Collection.

6. For a fuller account of the Berrymans' stay with the Lowells at Damariscotta Mills, see PM, 175–77. For an extended firsthand account of that stay, see chapter 6 of Eileen Simpson's *Poets in Their Youth: A Memoir* (New York: Random House, 1982), 115–46.

7. Lowell to Peter Taylor, 18 February 1948. Quoted in Ian Hamilton, *Robert Lowell: A Biography* (New York: Random House, 1982), 130.

8. Lowell to John Berryman, 19 September 1959, JB Papers.

9. Lowell to William Meredith, summer 1976, Berg Collection.

10. Lowell to Berryman, fall 1948, JB Papers. Cf. PM, 212 ff. As for misnaming books, Berryman himself does not escape blame. In the same letter asking Lowell if he'd ever received *The Dispossessed,* he added, "Best to the Kavanaughs of the Mills." Berryman to Lowell, 28 August 1948, Lowell Collection, the Houghton Library, Harvard.

11. Lowell to Berryman, spring 1959, JB Papers.

12. Lowell to Elizabeth Bishop, 14 April 1962, Bishop Collection, Vassar College. Part of this letter is quoted in David Kalstone's *Becoming a Poet: Elizabeth Bishop with Marianne Moore and Robert Lowell* (New York: Farrar, Straus and Giroux, 1989), 223 ff. Bishop confessed to Lowell that she too found herself "pretty much at sea about that book—some pages I find wonderful, some baffle me completely. I am sure he is saying *something* important—perhaps sometimes

too personally? I also feel he's next-best to you" (Bishop to Lowell, 1 October 1964, quoted in Kalstone, *Becoming a Poet,* 224.)

13. Lowell to Berryman, 10 March 1966, JB Papers.

14. Lowell to Berryman, 5 November 1966, JB Papers.

15. Lowell to Phillip Booth, 10 October 1966, quoted in Hamilton, *Robert Lowell,* 351.

16. Lowell to Bishop, February 1967, Bishop Collection.

17. Lowell to Meredith, June 1967, Berg Collection.

18. Lowell to Berryman, September 1968, JB Papers.

19. Lowell to Berryman, September 1969, JB Papers.

20. Lowell, "John Berryman," 116.

21. Lowell to Berryman, 27 December 1970, JB Papers.

22. Lowell to Frank Bidart, February 1972, Lowell Collection.

23. Lowell, "John Berryman," 115–16.

24. Lowell, "For John Berryman," *Day By Day* (New York: Farrar, Straus and Giroux, 1977), 27–28.

25. Lowell, "John Berryman," 115.

26. Lowell to Elizabeth Hardwick, 19 March 1972, Harry Ransom Research Center, University of Texas at Austin.

Part 2
Berryman's Development as a Writer

Charles Thornbury

A Reckoning with Ghostly Voices (1935–36)

For more than three decades, John Berryman sounded out the intricacies of human personality. One by one his assorted characters take the stage: the poet and the boy in "The Ball Poem"; the nine characters in "The Nervous Songs"; the twentieth-century poet and Anne Bradstreet; Henry and his unnamed friend in *The Dream Songs;* and the personality of the poet in *Love & Fame.* He said, willfully misreading T. S. Eliot, that he strongly disagreed with "Eliot's line" on the impersonality of the poet: "It seems to me on the contrary that poetry comes out of personality."[1] No other poet in the generation after Eliot took up the cause of the personality—of the poet or of the creation of character—as Berryman did. Now, seeing the whole of his poetry, we encounter something more: he viewed character and self as discontinuous. Far from being consistent and unified, his characters are none other than who he or she is perceived to be, "is," at a particular moment. "How much change is compatible with a continuous identity?" Berryman noted as he was writing his autobiographical sonnets in 1947.[2] The answer was quite a lot. "I am less impressed than I used to be," he wrote nearly twenty years later, "by the universal notion of a continuity of individual personality" ("One Answer to a Question: Changes," *FP,* 323).

Apart from matters of the discontinuous personality, the individual voice in poetry—the insistent dramatic mode it calls for and the ambiguous presence of the poet—was, according to Berryman himself, the most important discovery he made in his development as a young poet. ("One Answer to a Question: Changes," *FP,* 323–31). "Her & It," the opening poem of *Love & Fame* (1970), seemed to him emblematic of his "obsession" since "The Ball Poem" (1942): "the dissolving of one personality into another without relinquishing the original" (*CP*, 291). His published poetry suggests that his interest in personality dates from "The Nervous Songs" and *Homage to Mistress Bradstreet*—"Narrative!" he said of *Homage*, "let's have narrative, and at least one dominant personality" (*FP*, 327)—but in his earliest writing in the mid-1930s, the enigma of the creation of personality engaged him. During his last year at Columbia College and his first term at Clare College, Cambridge, his thinking about the creation of personality in a dramatic mode framed the subject, spirit, and temper of his later views. And it was his first attempt at writing a play, *The Architect,* the day after Christmas in 1936 in Paris, that instructed his later notions of voice and the discontinuous self.

Berryman spoke of himself as having a double nature and a seriously bifurcated personality, but his view of character in poetry and drama—and I believe his understanding on this point more accurately explains the man himself—was not consistently binary as though one Janus face warred against the other. He perceived character as being neither logically nor psychologically accounted for in the sense that the individual personality is neither linear nor cast; one simply is at a point in time. One has a history to be sure, but one's history may or may not account for who one (or a character) is or how he or she acts at any given moment. When Berryman attempted an autobiography in 1962, he raised an essential question about the impossibility of knowing and portraying a continuous character: "Who knows himself as he is, much less as he was?" "What then," he continues, "am I doing at the typewriter? Perhaps I may find out if I go on."[3] He valued the going on as much as the finding out, perhaps more, for one was certain to move on—having to move on, willfully moving on—in a world of change. He believed this sense of movement and slippage is manifest in human experience which the natural world confirms daily: "The sense of change, suns gone up and come down," he wrote in 1939, "Whirls in my tired head, and it will abide" ("At Chinese Checkers," *CP*, 29). Change may be willed (or is it that change is disclosed in the will?). Berryman said he did not believe Yeats's pronouncement "A man's mind at twenty-one contains all the truths that he will ever find," because it does not allow for "the self-transformations that many men active emotionally and intellectually achieve during their thirties" ("The Case of Ring Lardner,"

FP, 213). Even death, he said in the last year of his life, is a discontinuous moving on: "Someone is changed, simply, into someone else" (FP, ix).

In his own experience, Berryman believed the death of his father—John Allyn Smith, who was found shot to death, ruled a suicide, on 26 June 1926 when Berryman was eleven—profoundly informed and proclaimed discontinuity. His death did not account for discontinuity; grievous and shocking, his death confirmed it. "In torn images," Berryman wrote twelve years after his father's death, "I trace"

> The inexhaustible ability of a man
> Loved once, long lost, still to prevent my peace,
> Still to suggest my dreams and starve horizon.
> Childhood speaks to me in an austere face.
>   ("World's Fair," CP, 24)

His childhood, threatened by extinction and distinguishable from the child he actually was, speaks to him as other. "The fox-like child I was or assume I was / I lose," he wrote a year later, "the abstract remember only"; he remembers only signs of the actual setting—"lightness," "the passion for running," and "all my terror" ("At Chinese Checkers," CP, 28). He remembers emotionally and fiercely. Although, as Henry says, he wished to "kill" what his father began (DS, 235), the effect upon the young boy was a "splitting" of his "manward chances, to his shame" (DS, 43). His childhood was dispossessed before he possessed it. He felt afflicted by a "disappearance of continuity & love," and "a sense of total LOSS" (DS, 101). Throughout the Dream Songs, Henry vacillates between avenging his lost childhood (as in DS, 143) and forgiving his father (as in DS, 145), but during the eleven years of his songs, Henry discovers as he moves on that his contradictory actions and feelings are momentary. His actions and feelings simply are what they are at any moment in time, and the memory of his loss calls for a description of its effect rather than an explanation of its cause. Henry at another time imagines himself at his father's grave, and in a harrowing moment of vengeance, insight, and renewal, he digs down, axes open the casket, raises the ax a last time, and kills his bad start (DS, 384).[4] But the pistol blast had tethered Berryman to his father's soul for life, and he never laid his father to rest. Almost a year to the day before Berryman leapt to his death, he spoke of "a chatter of ghosts": "We're running out / of time & fathers, sore, artless about it" ("Tampa Stomp," *CP*, 247–48).

The loss was broad and its nuances complex in both his life and poetry. The expectation of closure was never this theme or temperament, and his passion for ritual and form was equaled by his passion for violating them. The ghostly figure of his dead father gave notice to Berryman's imagination when he first started writing poetry seriously in late 1935 and 1936, the tenth anniversary of his father's death. Berryman would discover, some twenty-four years after his first attempt at writing poetry, that his father's suicide decisively influenced his becoming a poet: "I suppose my father's suicide made a poet of me, no?" Berryman wrote in 1958.[5] Certainly imagination, talent, and a love for the sound and feel of words made him a poet as well, but he was persuaded that his father's suicide authored passion, will, and drive in him.

How frequently Berryman's speakers stand over a grave to summon a dead figure: in *Homage* the twentieth-century poet summons "from the centuries" "out of maize & air" the body of America's first poet (*Homage to Mistress Bradstreet, CP,* 133); in two of the concluding Dream Songs the ghostly dancer dances Henry away (*DS,* 382), and he stands above his father's grave "with rage" (*DS,* 384); in "Beethoven Triumphant," one of Berryman's last poems: "They said you died. . . . It's a lie! You're all over my wall! / You march and chant around here!" (*CP,* 242). Clearly Berryman had recast his own need to recover his voiceless and unfulfilled father into poems that stand quite apart from that need.[6] But it took him more than a decade to transfigure imaginatively—not simply sublimate or transfer—the figure of his father in his poetry. Played out in several contexts over a number of years, his personal urgency embraces the larger theme of the son's search for himself through the father.[7] The habit of mind and the situation that fascinated him most takes the form of an unresolved ritual, similar to Berryman's description of the dramatic construction of *Homage to Mistress Bradstreet:* the exordium by the poet—the invocation of a lost figure, usually a ghost; then the poet's voice merges with the figure and "allows" him or her to speak; the "new" character, now a living presence and merged with the speaker, undertakes or undergoes several trials or conflicts with the hope of overcoming them—he or she rebels against society, its values, the environment, the body, God; the drama ends with a coda in which the recovered figure is laid to rest but may still be omnipresent— "nobody is ever missing," as Henry says (*DS,* 29).[8]

While he desired to recover and forgive his father, and while personality and character in general were his subjects, as a young poet he learned most about them in resisting and claiming his dead father. Berryman seemed to work in the margins of the poems he published about his father in 1936. His laconic voice—circumspect, prophetic, world-weary, and disembodied—resists naming his subject and admitting his own feelings. It is also a voice that seeks certainty, purification, and redemption: "the words here," Berryman wrote in 1937, "are / At work upon salvation" ("Caravan," *CP,* 15). The salvation he sought in 1936 he saw in Yeats's example in which past experience is expiated, removed, and made independent through form, masks, and craft. But Berryman was also exhilarated by *words,* perhaps more than the independent experience they evoked. Henry Vaughan's "continual marvelous energy from line to line"; Shakespeare's "active continual joy" in language;[9] Blake's "splendid original poetic power"; and a line from Donne like "Hither with christal vyals lovers come," Berryman said, "lifts a tower": "I want to get down and bite a large piece from the poker when I see that."[10] But how to bring together his passion for words and his emotions surrounding his father? In his unpublished poems about his father in 1935 and 1936, he is caught between what he should or should not reveal. His dilemma is how to allow his father to be who he was (thus a created character expressing and being himself) and, at the same time, how to express his unresolved memory of his vanished father. The expressive personality, how the writer responds to a character, calls for tactics and a point of view quite different from the personality as subject; to understand the difference between the two meant the difference between lamenting the loss of his father and creating a relationship with him.

As an unfledged writer, he was uncertain as to whether to grieve his loss publicly or privately. Emotionally, Berryman needed to overcome the loss of his father and to displace the powerful example of his suicide (as he did by seeking out surrogate fathers like Mark Van Doren, whose example and encouragement inspired him to be a poet). At times the ghostly father seemed so much a nightmare-

reality that he "hounded" his son and "Intertangled all—choking,
groping bodies" ("Matins," *CP*, 226).[11] Berryman and his alter egos
seem possessed by the fear of some ghost; they, like Henry, often
"reckon up" ghosts in the dawn (*DS*, 29). *Reckon* is the precarious
and pivotal word, for he came to reckon with ghosts in several repre-
sentations: he counted them up; he brooded upon them; he relied
upon them; he settled accounts with them.

His air was "flung with souls which will not stop / and among
them hangs a soul that has not died / and refuses to come home"
(*DS*, 127). In Berryman's poetry the presence of the father's ghost
was required and relied upon, at once enacting a personal urgency
and satisfying the dramatic demands of character interacting with
character—or the poet, also a character. The actual experience of his
father's death—what he felt at the time—quickly became his emo-
tional memory of it. Berryman's personal need to recover (and, at
times, join) his father persuaded him to create not only his father's
voice and speech but also to *become* him. He must speak for his
father (or imagined subject); he must create a dialogue between
them; he must speak for himself and his father (or imagined sub-
ject). He must, in short, create himself in relationship with his
absent father, thus his attraction to a dramatic mode that evokes the
feeling of lived experience.

Any autobiographical account of the character/self is paradoxi-
cally continuous and discontinuous, continuous in the persistence
of a particular emotion and discontinuous in that one writes,
later, "impressions, structures, tales." "It's not my life," Berry-
man said in 1970, "That's occluded and lost" ("Message," *CP*,
201). As Joseph Wood Krutch observes of Pirandello's view of
character and self, Berryman's question is "not so much psychologi-
cal as it is metaphysical"—that is, not so much a question of
whether or not the character/self is unified or continuous, but
rather a question of the nature of the way one views reality.[12] The
memory of reality is "occluded," reshaped as impressions, struc-
tures, tales that are remembered but never again experienced as they
were. The character/self, it follows, is that which we perceive him
or her to be at a particular moment in time. "What . . . can a 'self'
be," Krutch suggests, "except what it is being from moment to
moment?"[13]

Superstructure Skill and the Rumored Heart

From the fall of 1935 through the summer of 1936, the period of testing his resolve to become a poet, Berryman "thought much" about his father's death. When he visited friends' homes, he recalled later, "with fathers /universal & intact," he thought of "perforated daddy, / daddy boxed in & let down with strong straps" ("Freshman Blues," *CP,* 173). He pored over the lives and works of poets and dramatists, wrote poems about them, and, in the process, discovered what was to become a familiar script of summoning the presence, almost simultaneously, of dead heroes and his father. At age twenty-one, in the spring of 1936, his father's suicide was his deepest secret, and he almost stoically subdued his grief and shame in the superstructure of symbolical poems. He aimed at a sort of Yeatsian art that simultaneously kept his secret and revealed it, as he suggested in the opening stanza of "To an Artist Beginning Her Work," written 17 April 1936:

> Show but the part that will
>   Prepare another part,
> The superstructure skill
>   Infers, the rumored heart
> That never can be known
> And must be counted on.[14]

While he affirms the "superstructure skill" that separates personal and public concerns, at some level he must rely upon the heart. The superstructure skill of art unifies experience, gives it an aesthetic and independent existence, but, as though he would guard against discontinuity, he is anchored to the paradox of the known and unknown heart.

Four years earlier, as he anticipated his first year in college, Berryman was concerned about writing in a more personal and passionate way. After he discussed his "rather cold and calculating" prose style with one of the English masters at South Kent School, he resolved to "get away from this impersonality" in his writing.[15] In risky, personal matters, he feared he might reveal himself too much. In his third year at Columbia, the editor of the *Columbia Review* persuaded him to submit two poems, one of which was published.[16] At first he refused because, he wrote to his friend Milt Halliday, "the *Review* prints so much shit," but, he added, "I'm glad enough now, since both of the poems are sincere, as skillful as I can make them, and sufficiently impersonal so that they won't bother me being read."[17] At times the separation of the private and public self gave him a sense of personal strength and control. In February 1936, he wrote to Halliday that Jean Bennett, to whom "To An Artist" was addressed, was in love with him: "She hadn't a chance, my record and position in the college being what it now is—I am extremely well known, incredibly, and even when disliked, respected. My double reputation renders me fascinating, of course—you know, rake and genius, that sort of thing . . shit, obviously, but it works as though it had validity" (23 February 1936).

The separation of the private and public self seemed less important in his relationships with some friends. "It's perfectly all right, of course, your telling Jean [Bennett] about my childhood," Berryman wrote to his mother in late December 1936, "but from this moment I wish, Mum, you'd give no information whatever about me to *anyone* (outside the family), Mark [Van Doren] & Halliday only excepted." "I am really absurd on the point," he added, "I simply *will not* have anything known about me if it can be helped (27 December 1936). "It's curious," he wrote to his mother less than two weeks later, "I want in general so little known about me, [but] I am passionately anxious that a few friends know as much as possible" (7 January 1937). He was also considering separating his "formal literary 'personality'": "I've practically decided," he wrote to his mother, "to use simply JOHN BERRYMAN for all verse or dramatic publications, and J. A. M. BERRYMAN for everything else" (27 October 1936).

All the while, his father's ghost had been brooding in the margins of his first attempts at writing poetry. Although he had written poems for his family's entertainment as early as 1932, the earliest extant poems—four sonnets to his mother and a villanelle on death two months later—were written in 1934.[18] The sonnets for his mother's birthday on 8 July speak in the third person of the love of a mother for her son: the first praises her unselfish devotion to her son, but she acknowledges "his own will, his own life path"; the second praises her tenacity, her sense of purpose, and her pride "In the hard-won center stretch of an uphill road"; the third praises her physical beauty as a sign of her inward virtues; and the fourth praises her wit and "verbal brilliance."[19] He was distressed over his father's failures (his suicide and his losing his position as a banker in 1925), which his mother subtly and repeatedly made him aware of. "Mother," he wrote in his diary in late December 1931, "gave me a long talk about a trait I've inherited from Dad."[20] He was engaged in an ongoing battle with his mother—at first repressed, later in outbursts—because her fierce pride and possessiveness forced him to choose between his feelings for his father, ambiguous as they might have been, and his loyalty to her.[21] The presence of his father is suggested in the second sonnet: "She found, too, how the winds of men are cast." (The image of the fateful winds would reappear in reference to his father nearly two years later: "The complicated catastrophe of this man / Came when winds crossed, with darkness at the centre.")[22] Berryman wrote "Villanelle: 1934" nearly two months after the sonnets.[23] While the voice speaks impersonally, muffled in the villanelle form, his father paces underground. The resolute repetition of "I thread ethereal paths alone" and the concluding stanza give quite a different image of the independent "lifepath" he wrote for his mother:

In this harsh dark a never-known
And forgotten doom is sped,
Silent as Death and sere as bone . . .
I thread ethereal paths alone!

The silence of death and the silence of the dead father continued to beckon in his poetry. In the spring of 1936, several months before he wrote "To an Artist Beginning Her Work," he published "Trophy," a short poem that obliquely and ambiguously refers to his father. Perhaps he was anticipating his father's birthday on 22 March, the second day of spring, for he took pleasure, as he did throughout his life, in writing poems for his family and friends' birthdays. (His father's birthday would also mark the beginning and completion of his writing *Homage,* 22 March 1948 and 22 March 1953). The unidentified speaker says at the outset that the winter night is "apt to awaken / Ambiguous memory" of "a man who is gone."[24] The man has been absent, rather than dead, for "nine years of peace constructing calm." It had been nine years since Berryman's father's death (in June he would write another poem on the tenth anniversary), but the reference is unclear as to whether the speaker or the man experienced the calm, perhaps both did. In the concluding stanza, the calm is disrupted; the man

> Throws up a hand
> Where a bird sings in
> An ash in spring, a shadow in the sun.

In throwing up a hand—like Hamlet's father's ghost, does he beckon or is he coming to aid his son?—the obscure father enters the scene, set in the spring. The singing bird, rising like the phoenix from his ashes, is ambiguously and simultaneously emblematic of the man (father) and the speaker (poet). The bird is a "shadow/shade" in the "sun/son"; the man is as much a double of the speaker as the speaker is of the man. Like the merging of the speaker and the boy in "The Ball Poem"—and later the merging of the voice of the poet and the voice of his subject in *Homage* and *The Dream Songs*—the man and the speaker are ambiguously one.[25]

The title, "Trophy," portends a memento, achievement, or legacy, something taken from an enemy and kept as a memorial of a victory. Seen as more of legacy than a victory, the singing bird suggests the poet-singer whose song is the poem itself, but, perhaps it is a triumph after all in Berryman's projection of his absent father's response to his son. In that sense, the song at once conjures up the soul (suggested in the bird image) and the physical presence of his dead father ("Throws up a hand" in response to the seasonal spring ritual). The *I* of the poem, so resistant to naming the man/father, strains to identify with his subject. In that sense, too, the poem is an achievement, for it is the first of Berryman's extant poems to present an imagined relationship with his dead father. As a legacy, "Trophy" signals the beginning of his ritualistic return to his father's grave in which and through which he attempts to rise out of his father's ashes.

All the while, Berryman was pondering the legacies of poets, his heroic, surrogate fathers. In the 1935 winter-spring issue of the *Columbia Review,* he published "Blake" and "Ars Poetica" (among his first published poems). He suggests that Blake's poetry can almost "distill in me a liquor like his," but he (Blake) cannot because "I am no vessel fit for fire." "Doubt is mine," the speaker concludes; he can write "no missle" like Blake's "Arrows of desire /

For the Lord." His doubt prevents closure to an infinite and omnipotent God the Father, which mirrors his emotional memory of his lost father and is linked with his loss of faith. His father's death, he wrote later, "blew out my most bright candle faith" ("Eleven Addresses to the Lord" #6, CP, 219). "Ars Poetica" speaks cryptically to Berryman's view of poetry at the time. Poetry may be many things—simple, concerned with love, complex; it may even "sharply swerve / Into perfection." But the opening links him with the idea of his presence in the poem: "I stumble strangely over my name," as indeed he had eight years before, and thereafter, in taking his stepfather's surname.[26]

"Elegy: Hart Crane," published in the 1935 summer-fall issue of the *Columbia Review,* is likewise crabbed and syntactically compressed, perhaps imitating Crane's style. But in it, Berryman draws upon the real and imagined experience of his father's death. He imagines Crane, who jumped from a ship in the Gulf of Mexico on 27 April 1932, "obscure in ocean." Similarly, Berryman associated his father's death with the sea. (His father was found shot to death in an apartment building two hundred yards from the Florida Gulf at Clearwater Beach.) The speaker meditates upon the poet dead at sea,[27] and the elegy ends:

> Cantlets of speech: beyond the reach of light
> Beyond all architecture, the last ledge,
> He is obscure in ocean in the night—
> Monstrous and still, brooding above the bridge.[28]

Berryman's saw his father, too, as "obscure in ocean." In 1954, as he analyzed his dreams, he noted his father's "Death *by* water."[29] His father had threatened, a day or so before his death (according to Berryman's mother), to swim with one of his two sons out to sea and not to return. How frequently Berryman imaginatively returned in his poetry to something lost in the sea, from the early "The Ball Poem" (the boy and the poet seek the ball lost in the harbor) to the late Dream Song "Henry's Understanding" in which Henry imagines himself descending a bluff by the sea and "into the terrible water" and walking "forever / under it" ("Henry's Understanding," CP, 256). In 1946, Berryman made the connection between himself, his father, and the sea more explicit:

My father still in my dreams uneasy I see
Still tramping the dark beach and down at me
Strangely looking. O my father! rest,
For if you cannot rest
I must rejoin you by the shameful sea.[30]

His references to death and water were "Corridors deep, near water,"
and there, as though he were looking into his father's grave, "The
surgeon looks over the parapet / & looks straight down in the water"
("In & Out," *CP,* 182). In "Elegy: Hart Crane" the father, the poet,
and the poetry begin to coalesce; in this early phase of his writing,
Berryman's imagination seems most alive in brooding over the ghost
of the lost poet.

Berryman would write elegies on a number of contemporary
poets later, but "Note on E. A. Robinson" was his first. Written
shortly after Robinson died on 4 April 1935, he "comments" on
Robinson's legacy of the cool and unemotional voice:

He was forever walking
A little north
To watch the bare words stalking
Stiffly forth,
Frozen as they went
And flawless of heart within, without comment.[31]

Like Robinson "forever walking / A little north," Berryman associ-
ated his father with the north, where he was born in South Stillwater,
Minnesota. The connection is more transparently seen in *The Dream
Songs,* where the father's ghost stalks in the cold north (Berryman
was living in Minneapolis, about forty miles west of South Stillwa-
ter—now Bayport—when he wrote most of the Dream Songs). At
sixteen below zero, Henry says, "Icy dungeons... / have much to
mention to you"; there he contemplates forgiveness of his father:
"Pardon was the only word, in ferocious cold" (*DS,* 108).[32]

Privately Berryman edged closer to his father's grave. On 15
June, about a week after his graduation from Columbia, he began to
explore a passage to his father, perhaps anticipating the tenth anniver-
sary of his death. For the first time, his speaker clearly identifies a
relationship with his subject and imagines the grave of his father:

> Perhaps a cottonwood leans to the wind
> Above my father's grave,
> Sustaining the pliant, thin tradition of those
> Who were as the wind was lonely and obedient.[33]

Unable to be present at the grave (compare the later Dream Song 384, where Henry imagines digging down into his father's grave), his emotion is transferred to the cottonwood tree, rooted in the grave, that bends to the wind. The wind is emblematic of those who, in the second stanza, "set their feet toward no destination / That could not be revised, if the wind would" (compare Dream Song 282, "the wind blows hard from our past into our future / and we are that wind"). Like the bird singing out of its ashes in spring, these uncertain ones "let the season regulate" their destiny. The concluding third stanza, like Robinson's bare words without comment, shifts from "my father" to the more removed "this man":

> The complicated catastrophe of this man
> Came when winds crossed, with darkness at the centre;
> Allegiance frayed then, tension fell away
> And the insane arms were ready for the ground.

Berryman was finding his imaginative direction in seeking out his father's ghost, but he was neither ready to acknowledge his grief nor to go public with explicit references to his father's death.

"Ritual at Arlington," an unpublished long poem of 359 lines written in July 1936 for a *Southern Review* poetry contest (Allen Tate and Mark Van Doren were the judges), was Berryman's most sustained poetic exploration of his passage to his father.[34] The poem owes something to Tate's "Ode to the Confederate Dead," but he attempted to make the experience real for himself in visiting Arlington in late July and marking a map of the grave sites as he walked among them. As the speaker meditates upon the dead soldiers at Arlington, he is periodically drawn to a grave elsewhere. The speaker does not reveal that it is the grave where Berryman's father is buried in Holdenville, Oklahoma. As the speaker broods over the "authoritative dead" soldiers in a rough blank verse, the force of another ghost speaks of "a distant grave / At Holdenville" in short, unpunctuated lines of two and three beats:

> the wind speaks
> In a cottonwood
> Where no man has spoken
> Since that time.

The alternation of two different verse forms suggest two voices, the voice of the poet grieving over "a distant grave / At Holdenville" and the voice of prophecy speaking sagely about the silence of the dead (as in "Villanelle: 1934"). At the outset, the speaker has declared that he will conceal his anguish and "return only / With the wind to grieve." The wind is no longer an emblem of destiny as in the cottonwood leaning to the wind above his father's grave, but the voice of a more personal fate. While both voices are meant to be impersonal, like those of Robinson's frozen words, Berryman was moving towards the creation of separate voices in a poem, voices that are impelled by the voiceless memory of his father. Once he imagined himself standing over his father's grave, he began to engage in a dialogue with him.

The dead at Arlington—and, implied, the grave in Holdenville—are "sustained / By liturgy," a liturgy that "they impose with blind / Incontestable severity on their sons." Although "no man has spoken / Since that time," these "forgotten members of the ritual" are the "authors of our dismay." The dead speak:

> Listen! can you hear
> Their tenuous invective, the bones' compelled
> Restraint in the ground?

The dead are "authors," and throughout the poem the speaker attempts to read and hear the word signs: "History is *written* / In tombs"; the dead leave "*signatures* of action"; "The sharp silhouette of a man's face / Is inimitable *idiom*"; a "Random boulder obliterates the *text* / And tenor" of a dead man's face; the dead's tongues are "a *document*" (italics added). Similarly, Berryman would say of his father in Dream Song 145, "I cannot *read* that wretched mind, so strong / & so undone" (italics added).

It is but a short step from "reading" experience and "reading" a text, or at least it was in Berryman's reading. As he intensely studied poetry and drama at Clare College in 1936 and 1937, he listened, literally, for the ghosts to speak, as in another poem on Blake written on 29 November 1937. The previous day, he had noted in his diary: "Blake born 180 years ago today—where now?" The next day he replied in a poem, "Where now he is I do not know":

> But know that if unfriendly doom
> Confine him ashes in a place
> Where is no living or dead face
> He has a place within this room.[35]

Berryman's portrayal of the dead in "Ritual at Arlington" as "sustained / By liturgy" owes something to W. B. Yeats, his most important poet father figure at the time. The preceding spring (1936) in a review of Yeats's *Collected Plays,* he defined ritual as "signify[ing] a code or form of ceremonies, the formal character imposed on any experience as it is given objective existence by the imagination working in craft" ("The Ritual of W. B. Yeats," *FP,* 248). That poetry plays out private experience in a public way perhaps owes something to Eliot's notion of the objective correlative; in any event, Berryman was attempting to impose a formal character upon his experience. Form and ritual, he was learning, may order experience so that it is at once personally vital and publicly encoded, the former satisfying his need for enacting and veiling his private ritual and the latter keeping with the frozen words of an impersonal poetry.

At Clare College, Cambridge, that fall the shades of writers seemed living presences to him; even the figure of Yeats, still living, appeared to him in a hallucination. On 21 October in "Nightmare, 1936," he was equally preoccupied with the ghosts of his ancestors who beckon him to a "contemplation of the intense" and an "unalterable place":

> those men the fathers of our eyes
> Have grown accustomed to the silence and
> The undifferentiated darkness there,
> Toward which all angers turn in their good time.[36]

Four days later, on his twenty-second birthday, he celebrated once again the impersonal order created by ritual:

This anniversary erects a pattern.
Angers and the small fears
Fall into place, endowments
Are justified in this impersonal order
Or so seem and the love and the long failure
Likewise are caught in the strict wheel and turn.[37]

The next day, still thinking about "angers and the small fears" and "the love and the long failure" (surely alluding to his father), he turned to his grandfathers in an untitled poem:

Now as always catastrophe and tumult
Of my grandfathers rises in my throat
Throbbing upon my tongue.[38]

Berryman does not name him, but he alludes to one grandfather in particular, his father's father, Jefferson Leonard Smith, who was a lumber foreman in the late nineteenth and early twentieth centuries in Minnesota. That grandfather, unlike his son above whose grave a cottonwood tree bends to the wind, was "sturdy as an ancient elm against / Whatever breed of wind / He knew." Berryman's other unnamed grandfather—his mother's father, Alvin Horton Little, who left Berryman's grandmother in the early 1900s—was "impetuous," and his "patience was a progeny of thunder." Both grandfathers are part of the "spectral company / of ancestors." The speaker is "shaken with shouts from [his] unburied past" as the specters

Leap from where they have lain
Embedded in the moral memory
And cry me to justify my birth and land.

The emotional force of these lines, as distinguished from the "moral memory" described in them, speaks of Berryman's charge to redeem something lost, perhaps "the love and long failure" of his birthday poem. Years later, in 1971, Berryman was asked, "Of what use do you think art is in the moral world?" He replied that he did not know about how feelings may affect conduct, but certain poems—on the death of a son, for example—may issue in feelings that are "refined,

and sort of exploded" by such a poem.[39] At age twenty-two, Berry-
man would have suggested that feelings greatly influence conduct.

In a letter to his mother the next day, 27 October, he was still
preoccupied with the rising of another spectral company, the heroic
figures of the wise, "white-haired men" through whom he might
justify his birth and land, and in whose passionate example was his
view of himself:

> I saw the white-haired men go one by one
> Up a great stair: the whiteness of the sun
> Showed crimson blood pounding beneath the hair.

These men exemplify, Berryman suggested in the letter, "the strict
majesty of ritual." During the week of his twenty-second birthday,
his fathers, grandfathers, and heroic poet figures ("Fathers of the
language I use," he would write the next spring)[40] were becoming
part of his dramatic imagination, an imagination that authenticated
his desire to relocate himself in another. He had yet to learn how to
portray his spectral company other than in alternating forms and a
single voice brooding upon them. He recognized the power of ritual
and the authority of language in a form, but how to bring the two
together without abstracting the individual voice? "Great plays *can*
be written," he wrote in the same letter; in drama he would discover
alternative ways of creating individual voices.

Drama at Its Simplest and Best Power

In late December 1936 in Paris, Berryman attempted to write *The
Architect,* his first play. He wrote to his mother, "I want to get a
strong play, and in doing it, to learn a hell of a lot" (27 December
1936). His attempt etched for him more clearly the questions he had
pondered during the past year: What subject to write about? What
form to use? What language or style? For what audience? To what
end and for what use? As Berryman studied plays between 1936 and
1938, he was greatly interested in how they were put together. "I've
been reading perfect reams of plays," he wrote to his mother, "in the
hopes of imbibing, so to speak, the business of dramatic construction
etc." (18 January 1937). But he was most interested in dramatists' use

of language. Shakespeare's language in a dramatic context was a standard: "nearly all pitch and accent of poetry is in Shakespeare somewhere, the body of language not revealing but creating passion" (6 April 1937). Language in both poetry and drama, he discerned, is fastened to and is expressive of the life of the writer, and it reveals, directly and indirectly, the writer's personality.[41] Although he did not complete *The Architect* (and most of the eight plays he attempted during the next twenty years), his failure as a dramatist was the fertile ground of the more successful direction he would take as a poet—a direction that broke with the 1930s New Critical mode of the impersonal poem, a direction that called into question the role of the poet in the poem, a direction in which the poet's personality shouldered more boldly into the poem, a direction that led to the dramatic mode and language of his poetry.

We have seen how Berryman's meditations upon his father's ghostly figure directed him towards a particular framework of ritual and drama: the invocation of the ghost calls up his presence; the speaker interacts with him; the scene ends with the ghost being laid to rest but still omnipresent. In his first poems, the speaker merges with the subject through imagery and symbol, and, later, in an implied dialogue of voices. We have seen, too, how the creation of character and voice, primarily through the ghosts of his father and father figures, was becoming central to his imagination. It seems inevitable that Berryman would turn to drama, for it would open up the possibility of creating individual voice and speech.

In the fall of 1936, shortly after taking up study at Clare College, Cambridge, Berryman began bracing his confidence to write a play. The day after his twenty-second birthday he wrote a prose prologue (what the play is about, he does not say), and at midnight he wrote to his mother. "Great plays *can* be written, and I'm positive—I must be positive for I hope so greatly, so intolerably—that I can write them" (27 October 1936). His resolve to write plays owes something to his taste for both popular and serious theater, which was greatly influenced by his mother's. (That he attempted to write *The Architect* at the end of 1936 owes something to her attempt to write a play the preceding summer.) He delighted in popular movies and musicals. Even during the time he was most absorbed in classical poetry and drama during his two years at Cambridge (he commented to his mother, "It's awfully silly, I think, ever to do anything but read

Shakespeare—particularly when we've only one lifetime" [6 February 1937]), he had "to confess a considerable pleasure" in seeing Pat O'Brien and Humphrey Bogart in *San Quentin*, "a tough hero film."[42]

When he was seventeen and in his last year at South Kent School in 1932, he was equally enthusiastic about serious theater and popular shows: "Dietrich's and Chevalier's pictures look good & of course I'll have to see Bing Crosby's picture," he wrote to his mother anticipating the summer vacation: "'Show Boat' should be wonderful.... Awfully glad you enjoyed 'The Wet Parade' and 'Crazy Girl.'"[43] Four weeks before, he had proudly reported to her that he was reading *The Stage,* a magazine on current theater: "very interesting photographs of scenes from plays," he said, "excellent critiques, etc.—it said that 'Mourning Becomes Electra' is sure to be the Pulitzer Prize-Winner" (1 May 1932). But the dramatic power of *The Emperor Jones* had impressed him more: "The gradual break-down of the veneer of civilization is grippingly portrayed. Perhaps it cannot be compared to 'Mourning Becomes Electra'..., but I enjoyed it more.... [T]he action is more vivid" (20 April 1932).

Berryman's preference for classical representations of character, form, and verse in drama was decidedly set by his senior year at Columbia. He had experimented with the dramatic and narrative possibilities of the sonnet. "To my knowledge, and Van Doren corroborates me," he wrote to Halliday in October 1934, "there are no single sonnets which even pretend to the narrative. The form in this use corresponds to a one-act play or the short-short story—and its action is necessarily limited, I think, to a single action." He went on to give an example of how, dramatically, he wished to bring together subjective and objective points of view: "The octet is a soliloquy of a condemned man, with his thoughts inter-parenthesed [*sic*] ... and the sestet is objective narration of his hanging."[44] He was discovering not only the friction between the expressive personality and the personality as subject but also the nature of his voice, abrupt shifts in style, voice, and point of view—"the impression of strain, torsion," he said in 1940 in his first public statement about the craft of poetry, "useful to the subject" ("A Note on Poetry," *CP,* 286).

Berryman later regarded himself "a clown, lazy to an African degree, frivolous and uncertain," as an undergraduate. There is something in Thomas Merton's view (Merton was a classmate) that he was "the most earnest-looking man on campus."[45] He was also "dead serious" about realism in drama. In February 1936, Berryman wrote to Halliday that he had argued hotly with some friends about the merits of Maxwell Anderson's *Winterset,* currently playing in New York:

> It really is a hell of a bad play—wretched as drama and unspeakable as poetic drama, confused, dull, cheap, overwritten and over-acted. I completely fail to see how anyone at all could make out any case for it; its popularity and acclaim I attribute to the fact that people leave their minds at home when they go to the theater, and read and see nothing but shit, so they have no standards of comparison. I have gone dead-serious, Halliday, but I am pretty fed up with the spurious and the superficial. (11 February 1936)

When *Winterset* won the first Drama Critics' Circle Award in April, Anderson said in his acceptance speech that he was "aware that *Winterset* is far from a perfect play. It's an experiment, an attempt to twist raw, modern reality to the shape and meaning of poetry."[46] Berryman was attempting the same kind of experiments himself in giving shape and meaning to his own experience. He too wanted to go beyond realism, to evoke, rather than mirror, lived experience. He wrote his mother from Paris, the day before he began writing *The Architect,* that he had seen *The Witch of Edmonton* "magnificently done" in London:

> It taught me that the Elizabethan aim was not character not consistency not persuasion, but *drama* at its simplest & best power. Also I think blank verse can still be used to great effect, that magic . . . is still available, and that the entire course of drama (comedy, which scarcely interests me, excepted) since the Restoration is absurdly misguided, save for Synge, O'Neill, Yeats, Dryden & a few others. Strength, terror are what count—get them how you will. But they can't be got by maundering, insipid realism. (25 December 1936)

Realism neither ignited intensity nor summoned the ritual of the personal urgency Berryman desired.

Berryman's interest in intensity and form were but aspects of the larger problem of the creation of character and personality. Shakespeare and W. B. Yeats were two very different models, but each, like Robinson, Crane, Donne, Blake, Vaughan, and his lost father, was the elusive and absent author. He learned, he said many years later, "an immense amount from Shakespeare": "How to be, or try to be, gorgeous. You know, lyric grandeur. But the main thing I learned from him is that you put people in action and see what happens."[47] Berryman actually learned firsthand about putting people in action and seeing what happens—thus his later view of the discontinuity of character—in attempting to write *The Architect*. Yeats the modern had addressed the problem of realism in his belief, Thomas Parkinson has observed, "in the essentially religious function of drama, and his attendant sense of theater as ritual"; Yeats's characters were, therefore, "evocation[s] of a sacred presence."[48] In 1936, Berryman responded in much the same way: "It is clear that Yeats has not been concerned," he wrote in a review of Yeats's *Collected Plays,* "as Shakespeare (we assume) was concerned, with the creation of recognizable and individual character. The people in his plays are typical or symbolic or mythical . . . or they are necessary figures to speak his lines in the interests of presentation and description. . . . They are, in fact, simple as a morality mask is simple" ("The Ritual of W. B. Yeats," *FP,* 245).

Berryman went on to suggest why Yeats wrote plays: "He wanted, first, to hear his poetry spoken, and spoken under the most emphatic conditions obtainable—those of the theater. . . . And he wanted . . . to dramatize his beliefs and doubts and preoccupations" (*FP,* 246). Perhaps he recognized in Yeats's drama his own disposition to dramatize his beliefs, doubts, and preoccupations—loss, death, abandonment, dispossession, fear, and betrayal—themes that would be central to his poetry. In Yeats's plays, Berryman had discovered two notions he had been investigating: first, Yeats's use of Japanese Noh plays, in which, in Parkinson's words, "the crises often came with the revelation that one of the characters was in fact a god or ghost" (perhaps the model for Berryman's experiments with the ghosts of soldiers and poets?), and second, that "by the use of the mask [Yeats] could present . . . remote, stylized, and supernatural reality."[49] Masks and rituals as evocations of reality interested Berryman most. In the fall of 1936, he recommended to Van Doren the film *Wife to Secretary* starring Clark Gable and Jean Harlow, and he observed that in the film "no definite characterization is attempted, the players can be considered as masks": "Even symbols (film symbols, I note, not verbal) are used to great effect; e.g. the couple Harlow sees when drinking alone at the table in Havana—purely sensual love, more love than lust because it produces the result of ritual—movements, gestures stylized." Ritual may also repress a character's emotion. The film fascinated Berryman in its "preventing, by household ceremonies, of the expression of grief." "The film's serious limitation," he added, "is a lack of proper speech—speech proper, in intensity and depth and range, to the action. . . . I begin to know what action can give to poetry" (27 October 1936). He felt speech in drama is a function of situation and action. Likewise, action and the act of speaking resonate in one another and create intensity and depth in character.

Berryman's effort to achieve an individual texture in his style and his ambivalence about the limits of consciously revealing himself are parts of the same question: What is the function of language in the creation of—perhaps even the revelation of—the personality of the poet? One answer at the time was that language in poetry is stylized, "unnatural" he would write to Van Doren, a sort of stylized verisimilitude. If the artist attempts to write objectively, he or she wars with "natural man." Rather than choose between the two, Berryman seemed to want the war itself in his drama and verse, a fight in the streets, in Keats's phrase, in which verisimilitude, perhaps even personal life, is most vividly and expressively portrayed. His aim, was "magnificent vitality through control." He had written the prologue to a play, he told Van Doren, "a five-page ironic speech in prose," but he could not get on with it because of his excitation in writing poems continually. He said he needed more self-discipline. Like the stylized characters of ritualistic drama, he wanted "a mask for my life, a discipline, a stylized order" (28 October 1936).

Much of the fall of 1936, Berryman was rethinking the function of language in a dramatic context. A dramatic situation calls for a patterning of language. Verisimilitude was not to be found in realism as much as in the alternations of tone and voice in poetic drama, as Anderson had not apparently done in *Winterset* and as Berryman realized he had not done in "Ritual at Arlington" (his "failure to secure emphasis," Robert Penn Warren had observed, "by alternation of intensity, relaxation, etc.).[50] What Berryman heard in his characters' language as he began writing *The Architect* was a "nervous, mechanical accent, giving way only infrequently to full passion."[51] A fragmented and minimal speech, he perceived, may heighten language without being either "poetic" or naturalistic; minimal speech may accommodate the poetic, slang, and speech rhythms, which became the distinctive inflections of his voices. In his critical theory, if not yet in practice, Berryman was discovering the possibilities of a vitality of language in drama, the interaction of several modes of language and form in which one might expect an interaction among minimal, "real," and theatrical kinds of speech. Some characters may "naturally" speak in a minimal, poetic language; others in a sort of prose. The result—the "magnificent vitality through control"—would be, as Berryman said of *Homage,* a form, a style, and a dramatic mode "at once flexible and grave, intense and quiet, able to deal with matter both high and low" (*FP,* 328).

On his way to Paris during the Christmas break in 1936, Berryman wrote to Halliday from London:

> I've just seen a hell of a good play beautifully done, Halliday, and it's confirmed my plans for us—plans I've been thinking about all fall and longer: You and I, my boy, are going to produce (by the mingled mangled might of our masterful minds) the best damn plays the western world has seen for three centuries. They're going to be unutterably tragic, because nothing exists in this hysterical time but tragedy, and when the stuff is too ghastly to do straight, we'll use irony—and they're going to be magnificent (22 December 1936).

Four days later (Saturday, the day after Christmas), lonely but greatly stimulated by being in Paris (to Halliday he remarked, "Paris, my boy, is not a city: it is a process" [2 January 1937]), just before noon he began writing *The Architect* in a "fury of excitement." His mind would "go like a race-course" during the next thirty hours.

"Joy, joy, I am marvelously ecstatic," he wrote to his mother at noon in what was to become one of two journal-letters to her that day and the next. The process, rather than the product, absorbed him most, and as he wrote *The Architect,* his interest in the interaction of styles and forms seemed almost like new discoveries. "I've been lying

in bed for half-hour," he said, "and suddenly scenes began to come
& I watched & planned and lo, a whole damned play is in shape in
my head and I've just written two short speeches for one of the
characters; it wants a lot of thought, but the outline & some detail &
the four main people are almost clear." After working several hours,
he wrote to his mother: "To hell with being 'contemporary', but I'm
going to keep [my play] from being 'pseudo-Elizabethan' if I can—
want a nervous, mechanical accent, giving way only infrequently to
full passion." He did not want to "pander" to his audience's taste for
"realism," and, he added: "The little I've written is verse but it is
notation for very important moments—there'll be a lot of prose. My
great difficulty will be . . . in keeping the general tempo & emphasis
down, in order to get the power when it's needed" (26 December
1936). The next day, after writing in a "valuable heat" for nearly
fifteen hours, he wanted the surcharge of different kinds of speech—
"contemporary cocktail inanity," "tight, formal, non-dramatic
verse," and "the free, large, general rhetoric of the Elis[abethan] &
Jacobean dramatists."[52]

Berryman was also learning to thrash happily about in the uncer-
tainty of knowing precisely the direction the play was taking (as he
would do later in writing the Dream Songs). He seemed to feel liber-
ated in a peopled world, and, like Pirandello's *Six Characters in
Search of an Author,* his characters seemed to have a life of their own:
"Curious," he wrote to his mother, "the situations, scenes, came
first (from nowhere), then people for them, then the scenes faded
and I'm already left mainly with the people, to do with as I will, or,
rather, *can*" (26 December 1936). He was discovering, too, that, un-
like writing the impersonal poem, writing a play "for other people"
gave him a sense of the "near sensibility" he needed in writing let-
ters.[53] As he had noted how Yeats seemed to profit from the disci-
pline of dramatic verse, Berryman realized more than ever "the mon-
strous ambiguity in all verse & *most* in dramatic verse" (26 Decem-
ber 1936).

After working on the play for nearly eight hours, Berryman's
limitations seemed to counterbalance his confidence; he reported to
his mother at 9:30 P.M. that he had finished a soliloquy and that it
seemed good, but it was "difficult to tell, because I must say the lines
aloud and I've never done any acting." He was writing in a roughed-
up blank verse, and although the meter was "terribly broken, [and]

the tempo slow," he felt he had "enough concentration & tension to justify using verse." By midnight he had the two scenes of act I plotted. He planned to observe the classical unities of time (5:30 P.M. to midnight), action (the protagonist's revenge), and place (New York City). When the heat of composition continued until 2:45 A.M., Berryman seemed at once elated and puzzled by the peopling of his play: "it's uncanny how all my people want to get together from time to time, and how everything helps in at least two ways" (26 December 1936).

Berryman had a sense of the play writing itself, as though he were an observer to the characters. Apart from mastering "dramatic poetry" and "the putting-together and sequencing," "all else invented itself marvelously," he wrote to his mother; "it is very exciting to watch things go, isn't it?" (26 December 1936). In the light of the next day, he began to think more about where he himself was in the creation of characters: "I am beginning to see a certain justice in the references to characters' being free agent[s]. . . . I see what even cheap novelists and poor actors are getting at when they say 'This Character I am creating or playing is *real* & makes his own destiny: I but fulfill it.'"[54] Like Keats's idea of the chameleon poet, a touchstone in Berryman's later notions of the ambiguous presence of the poet in the poem, he implies that he has no identity in the play, or, at least, no sense of his being present in the play. His characters and his main character "H.," he insisted, were not merely himself in disguise: "The people literally possess one, and since we've no idea where ideas come from, it seems crude, mechanical, to call them deliberate attributions." The heat of composition seemed to refine the near fury of his reading and seeing plays and movies during the previous three months. He was mainly concerned about the "strictly dramatic effect" of his play (27 December 1936)—"the Elizabethan aim was not character not consistency not persuasion, but *drama* at its simplest and best power" (25 October 1936). He believed that "H. himself is too damn clear—he wants controlling," and he wanted controlling because he was modeled on Berryman himself: "I ought to say at once," he protested to his mother, "that the play is not about me or anyone else I know, because certain persons & incidents remarkably resemble things in my biography; but no one is modelled except in incidentals, on any friend, and H. is most emphatically not me" (27 December 1936).

Berryman was protesting for good reason. Always a self-conscious writer, he needed his mother's approval and the authority of reasoned conclusions to buttress his confidence. But his mother as his audience suggests a further point: when one compares the two journal-letters to his mother with what he chooses *not* to tell her, his writing of the play amounts to a defiance. He did not tell his mother what he was writing in his notes: that "H.'s" father had been dead for ten years, the same as Berryman's father, and that "H.'s" father committed suicide "thru social hysteria," which was one of his mother's explanations for his father's suicide.[55] "H. seeks '*revenge*,'" Berryman wrote in his notes, for three things in his life: the loss of his father, the loss of his first love Jean, and the unfaithfulness of his wife Christine (sublimating perhaps Berryman's awareness of his own mother's infidelity). "H." feels trapped and exhibits "irresponsible fury" in his behavior.

And there was more he did not tell his mother. At one point in his planning, Berryman noted that Jean's father, "B." was H.'s friend, "as, Mark [Van Doren] to me" and that "H.'s father" was "roughly, J. A. S." (John Allyn Smith, Berryman's father). At another point, he noted that the protagonist "H." is like Hamlet and that the ghost of his father would appear to him several times. The previous February Berryman had written to Halliday that suicide "seems more and more to justify any system," the question being provoked in *The Red and the Black* and *Hamlet*. He especially wanted to discuss *Hamlet,* which he had read recently: "For the first time, I think I really know something about it. Read very carefully and ecstatically the Dover Wilson edition, which is wonderful. The problems of the play have been, I'm certain, overestimated."[56] Now the ghost of Hamlet's father would appear in his play, and the climax would be not so much an imperative to take revenge as an explanation of his death. The ghost would appear at a climactic moment in H.'s office and say to him:

> I studied what I could—for your mother
> I tried to be what I was not—a solid man,
> Resourceful, sound—
> I had no force, yet I was honest
> (And so again are you)
> Yet circumstances tired me, & I died.

The ghost's speech was unlike anything Berryman had written. He was reworking what he had seen in film and plays, how action gives force to poetry, how one character calls for interaction with another, and how action and the act of speaking in a context call for an individual voice. Removed from a dramatic context, the speech would be like Robinson's voice speaking without comment. As he planned the *The Architect,* the most revealing note about his personal connection with the voice is that "H.'s father has two voices—one the voice of his function as memory (Join me, Join me) & the other his natural voice, telling H. to study perfect vigor in his work."

At noon the next day after breakfast in bed, "where I still am and shall stay all day," his mind continued racing: "have written nothing [more] so far, but think & think & shall soon begin" (27 December 1936). A half hour later, he started a new letter to his mother. Like his letter of the previous day, he was most absorbed in describing his plans and conveying the passion of writing, but he was curiously general about the contents of the play. He told her he did not yet have names for the four male characters and was using initials; he mentioned only "H.," the protagonist. The three women had provisional names, only one of which he revealed. He had told her the previous day one was modeled on his American fiancée Jean Bennett, but the other named woman was Christine, H.'s wife and apparently modeled on Christine Elliot Bell, Berryman's recent mistress—H. is "trapped (also by circumstances) into sleeping with Christine."

The main character H. seemed most clear: as an architect, "the action & his relations to the others demanded that he be a public as well as private artist, a man with social power & responsibility as well as acuteness & integrity."[57] Three scenes were set in the bar of a New York hotel, "requiring a name, no sooner did I realize the necessity, than 'Random' popped into my head—I think it perfect, for sound and several trains of implications." He continued to work on the play that afternoon: "Have done 20 lines or so of the third scene of Act II, made many more notes, and a new character has reared, H's assistant—he looks to be important; the method of disaster is clearer now. 5 men & 3 women, I think that's all I need—one of the men has shifted his role somewhat, from older friend & critic to ironist" (27 December 1936).

Berryman was "magnificently filled" after thirty hours of fury and excitement. But he continued to think about how the play might develop; he wrote to Halliday on 2 January 1937: "Poetry, poetry—I merely communicate to you my most profound emotion and it turns out to be iambic pentameter. Truth in cadence! What ecstasy! Poetry it obviously is, but of what kind? Dramatic, lyric or epic? Looks like dramatic." He said he had planned a play, the characters were set, the first two acts outlined, and some forty lines written, but he had "since got interested in Paris & done little more but I'm a-thinkin', Jasper, I'm a-thinkin' and I'm going to write it" (2 January 1937). He returned to Cambridge a week later, and, after seeing his tutor George Rylands, who said he would help him with the play, he resolved to write it "because," he wrote to his mother, "I obviously want practice" (18 January 1937). By the end of the month, however, his first play was "vaguely ill" (27 January 1937). Although Berryman said he was serious about writing plays—"it's just possible that I might make a living writing plays" (18 January 1937)—by February he was preoccupied by his social life and scholarship on Shakespeare—"principally on *Twelfth Night* . . . comparing texts and notes, going into accounts of sources, data as to chronology . . . , and textual and dramatic history" (6 February 1937). He spent a nerve-frayed week preparing a lecture he gave on the life and poetry of Yeats on 11 February to the Dilettante Society at Clare College—"I slept little," he told her, "broke all engagements, read and wrote nothing but Yeats, working five or six days as I have not worked before" (14 February 1937). After the lecture, he resumed his study of Shakespeare with the plan that he might take the examination for the Charles Oldham Shakespeare Scholarship the next fall. But perhaps his self-consciousness was as much a barrier in completing the play. Nearly a year after he had attempted *The Architect,* Berryman admitted to his mother his "excessive, premature use of the critical faculty in composition" (7 December 1937). When he began writing *The Architect* in late 1936, the rhetoric and obscurity of his early poetry had dogged him. By January 1938, he seemed more confident: "Far greater effects can be had by tapping in the right place than by sledgehammers or thunder" (8 January 1938).

He revised *The Architect* two years later but completed only the first act and rough outlines for two and three. The ghost of the father does not appear to the son; the dilemmas of the architect/artist, now named Blake Puritan, become more immediate, his work, his marriage, and his friendship. Puritan is forced to choose between his

artistic integrity and the conservative demands of government fund-
ing for public buildings; his wife is unfaithful and she does not under-
stand his creative nature; his older friend and "the man he built on"
fails him at a crucial time. His younger friend, Hugh Severance (the
surname Berryman used later in *Recovery*), a journalist with an ironic
turn of mind, now takes the speech of the ghost of H.'s father:

> I tried to be what I was not—
> A solid man. I tried to be resourceful,
> Sound, to keep aside, merely to report.
> But circumstances tried me, and without
> That force—no fault of mine—I was condemned.

Realism wins over evocation; the dramatic moment of the ghost
appearing to his son in the Paris version is gone:

> I had no force, yet I was honest
> (And so again are you)
> Yet circumstances tired me, & I died.

Circumstances "tire" the father's ghost; they "try" Severance. And
yet one speech from the Paris version remained consistent in the
revision. "Throughout the course of the play," Berryman noted in
the revised version, the architect's "sacred things crumble from him,
until he can say at the end":

> I knelt among the rafters of my years
> And saw the fire consume from under me
> The house that has been mine.

All of the white-haired men Berryman had written about during the
fall of 1936 seem to speak in a chorus, like his grandfathers rising "in
my throat / Throbbing upon my tongue."

Had Berryman followed his Paris plans for *The Architect*, he
might have committed himself to an imagined action he himself
could not carry out. He might have revealed his commitment to his
father to his mother, and, as he did later, he might have had to face
the possibility of his mother's role in his father's death. Did she pull
the trigger? Did the "Uncle" (John Angus Berryman, who was called

Uncle Jack) murder him? Did she drive him to suicide? Nevertheless, the young Berryman was observing the "perfect vigor in his work" the ghost had asked. Throughout his writing of *The Architect*, he insisted that the play must be "*honest*," and although Berryman maintained that his characters were not "deliberate attributions" of his experience, he had edged closer to passionate center of his memory. The creation of H. and the ghost—the initial and the ghost double would seem to foreshadow Henry and his unnamed friend in *The Dream Songs*—was not so much an evasion of emotion, as one finds in his first poems about his father, as it was a momentary enactment of emotion. Poetry does indeed come out of the personality of the poet, but the character/self the poet creates, incomplete or discontinuous, may come closer to the self the poet is.

Repression and sublimation might be a psychological explanation of Berryman's relationship to his work. In the setting of his personal history, however, and in the context of his earliest attempts at writing poetry and drama, we witness how he discovered the monstrous ambiguity, to use his phrase, of the creation of dramatic language and character. Berryman's characters—forever present, forever in conflict, forever in dialogue with the past—are always now. The poet is who he or she is at a point in time, but the characters the poet creates demand that they be themselves. (Berryman insisted that the characters he creates, Henry for example, persist in being themselves.) They may even require an actual dialogue with past history.[58] He was not so much speaking from behind a mask as he was becoming another voice, an "other" in the work itself. How much he personally needed to *become,* in all the ambiguity the word touches, his father is part of his psychology; how much he relied upon the figure of his father's ghost is part of the history of his imaginative life. A comparison of the two plans for *The Architect* and a consideration of how frequently he responded to the ghostly father figure in his poetry invites a strange paradox in Berryman's use of the memory. He seemed to want his father to survive, consciously or unconsciously, as powerful and mysterious so that he would continue to be active in his imagination.

Later, Whitman would be one of his models for the self merging with character. "One always wishes to identify oneself with the loved object," Berryman said, but in relocating himself in that way, the poet is "out of sight, coming closer and closer into the experience, which is his [own]" ("*Song of Myself:* Intention and Substance," *FP*, 232, 240). The poet has no identity in this process, for he or she is, in Keats's phrase, "continually in—for and filling some other Body." Berryman's unresolved ritual approaches Pirandello's ideal of dramatic dialogue: "words, expressions, phrases impossible to invent but born when the author has identified himself with his creature to the point of seeing it only as it sees itself."[59] Herein lies the formative habit of mind in Berryman's first attempt at writing a play: he experiences creating and becoming a voice of and for voices, the speaker for others and for himself. In his imaginative attempts to see his father as he sees himself, he formulates a ritual of memory and creates a liturgy of immediacy. He is the celebrant of dispossession and the communicant in a rite of discontinuity. While he never made peace with his father's ghost, he imaginatively reckoned with his ghostly voice. As it turned out, he settled accounts in *Homage* and *The Dream Songs* in quite the same way he had improvised in 1935 and 1936.

In 1957, Berryman expressed his frustration that his attempts at writing plays had come to nothing: "The worst disapp't of my life," he wrote, "*if I should die tom'w:* no plays."[60] But his work on *The Architect* had come to something; he had discovered the two voices of his father—"Join me, Join me" and "study perfect vigor in your work." Over thirty years after his work on *The Architect* had dropped into time and long after he would not remember what he wrote in 1936, Berryman retold the story of the two voices once again. The story, he said, is from Hamann, quoted by Kierkegaard:

> There are two voices, and the first voice says, "Write!" and the second voice says, "For whom?" I think that's marvelous; he doesn't question the imperative, you see that. And the first voice says, "For the dead whom thou didst love"; again the second voice doesn't question it; instead it says, "Will they read me?" And the first voice says, "Aye, for they return as posterity." Isn't that good?[61]

NOTES

1. David McClelland, et al., "An Interview with John Berryman," *Harvard Advocate* 103 (Spring 1969):5.

2. *Sonnets,* file 3, JB Papers. I wish to thank Kate Donahue for permission to quote from Berryman's unpublished papers.

3. "Toward 48," an autobiographical fragment, JB Papers.

4. Berryman also felt ambiguous about whether to express grief or anger. When he was angry, he felt guilty that he was not observing obsequies for his dead father. When he grieved, he felt his anger was repressed. He frequently wavered between admiring his father's courage and disparaging his cowardice. In one time (1962) and place he would say, "Suicide takes courage," ("Toward 48"); in another (1971) he would write, "I thought I was in private with the Devil / hounding me upon Daddy's cowardice" ("Matins," *CP*, 226). These contradictory attributes of courage and cowardice were multiplied by contradictory fears—fear that he could not live up to his father's honesty and integrity and fear that he would follow his father's example of cowardice.

5. Diary fragment, 12 April 1958, JB Papers.

6. One outcome of Berryman's dramatizing voices is his identification with heroes in his poetry. Some heroes were overlords; some mentors and sponsors; many were, in his own phrase, "fathers and grandfathers." The paternal metaphor suggests that he was conscripted by his heroes, that they chose him and not the reverse. Like Hamlet's ghostly father, his heroes sought him out, and like Pirandello's notion of theater, he is the author whom the characters seek.

7. Berryman's search for his father, though individual and particular, belongs to a long tradition of sons in search of their fathers. The stories have several variations: the father initiates his son into the adult world and enhances his skills and intellect; the father has been lost and the son sets out to find him, as Telemachos in *The Odyssey;* the father rides the back of the son, who, like Aeneas, carries into the present the values and beliefs of a society's past.

8. For Berryman's description of his dramatic form, see "One Answer to a Question: Changes," *FP*, 328–29.

9. Berryman to his mother, 17 January and 6 February 1937. All references to Berryman's letters to his mother are taken from the originals in the JB Papers. Subsequent references are given by date. A large selection is in *DH*.

10. Berryman to Mark Van Doren, 28 October 1936. All quotations from Berryman's letters to Van Doren are taken from the Mark Van Doren Collection, Rare Book and Manuscript Library, Columbia University. I wish to thank the Columbia University Libraries for permission to quote from Berryman's letters. Subsequent references are given by date.

11. The same image of the intertangled dead appears in *Homage to Mistress Bradstreet* and the Dream Songs. The twentieth-century American poet in *Homage* "trundle[s] the bodies, on the iron bars, / over the fire backward & forth," and he wonders if "*I* killed them" (*CP*, 141). Henry has nightmares of violently killing a woman in Dream Song 29. Henry knows rationally he did not kill anyone, but like jackboot soldiers, his ghosts "shout commands" (*DS*, 12). The commands also call up Henry's resources: after he determines that "nobody's missing," rather than hide in fear, he *summons* his ghosts: "Often he reckons, in the dawn, them up" (*DS*, 29).

12. Joseph Wood Krutch, "Pirandello and the Dissolution of Ego," in *Modern Drama*, ed. Anthony Caputi (New York: W. W. Norton, 1966), 487.

13. Krutch, "Pirandello," 489. Berryman suggested his version of the "being

of a character from moment to moment" as he completed *The Dream Songs:* "All the people [besides Henry and Mr. Bones] who speak in the songs are people with voices and personalities and fates of their own, which get into the poem by the instrumentality of the twentieth-century poet, who begins in the opening song, 'Huffy Henry,' by subordinating his personality, so that by the end of the song it has disappeared" (Jonathan Sisson, "My Whiskers Fly: An Interview with John Berryman," *Ivory Tower,* 3 October 1966, 34.

14. "To an Artist Beginning Her Work," *Columbia Poetry 1936* (New York: Columbia University Press, 1936), 11. *Columbia Poetry 1936* was published 1 December 1936; my dating of the composition is based on Berryman's manuscript in Unpublished Poetry, file 32, JB Papers. Despite the poem's teacherly voice, it does have a more personal reference; the manuscript version is addressed to "Jean" [Bennett], who would become his first fiancée.

15. Berryman to mother, 20 April 1932.

16. "Essential," *Columbia Review* 16 (March 1935): 19.

17. Berryman to E. M. ("Milt") Halliday, 14 February 1935. All quotations from Berryman's letters to Halliday are taken from JB Papers. Subsequent references are given by date.

18. The four sonnets to his mother, a few poems he sent Milt Halliday in letters, and "Villanelle: 1934" are the only extant copies of Berryman's first poems. The four sonnets, handwritten, are in Unpublished Poems, file 11, JB Papers. The villanelle is in Unpublished Poems, file 32, Papers.

19. See *DH,* 33–35, for the four sonnets.

20. Diary, JB Papers.

21. In 1947, he would suggest an Oedipal explanation: "Father I fought for Mother, sleep where you sleep" ("Fare Well," *CP,* 12).

22. Unpublished Poems, dated 15 June 1936, file 30, JB Papers.

23. "Villanelle: 1934" is dated 31 August 1934, Unpublished Poems, file 32. JB Papers.

24. "Trophy," *Columbia Review* 17 (April 1936): 7.

25. This sort of ambiguity, the poet in the poem and not, is similar in kind—perhaps the seed of it—to Berryman's famous "ambiguous pronoun" in which the poet's identity is "reserved." The ambiguous pronoun was one of his major discoveries, his imaginative variation upon the poet's identification with his subject (see "One Answer to a Question: Changes," *FP,* 326–27). In his longer works, it was the means whereby the "I" of the poem "is gradually expanded, characterized, and filled with meaning," as Berryman said of Whitman's passionate sense of identification ("*Song of Myself:* Intention and Substance," *FP,* 232).

26. "I dreamt at times in those days of my *name,*" he said years later, "blown by the adoring winds all over" ("My Special Fate," *CP,* 175).

27. Compare this reference to the sea with his short story "Wash Far Away," written in 1947, in which the ghost of a poet-friend appears in his imagination as he teaches a class on Milton's "Lycidas," which in turn meditates upon a poet and friend dead at sea ("Wash Far Away," *FP,* 367–86).

28. "Elegy: Hart Crane," *Columbia Review* 17 (November 1935): 21.

29. St. Pancras Braser, file 9, JB Papers.

30. Unpublished Poems, file 28, JB Papers.

31. Note on E. A. Robinson, "*Nation,*" 10 July 1935, 38.

32. Henry also dreams of his dead father as an arctic bear with whom he must make peace; see *DS,* 120.

33. Unpublished Poems, file 30, JB Papers. The only extant copy of this poem is handwritten with changes and is dated 15 June 1936.

34. "Ritual at Arlington," Unpublished Poems, file 19, JB Papers.

35. Unpublished Poems, file 30, JB Papers.

36. Unpublished Poems, file 32, JB Papers.

37. "25 October 1936," Unpublished Poems, file 32, JB Papers.

38. Unpublished Poems, dated 26 October 1936, file 32, JB Papers.

39. Martin Berg, "An Interview with John Berryman," *Minnesota Daily,* 20 January 1971, 17.

40. Unpublished Poems, untitled, file 32, JB Papers.

41. In the winter of 1936, Berryman observed the connection between Yeats and his poetry: "All obtainable information [about Yeats's life] may be valuable to me as a critic, and particularly in Yeats's case, for many of the symbols in his poems are personal symbols, to be understood in terms of his history, and only when understood can they be appraised" (Berryman to mother, 14 February 1937).

42. Diary, 21 October 1937, JB Papers.

43. Berryman to mother, 25 May 1932. Nearly four years later (10 October 1936), after seeing *The Prisoner of Shark Island,* he would write in one of his best early poems, "Homage to Film": "This night I have seen a film / That might have startled Henry James." An uncollected poem, "Homage to Film" was published in the *Southern Review* 5 (Spring 1940): 773.

44. Berryman to Halliday, undated, JB Papers. Halliday, in his *John Berryman and the Thirties: A Memoir* (Amherst: University of Massachusetts Press, 1987), suggests it was written in later October or early November 1934; see 50–54.

45. "Toward 48."

46. Lawrence G. Avery, ed., *Dramatist in America: Letters of Maxwell Anderson 1912–1958* (Chapel Hill: University of North Carolina Press, 1977), 295.

47. Bob Lundegaard, "Song of a Poet: John Berryman," Minneapolis *Tribune,* 27 June 1965, p. 2E.

48. Thomas Parkinson, "The Later Plays of W. B. Yeats," in *Modern Drama: Essays in Criticism,* ed. Travis Bogard and William I. Oliver (New York: Oxford University Press, 1965), 388–89.

49. Ibid., 388–89.

50. Berryman to Van Doren, 28 October 1936.

51. Berryman to mother, 26 December 1936. See Andrew Kennedy, *Six Dramatists in Search of a Language: Studies in Dramatic Language* (London: Cambridge University Press, 1975), especially his introduction, 1–37, and his discussion of T. S. Eliot, 87–129, for an analysis of the development of language in drama during the time Berryman was attempting to write his first play.

52. Berryman to mother, 27 December 1936. Compare this description of a fusion of styles with Berryman's later description of his stanza form in *Homage*

to Mistress Bradstreet: "I wanted something at once flexible and grave, intense and quiet, able to deal with matter both high and low" ("One Answer to a Question: Changes," *FP,* 328).

53. In mid-February 1937, Berryman wrote to his mother that the sense of addressing someone was necessary for him to write even prose: "Your suggestion of [my keeping] a journal is impossible, I cannot write into blank air, I must address some near sensibility" (14 February 1937.)

54. Berryman to mother, 27 December 1936. In 1948, Berryman wrote to Beryl Eeman: "You speak of the artist moving towards God and himself. I see him moving towards annihilation—towards becoming a *voice:* first a voice for the *object,* later (very rare, this) a voice for powers and passions and acceptances buried somewhere in men for good—Tempest, Magic Flute, Schubert c major Quintet, last works usually" (carbon copy, dated 8 September 1948, JB Papers).

55. All quotations of Berryman's notes are taken from Plays, *The Architect,* JB Papers.

56. Berryman to Halliday, 26 February 1936. Later in 1954, when Berryman was analyzing his dreams, he wrote that Hamlet's father's ghost "beckons" in one of his dreams, "as the ghost did to Hamlet—*also* killed by my Uncle, *Uncle Jack*" (i.e., John Angus McAlpin Berryman, his stepfather). And again in another dream: "I, young Ham[let], heard fr. the Ghost lately saying *Kill Uncle Jack* 'but not saying how he'd recom'd me to go about it'" (St. Pancras Braser, files 2 and 7, JB Papers).

57. Berryman to mother, 27 December 1936. The next summer, on 15 August 1937, Berryman would return to the themes of the public man and the man of acuteness and integrity in a poem to his father "Epitaph on a Banker—J. A. S."

58. Most of Berryman's attempts at drama were based on historical characters; so were his long poems and even the historical personality of the poet in *Love & Fame.*

59. Cited by Kennedy, *Six Dramatists,* 18.

60. Diary fragment, JB Papers.

61. McClelland et al., "Interview," 9.

Charlotte H. Beck

"Solely *The Southern Review*": A Significant Moment in the Poetic Apprenticeship of John Berryman

And the live magazines were gone,
The Dial, Symposium. Where could one pray to publish?
The Criterion's stories & poems were so weak.
Solely *The Southern Review,* not *Partisan* yet.
—"In & Out," *CP,* 183

Although John Berryman's (1937–41) relationship with the *Southern Review* was brief and relatively unproductive in regard to his major poetic achievement, it must nonetheless be considered a significant moment in his poetic apprenticeship. The *Review* had been created in 1935 as an aspect of Governor Huey P. Long's scheme to make Louisiana State University a center of academic and athletic excellence. Its principal creators and editors were Robert Penn Warren and Cleanth Brooks, whose earlier associations with the Nashville Fugitives had made them important figures in the Southern journals literary Renascence. In the absence of today's plethora of literary reviews, the *Southern Review* soon became a respected route to critical attention for experienced as well as fledgling writers of poetry, fiction, and criticism. At the outset of John Berryman's poetic career, he submitted his best poems to the *Review's* editors and, in the process, formed a crucial and problematic relationship with its editors. The letters exchanged between Berryman and Brooks, Warren, and John Palmer chronicle the role that the *Review* played in Berryman's earliest attempts to realize his vocation.

Berryman's biographers and critics have passed quickly over his publications in the *Southern Review*. Milt Halliday's *Berryman and the Thirties,* which chronicles that period in Berryman's life, mentions neither the journal nor its editors, possibly because, as Paul Mariani suggests in his afterword: "What Halliday wants to tell, in large part, is the story of a friendship. Let someone else, he says by his absences, talk of Berryman's sea change at Cambridge which left Berryman forever after altered as well as altared."[1] When Eileen Simpson takes up the record in *Poets in Their Youth,* it is clear that by the time of her marriage to Berryman, his *Southern Review* phase was past history. John Haffenden's *The Life of John Berryman* (1982) omits all mention of the *Southern Review*'s role in Berryman's career, while Paul Mariani, in *Dream Song* (1990), surmises that "those poems [that the *Review* published] merely bored him, and worse, they were surrounded by [what he called] 'contemptible company'" (PM, 119). The fact remains, however, that outside of student publications in the *Columbia Review* and a six-line "Elegy to Hart Crane" in the *Nation,* the two groups of poems, nine in all, that Berryman finally published in the *Southern Review* constitute his debut to the literary world. To Berryman in the thirties, unsure of his poetic vocation, there was "solely the *Southern Review,* not *Partisan* yet."

Berryman's first letter to Robert Penn Warren, on 4 February 1937, concerns his first rejection by the *Review*. Because "Ritual at Arlington" was inspired both by his own Southern roots and Allen Tate's "Ode to the Confederate Dead" (PM, 56), Berryman no doubt had expected that it might find favor in Baton Rouge. He entered the 360-line poem in the *Review*'s contest for the best long poem of the year, but Tate, one of the contest's judges, rejected it because of its resemblance to his "Ode" (PM, 61). From Clare College, Cambridge, Berryman responded with respectful deference:

> Your criticism of "Ritual at Arlington" is perfectly correct. Van Doren, Tate, and Rylands here say substantially the same things. I am now very glad that you did not print it, too many pleasant failures are probably floating about in ill-advised print. I ought probably to destroy the poem and forget it; but it cost me much labor, the abstract plan I still think valuable, and parts of it are worth keeping. So I'll put it away for a few months; then I shall re-work, and plague you again.

Enclosing his check for a two-year subscription, Berryman called the *Southern Review* "decidedly now the best literary medium in English" and added,

> I've written since last summer a fair amount of verse, but have been waiting until I had a group I could respect, before sending you anything. Which looks to be never. On the chance, however, that my judgment is decaying, as friends have inferred, I'll select some poems when I have time and send them, confident in your expert opinion.[2]

"Ritual at Arlington" was effectively doomed, but because Warren sent advice along with rejection, Berryman began sending large numbers of poems.

From its inception, the *Review*'s policy was, according to its letter to prospective contributors, not to publish "miscellaneous pieces," but rather to feature "long groups of poems by a single author, so that the reader may be able to get a real sample of the poet's work."[3] Berryman therefore wrote to "Mr. Warren," on 18 March 1937: "I am sending you under separate cover twenty-five poems; so large a number because Mark [Van Doren] told me you wanted to see more and more of his. . . . I rely on you to print nothing that is not good, and I'd like to know which you think worthless."[4] On 27 July, Cleanth Brooks wrote to Berryman that he was "highly interested" in Berryman's poems and "very definitely want[ed] to publish a group of them." But with characteristic editorial caution, Brooks added, "Whether we can find a group in this batch we are not at this time altogether sure, though I think several of the poems are something to be proud of."[5]

Such remarks were sincere and constructively intended since, although the review was relatively young, it was by no means lacking in submissions by well-known poets. Moreover, although the editors wanted a mixture of experienced and inexperienced writers within the covers, they readily rejected poems of poor quality from either class of contributor. John Berryman, who had already had his poems rejected by T. S. Eliot's *Criterion* (PM, 55), was understandably encouraged by Brooks's measured response.

By August 1937, the editors *seemed*, in fact, to be well on their way toward publication of a Berryman group. An excited Berryman wrote on 10 August that he was sending "four recent poems, one an hour old." He directed that the last line in the tenth stanza in "Last Days of [later "Night and] the City" be changed to read "The barriers were down, they fell afraid" and in the fifth stanza to change *deep* to *strict* (for "exacting"). With lordly superiority he characterized English poetry as "incredibly bad at the moment, even French is much better; were I a literary patriot I could be hated with just cause here," and, in a more modest postscript, he added, "I shall greatly appreciate comment on the verse, or suggested changes."[6]

It was autumn, however, before Berryman finally received commitment in the form of an unsigned letter in unmistakable Warren idiom:

> We take a mighty long time to make up our mind some time, and this has been one of those times. We have finally decided on keeping the following poems: "Note for a Historian," "Film," "Last Days of the City," "Frequently When the Night," and "Poem in May." We are planning to publish a group of your poems perhaps in the Summer issue. We should like to publish more than five pieces, and are very anxious that you let us have a look at whatever you have recently or will do within the next few months. Is this asking too much? By the way, I should like to say here that I like your stuff very, very much indeed.[7]

Thus reassured, Berryman replied, on 12 February 1938, that he was sending still more poems, including two "'Songs from *Cleopatra*' which seem to reinforce each other, either can be printed separately as 'A Song from *Cleopatra*'; *C* being a blank verse play I wrote last year." With sincere gratitude, he added that "more than anything else I appreciate your saying that you liked my verse."[8]

The 1938 summer issue of the *Southern Review* did include a group of poems by John Berryman, but Warren's letter notwithstanding, it consisted of only *four* poems: "Night and the City," "Note for a Historian," "The Apparition," and "Toward Statement." All are written in formal stanzas of four to six lines, metric but not always rhyming. Of the four only "Night and the City" has received any critical comment, most of it echoing Linebarger's dismissal of the poem as "perfectly fit[ting] the Auden climate."[9] Berryman himself later called it "a very bad poem,"[10] but Warren probably liked it

because in its formal structure, distanced tone, and metaphysical gro-
tesquery, it resembled poems that he himself was writing at the time.
The following stanza is typical:

> While worms in books held carnival and ate
> And slept and spurred their nightmares to the post . . .
> Speechless murderous men abroad on great
> Thoroughfares found the virgin and the lost.
>
> (*CP*, 273)

"Note for a Historian," now virtually forgotten, is a short but
rather interesting poem in three quatrains. The "historian" could be
Berryman himself, who later preferred to teach courses in "the
American character" and "the meaning of life" rather than literature
or creative writing.[11] "On that day" when "certain men . . . died . . . /
By violence as bits of lead," this traumatized protagonist makes a
Wordsworthian retreat:

> So he postponed his trip into the country:
>
> Made a great fire and burned his books and burned
> The animal part from him in contemplation
> By that fire, then he rushed upstairs and there
> Took out the children's blocks and built a castle.[12]

In retrospect, Berryman's debut was less than an auspicious
event. He must have been somewhat frustrated by the number of
poems and the editors' vacillation. Berryman was, however, still
eager to attempt a second appearance in the *Review*.

As earlier letters indicate, he had already sent a large number of
poems for this second group. Late in 1938, however, a serious break-
down in communication occurred between Berryman and the edi-
tors. Having recently returned from England, Berryman wrote to
Warren from 41 Park Avenue, New York:

> Our accounts are not quite straight. Some ten months ago, on
> your saying you wanted to print a group larger than five, I sent
> you about a dozen pieces, of which I have heard nothing except
> from Mr. Erskine, who said they were there, at any rate, in July.

"Meditation," in which I am still interested, was among them; what else I don't know. Also, something seems to have happened to "Film," which you said you were going to use but which didn't appear. . . . Mr. Tate tells me you are exceedingly busy, so I don't like to seem to harry you, particularly since I'm grateful for the good appearance of my group in what I think is so far as essays are concerned, the best issue of *The Southern Review* so far. But you will understand my perplexity.[13]

On 1 December 1938, Berryman's frustration crested in a short note to which a small metal sword was attached:

It has been 13 months since you wrote me last. During that time you should have had from me: a dozen poems and a letter; *A Vision* for Mr. Brooks; another letter; two months ago, another letter and two poems. The mails cannot so err from their true course but that you owe me something in reply. Sincerely John Berryman.[14]

The note elicited a quick and apologetic reply from Brooks:

We are ashamed of our long lapse in writing, and can plead only that we have not been busy but that our work is so confused—a little teaching, a little manuscript reading, a little conference, etc., etc.—that it is easy to let matters slip. This is not a real excuse we know, and we promise to do better in the future.[15]

Significantly Brooks added, "I need not tell you that we look forward to publishing a great deal more poetry by you. A follow-up letter (20 December) promised that Berryman's poems would appear in the spring 1940 issue.

As Berryman and the editors moved toward that issue, the relationship between John Berryman and the *Southern Review* climaxed. In a letter dated 13 January 1939, Robert Penn Warren listed the poems to be published and offered specific suggestions about "Meditation," the longest and most ambitious poem in the group:

The first five stanzas please us greatly, but the sixth stanza, which doesn't seem to advance the poem, reads almost too much like

an echo from Yeats. The last line of the eighth stanza raises the
same question for us. But the ninth, we believe, doesn't really
bring the prom [*sic*] to focus. We do not have, of course, any
specific suggestions to make for revision of the poem. That
would, indeed, be a piece of presumption. But we do hope that
if you ever find it necessary to do any more work on "Medita-
tion," you will let us have another reading on it. Meanwhile we
are very anxious to see more of your poems so that we can fill
out another and, we hope, a larger group.[16]

Commenting on such editorial "presumption," Brooks later wrote
to me:

> We may have suggested a writer to send us something on a
> particular topic and then found that what he actually sent was
> not satisfactory. We certainly never rewrote anyone's piece. We
> sometimes suggested changes but in that case the author was
> always allowed the final say. Unless he accepted our suggestion,
> what he had written went to press.[17]

Like other, more famous *Southern Review* contributors, Berryman
did act on such advice. On 16 January, he wrote that he was "aston-
ished and pleased to hear that you 'look forward to publishing a
great deal more' verse by me; I thought that *The Southern Review*
had given me up forever."[18] On 20 January he accordingly sent a
number of new poems, remarking, "Thank you for the comments
on 'Meditation'; I have known for some time that it wanted revi-
sion. I will return it to you as soon as I am able to work on the
poem again."[19] And eventually, on 11 April, Berryman wrote that
he was sending

> "Meditation" . . . finally, revised. I thought your criticism of the
> poem admirable and was very grateful for it; I wish you felt you
> could make the same kind of comment more often. The places
> you mentioned are precisely those I have substantially changed:
> what was the sixth stanza I have excised, the final line of the
> (now) seventh is entirely new, and the last stanza re-cast. Recall-
> ing and expanding the central mood (stated first in the second
> stanza), it seems now to provide a satisfactory major theme.

There are also some minor changes, toward clarity. I hope it will please you.[20]

The final version of the poem, in its fuller development and somewhat looser syntax, is a timid precursor of the later Berryman. More than the other four poems, "Meditation" dares to the autobiographical. Linebarger's identification of its speaker as "a young man who must be equated with the poet [who] sits in his Cambridge room on a rainy day and recalls his boyhood at school, his dedication to his craft, and a disquieting love relationship"[21] provides a capsule description of its author, with the last lines of stanza 7 gracefully blending Keats, Yeats, *and* Berryman:

> deserted walls for us
> One afternoon a lovely shelter, soft
> Grass where a floor had been, and when she laughed
> The sound could make a shelter for the mind.
>
> (*CP,* 271)

But if these "items to make a history" are Berryman's own, his "new" sixth stanza, in typical modernist mode, seems coldly artificial:

> The uncontrollable eye spins in the year,
> A curious harvest brings. Pieces of bread
> At twilight on a Dublin quay, and fear;
> The clenched lip, a wrinkle on the forehead
> Of hanging Christ;
>
> (*CP,* 270)

Berryman's satisfaction with the final version of "Meditation" is evidenced by its subsequent appearance in *Five Young American Poets.* As of May 1939, however, his relief at having survived the editorial process was mixed with irritation. Writing to the editors, he was "glad you now like 'Meditation'" but surprised at rejection of the last fourteen poems, about which he remarked testily, "I am told and know that my verse is improving, and I select with some care what I send you. I don't know what to think. If you don't like 'Winter Landscape' or 'The Disciple', I think I had better retire and try archery."[22] On 23 August 1939, "gratified" that his poems had not been "lost or burnt," Berryman sarcastically threatened to

> consider resigning my precarious status as *SR* contributor and [take] up normal life again. . . . As I wrote Mr. Warren in one of half a dozen unanswered letters, my principal aim in life at present is a large good group in THE SOUTHERN REVIEW, and I am now holding back my normal contributions elsewhere, to that end.[23]

Brooks's reply, on 30 October, is a scarcely speedy attempt at mollification:

> We have finally decided on the group with the following five poems in it, "Film," "II Song from *Cleopatra*," "Meditation," "Conversation," and "Desire [*sic*] of Men and Women." I think it is a fine group, and I hope that you will be pleased with it even though we are not including "Winter Landscape," and "The Disciple" [which Berryman had revised]. And please don't take up archery. Maybe we are making a mistake in ranking the poems and choosing as we do, but it is a very honest one if mistaken, and we are very happy and very much satisfied with the group which we have chosen.[24]

Berryman shot back, on 27 November, "I hope the group you and Mr. Warren have selected is better than I think it is; however, since I once committed the poems and you are kind enough to want to print them, I daresay I should hold my tongue."[25]

These decisions and indecisions portended a waning relationship between John Berryman and the *Southern Review*. Although he continued to submit poems, there was never to be a third, "larger" Berryman group in that journal. By then, it was not "solely *The Southern Review*" for John Berryman. His poems had appeared in other reviews, including the *Partisan* and the *Kenyon Review*, so that on 15 December 1939, he had good reason to ask, "When do you plan to use the group of poems: I may publish a selection with New Directions next year, and I would want these to appear before that."[26] Still desirous, however, of maintaining his relationship with the *Southern Review*, Berryman submitted one final poem, "A Point of

Age," sometime in 1940. His letter to Warren on 23 November re-
marks almost plaintively, "Several months ago you were kind
enough to hope I would send some new verse to the *Southern Re-
view.* . . . I hope you will like this more or less long poem. It was
written in April and has been seen by no one except, privately,
Schwartz."[27] But hearing nothing, Berryman repeated on a postcard
to Brooks, "Several months ago I sent you or Mr. Warren for the
Review, a poem of mine called 'A Point of Age'. I don't expect to
know your decision so soon as this, but I would like to know whether
you received the poem." The final item of his correspondence with
the *Review* was a poignant note from John Palmer dated 21 October
1941:

> After these many months, your manuscript has turned up in a
> general overhauling of the office files and I am returning it to you
> with our deepest apologies. We are, as you know, severely un-
> derstaffed and the result is, except for a few intervals, a state of
> near chaos. Various of our contributors have been exasperated
> to that same pitch of fury that you exhibited in your letter of
> inquiry, and while we can entirely understand and sympathize
> with your feelings, we must ask you, as we have asked the oth-
> ers, to bear with us.[28]

Not long thereafter, in the spring of 1942, the *Southern Review* would
suspend operations, mainly for financial reasons.

John Berryman's somewhat chaotic relationship with the editors
of the *Southern Review* was initially beneficial, if ultimately frustrat-
ing. It may well have led to his inclusion in *Five Young American
Poets,* since four out of five YAPS (as Randall Jarrell informally called
them), namely Jarrell, Berryman, George Marion O'Donnell, and
W. R. Moses, were *Southern Review* contributors. Both Jarrell and
Berryman thus owed considerable credit to the journal as a vehicle
of self-discovery and presentation before the literary world at a very
insecure time in their careers. Unlike Jarrell, Berryman was *not* a
Southerner and former Vanderbilt student of Warren's; thus his po-
etry had to appeal to the editors on its own merits. On the other
hand, Brooks's and Warren's judgments of individual Berryman po-
ems were far from faultless, as is clear from the relative permanence
of some such as "Winter Landscape," which they rejected, and the

near disappearance of others, such as "Film," which they accepted. Fortunately Berryman did not allow their opinions to shape irrevocably his attitude toward his poems.

As Berryman later recalled, publication in the *Southern Review* was an "In and Out" affair, a brief but significant moment in the crucial period of his poetic apprenticeship. Although the relationship resulted in few lasting poems, it may have reinforced in Berryman's poetics a fundamental sense of form that served him well even as his poetry underwent its eventual evolution beyond formalism. The eventual disintegration of Berryman's relationship with the *Southern Review* may, on the other hand, have played an even greater role in provoking that evolution, perhaps loosening his commitment to Fugitive-New Critical poetics and making way for the competing influence of Whitman and the poetics of open form.

After his period of apprenticeship, Berryman, like Randall Jarrell and Robert Lowell, began to break away from his Fugitive mentors. Delmore Schwartz and the *Partisan Review,* in combination with the Auden influence, constituted that "Other" with which to oppose the parental presence of Warren, Tate, and Ransom. The *Partisan's* iconoclastic Marxist ideology was a major attraction to the young poets, as was the panache of the northern literary scene. Clearly they were eager to address a national rather than regional audience. It is fascinating, however, to review how these fledgling poets continued to imitate their mentors—by forming a new network and by moving out of the South. But these acts of rebellion, often chronicled in friendly correspondence with the former Fugitives, *did* generate the creative energy that characterizes Harold Bloom's "anxiety of influence." It becomes evident, therefore, that Berryman and his contemporaries achieved success as poets, not *in spite of* but *because of* those exercises in letting go.

NOTES

1. Paul Mariani, afterword to *John Berryman and the Thirties: A Memoir,* by E. M. Halliday (Amherst: University of Massachusetts Press, 1987), 219.

2. John Berryman to Robert Penn Warren, 4 February 1937. All correspondence between Berryman and the *Southern Review* is collected in the *Southern Review* papers, Beinecke Rare Book and Manuscript Library, Yale University, hereafter designated SRP.

3. Form letter to prospective contributors from the editors of the *Southern Review*, 3 March 1935, SRP.

4. Berryman to Warren, 18 March 1937, SRP.

5. Cleanth Brooks to Berryman, 27 July 1937, SRP.

6. Berryman to the *Southern Review*, 10 August 1937, SRP.

7. [Warren] to Berryman, 29 October 1937, SRP.

8. Berryman to the *Southern Review*, 12 February 1938, SRP.

9. J. M. Linebarger, *John Berryman* (New York: Twayne, 1974), 34.

10. Peter Stitt, "The Art of Poetry," in *John Berryman's Understanding,* ed. by Harry Thomas (Boston: Northeastern University Press, 1988), 25.

11. John Plotz et al., "An Interview with John Berryman," *Harvard Advocate* 103, no. 1 (Spring 1969): 4–9; rpt. in Thomas, *Berryman's Understanding,* 15.

12. John Berryman, "Note for a Historian," *Southern Review* 4 (Summer 1938): 170.

13. Berryman to the *Southern Review*, 10 October 1938, SRP.

14. Berryman to the *Southern Review*, 1 December 1938, SRP.

15. Brooks to Berryman, 1 December 1938, SRP.

16. Warren to Berryman, 13 January 1939, SRP.

17. Brooks to Charlotte H. Beck, 12 April 1986.

18. Berryman to the *Southern Review*, 16 January 1939, SRP.

19. Berryman to the *Southern Review*, 20 January 1939, SRP.

20. Berryman to the *Southern Review*, 11 April 1939, SRP.

21. Linebarger, *John Berryman,* 30–31.

22. Berryman to the *Southern Review*, May 1939, SRP.

23. Berryman to the *Southern Review*, 23 August 1939, SRP.

24. Brooks to Berryman, 30 October 1939, SRP.

25. Berryman to the *Southern Review*, 27 November 1939, SRP.

26. Berryman to the *Southern Review*, 15 December 1939, SRP.

27. Berryman to the *Southern Review*, 23 November 1940, SRP.

28. John Palmer to John Berryman, 21 October 1941, SRP.

Lea Baechler

A "Deeper—Deepest—Acquaintance" with the Elegy: John Berryman and "Wash Far Away"

All the new thinking is about loss.
In this it resembles all the old thinking.

Self-referential and ironically revisionary, these opening lines from "Meditation at Lagunitas," by Robert Hass,[1] allude both to a curious feature of the modern sensibility—the self-conscious and characteristically elegiac disposition of our age—and to recognition that human history is a history of our sense of continuous loss punctuated by moments of specific loss. The two lines counterpoise acknowledgment of a "truth"—that loss and confrontation with mortality are inherent facts of human life—with an admission—that the twentieth-century appropriation of a presentiment of loss is a singularly modern tendency. Implicit here is the notion that the impulse toward elegy is itself an essential feature of the modern elegy, and that the elegy is thus both a text and a manifestation of the "work" involved in the process of mourning—that is, of the psychological, spiritual, and creative energy the poet/mourner must summon and enact in order to move from grief to consolation.[2]

Rich in its documentation of the impulse toward elegy, the poetry of John Berryman testifies to the elegy's function as an active work in the process of mourning—for certainly no modern American poet has more than Berryman so ardently and devotedly engaged in an unrelenting study of "the epistemology of loss" ("The Ball Poem," *CP,* 11). Berryman's persistent attention to that study spans his entire poetic career, from the earlier poems, often characterized by a presentiment of loss as perfectly captured in the brilliant early lyric "The Ball Poem"; to poems that address the loss of the father, beginning with the 1939 "World's Fair" (*CP,* 24) and continuing through *The Dream Songs* and later poems and epitomized in Dream Song 241, which begins, "Father being the loneliest word in the one language." They include, as well, laments for lost love and the equation of disappointed love with death; specific elegies occasioned by the death of a particular person—"A Poem for Bhain" (*CP,* 40–41), "In Memoriam" for Dylan Thomas (*CP,* 243–45), Dream Song 121 for Randall Jarrell, Dream Song 173 for R. P. Blackmur, and the Dream Song sequence (*DS,* 146–57) for Delmore Schwartz, among many others; and poems obsessed with an ever-present foreboding about the "dying" self and Berryman's extension of that obsession to an eventually realized preoccupation with suicide. Throughout, Berryman brings to "his complex investigation of death" (*DS,* 335) a stunning range of voices and perspectives: by turns he is audacious, unnervingly candid, melancholic, exuberant, self-deprecatory, outrageous, humble, wretched, grandiloquent, stingingly ironic.

Indeed, Berryman's poetry represents a number of the impulses toward the elegiac, which in his case are not discrete phases marking some sort of progression. Rather, from Berryman's lifetime movement through "pockets of grief" (*DS,* 358) arises a variety of articulations, reiterated, interwoven, and circled back upon as the poet examines and reexamines, excruciatingly lives and relives, any number of given points within the broad spectrum of response to loss and the subsequent experience of grief. Repeatedly evocative of an elegiac self-consciousness, the poems call attention to themselves as "works" of mourning informed by the social and cultural, personal, and aesthetic pressures brought to bear on the poet's imagination in relationship to the psychic disturbance and turmoil generating a particular poem.

Demonstration of those pressures can be found in Berryman's short story "Wash Far Away" (*FP,* 367–86), first published posthumously in 1975.[3] In this brilliantly complex and highly achieved short story, the central character, a Berryman-like professor at what appears to be a small Ivy League college, recalls an unsettling but profound teaching (and personal) experience, his rediscovery of Milton's poem "Lycidas," resonant of Berryman's own reverence for and attachment to the poem:[4]

> Long after the professor had come to doubt whether lives held crucial points as often as the men conducting or undergoing them imagined, he still considered that one day in early spring had made a difference for him. The day began his deeper—deepest—acquaintance with "Lycidas," now for him the chief poem of the world. (FP, 367)

As the story develops, the professor reflects back, from the unspecified present of the first paragraph, to that "crucial" moment some years earlier when, encumbered by a pervasive sense of deflation, ennui, and disenchantment, he had been revitalized while teaching the poem to his undergraduate students. The experience leads him to a new and inspired understanding of "Lycidas," his preparation and performance in the classroom underscored as they are by his intermittent drifts into reverie about his dead friend Hugh, the fictional counterpart to Berryman's friend, fellow poet, and colleague—Bhain Campbell. This narrative integration of a subtextual reading of "Lycidas" with the embedded and fictionalized reconfrontation with the early death of Bhain Campbell crystallizes Berryman's relationship to the elegiac tradition—and his own excursion from that tradition and its conventions. It provides, as well, a locus from which we can read backward to the earlier poems and forward to the more achieved elegies, most specifically the sequence of poems for Delmore Schwartz in The Dream Songs.

The two subtexts—the renascent interpretation of "Lycidas," through which Berryman apprehends that "magnificent" poem's impact on him both poetically and personally, and the elegiac movement in the story toward a life-affirming consolation with regard to Campbell's death—are intricately meshed in a narrative of chronological and thematic complexity. What is immediately discernible are the parallels between specific points of narrative time and specific events in Berryman's life. While the professor is preparing his lecture on "Lycidas," he recalls a more exuberant and less troubled time seven years earlier, when in his first year of teaching he and Hugh had together aspired toward a passionate engagement of their chosen vocations as writers, teachers, and scholars. According to both available biographies (JH; PM), Berryman began the first drafts of "Wash Far Away" (then entitled "Vain Surmise"—a conflation of two phrases from "Lycidas")[5] in April 1947,[6] a period that positions the story's genesis seven years after Berryman's 1939–40 appointment at Wayne State, where he had taught with Campbell. Other correspondences include the professor's tenure at an institution similar to Princeton University (where Berryman was teaching when he first began work on the story); Hugh's death five years before the central narrative time of "Wash Far Away" with Campbell's death in December 1940; and the professor's reference to marital problems with Berryman's first glimpse of "Chris" in February 1947, the woman with whom he would have his first extramarital affair later that spring and summer and for whom he would write the *Sonnets to Chris*.

Although narrative references to time after the epiphanic "Lycidas" day tend to compress the passage of time in Berryman's own life—for example, the professor's wife dies four years later though Berryman and his first wife Eileen (née Mulligan) Simpson did not separate until 1952—the figure of the wife is uncannily resonant in the story, and Eileen is herself seemingly inseparable from the experiences that generated the story. While "Wash Far Away" foregrounds the professor's grief in relationship to Hugh, he claims in the first paragraph that to "Lycidas" he owes, "as much as anything else, the survival of his *wife's* death" (italics added). This early but nearly buried admission, given the focus on the Hugh/Bhain Campbell figure throughout the subsequent narrative, is suggestive. Berryman's divorce from Eileen was finally granted in late 1956, and it may have been around this time that Berryman revised the various drafts, which he had begun in 1947 and returned to in the early 1950s, into the story we know as "Wash Far Away."[7] That Eileen and the "loss" of her are tied to the story and its basis in Berryman's life is further reinforced by a notable though coincidental series of events: Berryman's proposal in August 1942 to Eileen Mulligan (whom he had first met a few weeks after Bhain's death) ten days after his final break with Beryl Eeman, and the premature appearance a few weeks later of *Poems* (September 1942), which was dedicated to Bhain Campbell and which included, among the ten poems framed by an epigraph and an epilogue for Campbell, Berryman's "A Poem for Bhain."[8]

Firmly grounded in the experience and anguish of Berryman's

own life, "Wash Far Away" recreates through its intertextuality—
that is, the integrated reading of "Lycidas" with the professor's excur-
sions into his own grief and his restrained though empathetic
response to grief in others—the work involved in the process of
mourning. For the story itself employs not only the traditional ma-
chinery and conventions of the pastoral elegy as appropriated by the
text it seeks to explicate, but its structural, rhetorical, and imagistic
strategies as well. The double invocation—first, in the opening para-
graph, which calls forth a rarefied experience in the past, the profes-
sor's reacquaintance with "Lycidas," out of which arises yet another
invocation of an even earlier, even more pristine past, the years of his
youth and friendship with Hugh—parallels the double statement of
grief for both his wife and for Hugh and mirrors Milton's double
invocation: the biographical epigraph for Edward King followed by
the opening repeated lament for "Lycidas," which spirals out from
the central lines in the passage, "For Lycidas is dead, dead ere his
prime / Young Lycidas" (8–9). The traditional evocation of the vege-
tation deity (Hugh, like King in Milton's "Lycidas," died quite young
and before—to Berryman's mind at least—the promise of his genius
could be realized) are present in Berryman's allusions to Hugh's early
death, his vitality, physical fearlessness, the forcefulness of his pres-
ence.

Despite the modern and American setting of the university class-
room, the pastoral contextualization of the story is established early
on as the professor walks to class—"The small leaves of the maple
on the corner shook smartly as he passed" (*FP*, 367)—and is main-
tained by further allusions to the natural world, both in the profes-
sor's notice of it and in the classroom discussion on the poem's pas-
toral construct. The funerary flowers, which in the elegy are both
offerings and demarcations between the living and the dead, are dou-
bly present, doubly cataloged, when the professor asks his students:

> "How many of you know jessamine, crow-toe, woodbine—have
> visual images when you see the words or hear them?" . . .
> He went off to the windows. "I don't know myself," he said,
> looking out. Forsythia, daffodils, snapdragons. (*FP*, 379)

The last incantation—"forsythia, daffodils, snapdragons"—is itself
another doubling, evocatively mirroring the professor's observations

during his earlier walk from town to campus: "The Dostals' garden, anemones, snapdragons, crimson, yellow, rose-pink; colors swimming, the air sweetened" (*FP*, 368). Likewise, Berryman makes omnipresent the recurrent images of light, the hopeful figurations of possible consolation and resurrected life characteristic of the elegy: "Sunlight plunged to the pavement and ran everywhere like water, vivid, palpable" (*FP*, 367)—"the sunlight died, returned, died" (*FP*, 371)—"the sun streamed in afresh, glowing on the rim of Warner's glasses and white collar" (*FP*, 377)—"the trembling of light on the page" (*FP*, 386)—"the sun shone steadily in at the windows. The class was over" (*FP*, 385).

In "Wash Far Away" we also find the elegist's self-conscious sense of guilt for surviving and concern with his own death: "This was the superiority of aging one waited for: just to remember. True or false, evil or gay, never mind. The Nobel Prize for Memory. Recipient a suicide en route to Stockholm, having remembered all his sins at once, sitting in a deck chair sharpening a pencil" (*FP*, 371). Doubts about the integrity and very purpose of his endeavor and a recurring sense of defeat and resignation—"My life is in ruins. . . . I'm no further on than when we started—*I* started. . . . I am really dead. . . . . just a teacher . . . not a very good one, and stale" (*FP*, 368)—are interwoven with the need to call attention to his own surviving powers and believe in them: "He could determine to teach today as he hadn't for a long time, to swing the whole class to a fresh, active relation, an insight grave and light" (*FP*, 369); "he looked forward eagerly like a defendant facing the last day of a suit that had so far gone well: anxious and confident, pacing out the final hour of his imputed, fantastic guilt" (*FP*, 376); and "his difficult, morning sense of the poem as a breathing, weird, great, incalculable animal was strong on him again. He returned to the table excited" (*FP*, 385). Likewise, regret and disillusionment are counterpointed by moments of powerful emotion—"Warner's simple, uninflected question somehow moved the professor very much" (*FP*, 378)—and occasional outbreaks of anger: "Hugh, it seemed to him with the first resentment he had ever felt for his friend, kept steadily with him like a deadweight he could never live up to" (*FP*, 368), and, later, "The professor suffered a flick of rage" (*FP*, 381). All of these shifts in self-appraisal contribute to the overall tone of melancholy, most obviously characterized by lapses into lament and self-deprecation, as self-consciously highlighted by the professor's comment "exquisite melancholy" (*FP*, 372) in his preparatory notes on "Lycidas."

While development of the narrative in "Wash Far Away" is both associative, relying on flashes of memory for nonchronological movement in and out of time, and linear (loosely hung as the framework of the story is on the sequential events of a particular day), Berryman executes that complex progression with an eye to his model and with responsiveness to the psychic process the story seeks to elucidate. Essential to the work of mourning is the convergence of past, present, and future—when desire for the lost perfection of the past from the vantage of a painful present merges with the longed for, imagined fulfillment of the future. The narrative structure of "Wash Far Away" reenacts that convergence, beginning as it does with an informed moment in the future of the central narrative experience, which itself returns to a seemingly purer and lost past. That convergence is further reinforced by the way in which "Wash Far Away" appropriates the elegy's dependence on reiterated question, repetitions, and refrains in order to provide structure and to reveal the psychic tensions integrated into the story.

Berryman's use of a ceremonial structure—which in elegy modulates pace and direction and effects the performance necessary for encouraging active response to life—is perhaps no more evident than in the classroom passages, with the give and take between the professor and the students, the movement between his thoughts, both personal and pedagogical, and his articulation of them, his probing into the minds and responses of his students, a probing that, at times, turns inward. The dialectic of the classroom also vivifies what the professor, in the solitude of his office preparing for class, had worried over in Milton's linkage of Triton-Aeolus-Camus-Peter: "The testimony of Triton and Aeolus, and the speeches of Camus and Peter, actually made up a sort of a trial. . . . What on earth made Milton think of a trial?" In the relative security of his office, the professor contents himself with an academic analysis: "*Oh.* His [Milton's] own inquisition of the nymphs above! They had deserted Lycidas when he needed them: who then *had* been with him, for evil? Let a court find out" (*FP*, 373), a line of thinking he modifies for presentation in class: "The trial, I think gentlemen, continues the dramatic method of Milton's own inquisition of the nymphs, earlier. It's a way of clamping his material together" (*FP*, 384). But the answer and the professor's "deeper—deepest" understanding that the trial provides a context for the necessary, inevitable but unanswerable questions of the mourner—"Why the inquisition! What does a man think when a friend dies, what does he do? He *asks questions*—'not loud, but deep.' *Why? Where now? Why? Where?*" (*FP, 384*)—comes to him only when he poses the problem to his students, whose own "inquisition" of the poem (and of the professor's argument here) reenacts the "trial" in "Lycidas," a stunning moment when the questions tormenting the professor in his earlier reflections on his life, on Hugh, arise poised in the classroom, palpable and undeniable.

For, once the professor passes into the classroom, he and the students join, by their very interrogations of the text, in a performative trial of their own, one which, for the professor, dramatizes and activates his participation in confronting the losses that have so debilitated his imagination and energy. The students, then, become the "procession of mourners" who, like the various figures in "Lycidas," accompany the grieved, their presence necessary for urging the mourner to temper sorrow and rejoin the community of the living, their multivocality essential for effecting the dialectic movement from grief to consolation that the mourner must experience. The professor's charged interaction with the students is itself evidence of his return to that community of the living, the last paragraph signaling the moment at which he is revitalized through release from the paralyzing emotions of grief. The professor's acknowledgment earlier that "consistently Lycidas was Hugh" (*FP, 372*) is transformatively crystallized as he ponders, after class in the healing quiet of his office, "the transfiguration of Lycidas" (*FP, 386*), his meditation enabling him to move toward a tentative consolation vibrant with "the trembling of light on the page."

While the above examination merely highlights how the structure, images, and movement of "Lycidas" inform Berryman's conception of the story and suggests how the story reenacts the potency of transformative experience, "Wash Far Away" is clearly both an achieved work and an achievement of the necessary work of mourning. As such, especially given the pressures brought to bear on its creation, the text and its process of invention perhaps provided Berryman with a source of strength, formally, aesthetically, and psychically, for the "works" he would be compelled to wrestle into being:

what lay in his future were an astounding number of losses that followed one upon the other—the deaths of Ernest Hemingway in the summer of 1961, William Faulkner the following July, Robert Frost in January 1963, Sylvia Plath in July 1963, and Theodore Roethke in August 1963, followed by the deaths of Louis MacNiece later that year, T. S. Eliot in January 1965, R. P. Blackmur in February 1965, Randall Jarrell in October 1965, and Delmore Schwartz in July 1966. While only some of these figures were intimate friends of Berryman, the death of each constituted a devastating personal loss for a poet who stood in an uneasy relation—of admiration, envy, anxiety, need, even love—to his mentors and poetic forebears and contemporaries.[9]

Although Berryman wrote a number of poems for his fellow poets, what he ascertained critically, aesthetically, and intuitively from his "deeper—deepest—acquaintance" with "Lycidas" is perhaps no more evident than in the twelve-poem Dream Song sequence (*DS*, 146–57) for his friend and fellow poet of his youth, Delmore Schwartz, Dream Song 146 functioning as an epigraphic invocation and Dream Song 157 as an epilogue. Adhering to traditional conventions, Berryman provides a double invocation, Dream Song 146 naming the subject of the poems that follow—"Delmore specially, the new ghost / haunting Henry most" (cf. the 1645 addition of the headnote to "Lycidas")—and Dream Song 147 summoning the dead poet in a doubled chant that appears once in each of three stanzas: "Delmore, Delmore." Evocations of the vegetation deity come not only from the suggestion that Delmore died "too soon" (*DS*, 151), "fallen from his prime" (*DS*, 148), but from references to Delmore's virility—"he was young & gift-strong" (*DS*, 149), "Flagrant his young male beauty" (*DS*, 154), "the whole young man / alive with surplus love" (*DS*, 155)—and his sheer physical presence, which Berryman affectionately documents by allusions to the intensity of Delmore's "sudden appearances" (*DS*, 152), most vividly recounted in Dream Songs 154 and 155. Counterpoised to those evocations, however, is Berryman's considered judgment that his friend wasted, to some extent, that early promise "blazing with insight" (*DS*, 149). Though cut off in his prime, Schwartz did live long enough, Berryman reminds us, to have suffered the failure to achieve his enviable and youthful genius:

He hid his gift
. . . .
I'd bleed to say his lovely work improved
but it is not so. He painfully removed
himself from the ordinary contacts
and shook with resentment.

                                                    (*DS*, 150)

The opening lines of the sequence, "These lovely motions of the
air, the breeze" and Henry's "bird-of-paradise vestures" (*DS*, 146),
followed in Dream Song 147 by "High in the summer branches the
poet sang," all provide the initial pastoral contextualization conven-
tionally associated with the elegy. Except for the later line "His death
clouded the grove" (*DS*, 151), however, such allusions are rare in
these songs, and not surprisingly. Given the cigarette smoke settling
hazily over the late nights of talking, the long hours of coffee and
drinking, the dark and shadowy light of those Northern cities, in
which the two poets' habitual but constantly changing abodes were
more often than not shoddy apartments and cheap hotels, Berryman
appropriately replaces pastoral detail with evocation of those haunts
in which the early friendship between Schwartz and Berryman flour-
ished and suffered its numerous misunderstandings and enigmas. The
funerary flowers dismally absent in these poems become unexpect-
edly present as the poet gathers the verbal significations of place in
an incantatory integration of reference after reference to sites of
shared experience and the various modes of traveling, taxi and ambu-
lance, between them: Harvard, Manhattan, Brooklyn, hotel rooms,
Warren House, NYU, Bellevue, Providence, police stations, and
Cambridge. In accord with the interior settings of these poems, the
few allusions to light, with one notable exception (see below), come
not from the external, natural world but from the poet's summoning
the light of Delmore's creative genius: "the brightness of his prom-
ise," which the poet describes as "blazing with insight" (*DS*, 149);
the recollection of one of Delmore's "sudden appearances" and his
exclamation, "'My head's on fire'" (*DS*, 152); and the poet's com-
ments on Delmore's marriage, "white his devotion" (*DS*, 154), on
his gifts, "his electrical insight" (*DS*, 155). In fact, the overall "light-
lessness" of the sequence corresponds not only to its dark interior
settings but to the dark interior of Delmore's genius, "the awful years

/ of the failure of his administration" (*DS*, 151), his wasted talent itself a heavy and inexplicable darkness:

> we never learnt why he came, or what he wanted.
> His mission was obscure. His mission was real,
> but obscure.
>
>   (*DS*, 155)

The poet's despair over Delmore's death is (at the least) two-fold—that is, he is unable to differentiate decisively between regret for the waste brought about by death and the waste willfully indulged in *life*. Perhaps because of that mixed response, we do not find here the elegist's usual expressions of guilt, self-deprecation, or obsessive doubts about poetic potency, though repeated questions about the lasting impact of Schwartz's early work and the pleasure his brilliance may have brought him in life suggest, by implication, the questions the poet may be asking himself. In the one section testifying to the poet's belief in his own poetic powers appears Berryman's one allusion to natural light. After protesting in the first stanza of Dream Song 153 the god who has "gorged" himself, through death, on the best of Berryman's generation, the poet moves on to a singularly moving passage, his eye momentarily deflected by the living, affirmative here and now:

> Somewhere the enterprise continues, not—
> yellow the sun lies on the baby's blouse—
> in Henry's staggered thought.
> . . . .
> I hang, and I will not be part of it.

Likewise, expressions of the elegist's usual preoccupation with his own death are relatively rare. Besides several expected admissions early in the sequence—"only his heart is elsewhere, down with them / & down with Delmore specially" (*DS*, 146) and "This world is gradually becoming a place / where I do not care to be any more" (*DS*, 149)—an explicit desire for death occurs only once, and at that, in the last line of the penultimate Dream Song of the sequence: "and nearly would [I] follow him below" (*DS*, 156). Even so, the death wish is diminished by the qualifying "nearly" and subsequently over-

ridden by the next and final Dream Song of the sequence, which, like
the last paragraphs in "Wash Far Away," enacts the consolatory let-
ting go, the release from stultifying grief, necessary in the work of
mourning.

The overall tone throughout most of these poems is, nonethe-
less, one of melancholy and appropriately characterized by repeated
references to the poet's tears: "grief too astray for tears" (*DS,* 149),
"Bitter & bleary over Delmore's dying," and "my tearducts are worn
out" (*DS,* 151). Expressions of lamentation are pervasive in these
songs—"Henry's mind grew blacker the more he thought" and "Al-
most his love died from him" (*DS,* 147), "We suffer on, a day, a
day, a day" (*DS,* 153), and "O and O I mourn / again this complex
death" (*DS,* 156), though often these outpourings are counterbal-
anced by outbursts of rage—"He flung to pieces and they hit the
floor" (*DS,* 147) and as particularly evident in Dream Song 153,
which begins, "I'm cross with god who has wrecked this generation"
and closes with "And never again can come, like a man slapped,
/ news like this." Lament and anger, figures and images, all function
within a rhetorical structure whereby the convergence of past, pre-
sent, and future and the repetitive questions—"What matters is that
there *be* questions" (*FP,* 384)—construct a framework for the perfor-
mative trial Berryman has been conducting throughout the sequence
and which culminates in the entirety of Dream Song 156, where the
poet admits:

> There are all the problems to be sorted out,
> the fate of the soul, what it was all about
> during its being, and whether he was drunk

Nor has the poet neglected his procession of mourners; rather,
he has carefully gathered them into his "Ten Songs, one solid block
of agony" (*DS,* 157)—Berryman's mother and brother, the gossips
of Harvard, the police in Washington, the "Jews bereft, for he
[Delmore] was one" (*DS,* 151), the children Delmore never had, the
ambulance, the girls at NYU, the recently dead poets evoked in Dream
Song 153, Delmore's wife Gertrude, his friends Saul (Bellow) and
Dwight (MacDonald), the taxis, and the long-dead fellows Mozart,
Bach, the Buddha—their multivocality resonant, by their very pres-
ence as figures in the poems, and necessary to the performative experi-

ence the poet/mourner must engage if the words he writes are to achieve not only poetic transfiguration but psychic transformation.

The difficult and complex work of mourning requires an eventual substitution for what has been irrevocably lost if the mourner is to experience fully the grief itself and the movement toward consolation. Classically, that substitution would be Apollo's appropriation of the laurel leaves as an emblem of creativity after the loss of Daphne, or Pan's invention of the reed pipes, itself an instrument for assuaging sorrow, after the loss of Syrinx. In the case of the elegist, language itself is that substitution, though the symbolic substitution of language for the dead one requires the poet's submission to the constraints and inadequacies of language. The paradox of that substitution and submission is further intensified by the elegy's origins in the movement between two silences: the silence of loss, the absolute void of the grave, and the silence of complete presence, the consolation of fullness and union. Where in 1941 Berryman writes of Bhain Campbell's death, "Both of us at the end. / Nouns, verbs do not exist for what I feel" (CP, 282), in the later "Wash Far Away" and the Songs for Delmore we find quite different assertions. In fact, the achievement of the elegy for Schwartz, of the "Ten Songs, one solid block of agony, / I wrote for him, and then I wrote no more" (DS, 157), is perhaps made possible by the transformative experience recounted in "Wash Far Away": the professor, "once he read over the transfiguration of Lycidas, . . . was troubled by the trembling of light on the page; his eyes had filled with tears. . . . He felt older than he had in the morning, but he had moved into the exacting conviction that he was . . . something . . . not dead" (FP, 386).

In the course of the day the professor had moved from a possessively held but numbing grief to a transfigured relation to his loss, as crystallized toward the end of class when, while one of his students reflected on a question, he had "made a short excursion":

He climbed, dripping, under a blinding sun, up and up a sand dune. . . . He was laughing and calling up. Once he looked back, fearful. Hugh helped him at the top. . . . he knew Hugh was saying, "It's wonderful," running back toward the edge. "Just step as far as you can with each foot," then disappeared over it. Now he had to? Yes. He shuddered, cold, came toward the edge, shrank. Feet moved by strong love on. Fought. He leaned erect

off the world's edge, toppling, and stept! Through empty air
straight down, terror of the first, the bounce and astonishment
of the second. Pure joy the third, his eyes cleared. He rushed
through the sunlight wild with delight in deep jumps, foot far
to foot, touching the earth, down and down toward Hugh,
bounding far below. Far off, another world. (*FP*, 384)

From that "relived" terrifying and jubilant first letting go comes not
only the professor's "exacting conviction" that he is alive, healed and
whole, prepared to join the community of life, but also Berryman's.
And despite his lifetime waverings from that conviction, sorely tested
by an early presentiment of loss intensified by the devastating number
of losses he suffered over the years, Berryman is able in the final Song
of the sequence for Delmore to reenact that letting go:

> His sad ghost must aspire
> free of my love to its own post, that ghost,
> among its fellows, Mozart's, Bach's, Delmore's
> free of its careful body

He longs to join that company of "fellows"

> high in the shades which line that avenue
> where I will gladly walk, beloved of one,
> and listen to the Buddha

but concludes the song with that consolatory directive of elegy necessary to both the subject, Delmore, and the poet himself:

> I hope he's sitting with his peers: sit, sit,
> & recover & be whole. (*DS*, 157)

NOTES

1. Robert Hass, *Praise* (New York: Ecco Press, 1979).

2. Sigmund Freud, "Mourning and Melancholia" (1917), tr. Joan Riviere, in *General Psychological Theory*, ed. Philip Rieff (New York: Macmillan, Collier Books, 1963), is the primary source for discussion of "the work of mourning." Peter Sacks's *The English Elegy: Studies in the Genre from Spenser to Yeats* (Balti-

more: Johns Hopkins University Press, 1985) discusses in detail the notion of the elegy as a *work,* "both in the commonly accepted meaning of a product and in the more dynamic sense of working through an impulse or experience" (1). Although a number of sources delineate the various features of the elegy—the invocation, allusions to the vegetation deity, images of light, the role of the funerary flowers, the pastoral contextualization, the poet-mourner's self-consciousness, anger, lament, self-doubt, and struggle for poetic inheritance— Sacks's analysis of elegiac conventions, patterns, and images in relation to the elegy as both text and process is most relevant to my own approach. His discussion of ceremonial structure, the performative quality of elegy, the constraints of language, and the role of substitution is particularly valuable.

3. Before being collected by Robert Giroux in *The Freedom of the Poet,* "Wash Far Away" was first printed in *American Review* 22 (1975): 1–26.

4. In his biography of Berryman, Paul Mariani notes that in early 1934, the poet's second year as an undergraduate at Columbia University, Berryman read "Milton's 'Lycidas' [and] was so struck by the poem he read it through three times. It was, he [Berryman] wrote, 'magnificent,' and it remained a literary touchstone for him for the rest of his life" (PM, 34).

5. The title "Vain Surmise" is a conflation of the two "Lycidas" phrases "denial vain" (18) and "false surmise" (153). With these Berryman picks up on the opening lament—the vain denial of death (and the poet's "vain" wish for immortality)—and on the "false surmise" late in the poem that all can be recovered and made whole again. By doing so, however, he fails to respond to the poem's movement (from grief to consolation) or to delineate carefully the *context* of "false surmise." Although literal recovery is, of course, a false surmise that allows us to "interpose a little ease" (152) (the bones of Lycidas are, in fact, "wash[ed] far away"), the phrase "wash far away" signals the poem's gesture toward reconciliation and consolation. A purgative and cleansing expression of the letting go necessary in the process of mourning, the passage culminates with the couplet beginning "Look homeward angel" (153), itself a transition into the penultimate section, which begins, "Weep no more, woeful shepherds, weep no more, / For Lycidas your sorrow is not dead." In "Wash Far Away," the professor recognizes, at the end of class, the significance of "false surmise" in relation to the "wash far away" passage. Berryman's change of title validates his recognition that "wash far away" is fundamental to the story's inner direction and to his own engagement with the work involved in the process of mourning.

6. Since the manuscript of "Vain Surmise," if it still exists, does not appear in the Berryman archive at the University of Minnesota, the April 1947 date noted by Mariani (PM, 184) and Haffenden (JH, 168) probably derives from Berryman's notes in journals from that period. Although the journals and diaries from 1942–56 were originally housed in the archive, Eileen Simpson requested that they be returned to her sometime early in the period when Haffenden was working (1974–82) on his *Life of John Berryman.* Kate Donahue, Berryman's wife, graciously complied with this request and the materials are presently unavailable. What does exist in the archive, besides the final draft of "Wash Far Away," are several undated typed drafts, one entitled "The Lesson" (amended

to "The Lesson and The Light") and another, its title "The Professor and the Lesson and the Light" crossed out and replaced, in the author's hand, with "Wash Far Away." There are several pages of notes for revision, one earmarked as "Wash Far Away" and dated 18 August 1952. On one undated page of notes for revising the story Berryman queries himself, "(when written? 1946?) 1947?"

7. Although Berryman had as early as the summer of 1952 titled the story "Wash Far Away," the version known by that title is undated. In his preface to *The Freedom of the Poet*, Robert Giroux comments that he has included "'Wash Far Away,' one of his [Berryman's] best stories, of whose existence no one was aware until Kate Berryman found it among his papers" (*FP*, ix). In the notes Giroux adds that "it existed in draft form in 1957 and may have been written somewhat earlier" (*FP*, 390). Despite the problems with dating, Berryman first drafted the story the spring he met "Chris," returned to it during the last year of his disintegrating marriage, and apparently continued to work on it in the years following his separation from Eileen until their formal divorce.

8. According to Mariani, when Berryman saw the slim collection in a Cambridge bookstore he was surprised to see the book "with the simple title *Poems*. He had told [James] Laughlin the book was to be titled *Poems, 1939–1940*, to commemorate the years he had spent with Bhain. . . . Upset, he wrote Laughlin . . . that he was 'sorrier and angrier' than he could say that Laughlin had taken it on himself to change the book's title" (PM, 144).

9. Eileen Simpson's *Poets in Their Youth: A Memoir* (New York: Farrar, Straus and Giroux, 1990; Random House, 1982) recounts the early years and development of Berryman's poetic and personal friendships with Robert Lowell, Randall Jarrell, and Delmore Schwartz, among others.

Sharon Bryan

Hearing Voices: John Berryman's Translation of Private Vision into Public Song

In his introduction to John Berryman's *Collected Poems,* Charles Thornbury says that Whitman is the poet Berryman most resembles (*CP,* xix). But what I hear are echoes of and resemblances to Eliot, especially the Eliot of "Prufrock" and *The Waste Land.*

This comparison may seem to fly in the face of Berryman's criticisms of Eliot's poetics. In describing his work on *Homage to Mistress Bradstreet,* for example, Berryman says of its structure, "Let's have narrative, and at least one dominant personality, and no fragmentation! In short, let us have something spectacularly NOT *The Waste Land*" ("One Answer to a Question: Changes," *FP,* 327). And in response to a query about why he referred to the Dream Songs as one poem rather than a series of lyrics, Berryman responded: "Ah—it's personality, it's Henry. . . . The reason I call it one poem is the result of my strong disagreement with Eliot's line—the impersonality of poetry . . . I'm very much against that; it seems to me on the contrary that poetry comes out of personality."[1]

I would take issue with this response on several grounds: for one thing, Eliot didn't dispute that poetry comes out of personality, but argued that what comes out of that source must be transformed by the formal pressures of the poem; second, Berryman fails to distinguish here between the author's *personality,* which is extraliterary, and *character* which is a literary construct; third, just as negative space is defined by positive in a work of art, as any of us are defined by and

tied to whatever we rebel against, so Berryman's poetry is deeply
shaped by what he so passionately rejects; fourth, the terms *personality*
and *impersonality* seem far more muddying than illuminating. I would
prefer to substitute *temperament,* as used by David Kalstone, in his
book *Five Temperaments:* "I intend the word 'temperament,' of
course, in its nonpejorative sense, as Wallace Stevens used it when
he remarked that, '*Temperament* is a more explicit word than *personal-
ity* and would no doubt be the exact word to use, since it emphasizes
the manner of thinking and feeling.' Stevens, one of the least overtly
autobiographical of poets, understood exactly what part the personal
played: 'It is often said of a man that his work is autobiographical in
spite of every subterfuge. It cannot be otherwise . . . even though it
may be totally without reference to himself.' "[2]

The similarities I hear between Eliot and Berryman have to do
with their use of a range of voices in their poems as a means to
discover and construct their own poetic voices, and my sense that
these similarities in poetic strategy arose in part from similarities in
temperament. Both Eliot and Berryman were masters at creating a
specific voice with a few words, and using that voice to summon an
entire character. This enabled them to express strong emotions indi-
rectly, through their characters; when an *I* does speak, it is as one
voice among many. It's Prufrock, not Eliot, who says:

> For I have known them all already, known them all—
> Have known the evenings, mornings, afternoons,
> I have measured out my life with coffee spoons.

And:

> I grow old . . . I grow old . . .
> I shall wear the bottoms of my trousers rolled.

And in the "Game of Chess" section of *The Waste Land,* it's an un-
identified but specific character who thinks to himself, in response to
the querulous woman who badgers him with, " 'What are you think-
ing of? What thinking? What?' "—"I think we are in rats' alley /
Where the dead men lost their bones." And who follows, a few lines
later, with the scrap of song and dance: "O O O O that
Shakespeherian Rag— / It's so elegant / So intelligent."

David Perkins comments that the following lines from Berryman's *Love & Fame* might have been one of the fragments quoted in *The Waste Land:* "I drink too much. My wife threatens separation. /She won't 'nurse' me. She feels 'inadequate.' / We don't mix together."[3]

Berryman, too, was able to achieve the music and intensity he strove for through the creation of individual voices, from the personas of "The Nervous Songs," to the man addressing his lover in the *Sonnets,* to the two speakers in *Homage to Mistress Bradstreet.* It's almost as if Eliot and Berryman, both shy men in their different ways, are most comfortable and least tongue-tied in the company of imaginary friends. Even when Berryman and Eliot use an *I* that in some sense stands for the poet, it's a specific character, not the billowing, boundless *I* of Whitman's poems.

We speak of poets "finding" their own voices as if we knew what that meant, and I suppose that in a general way we do. But I'd like to define and explore that vocabulary in some detail as it applies to the procession of Berryman's poems from the earliest, which are often characterized as "stiff" and "academic," through the more distinctive *Sonnets* and *Homage* to the Dream Songs.

It's obvious that the public voice a poet finds and that we hear as his or her own need not be first person or autobiographical, but I make the point because so many poets from Berryman's generation—Lowell, Plath, Rich, James Wright, and so on—"found" their own poetic voices by moving from third person and relatively anonymous and general first person to a specific and autobiographical first person. This shared path had more to do with the literary climate of the time than with a similarity of temperaments. Poets who were writing their early poems when the influence of the New Criticism was at its height worked to keep the obviously personal out of the poems, to make the poem independent of its author, to erase or disguise ties between the work and the life. It's no surprise that any element so thoroughly suppressed would eventually reappear with a vengeance.

Voice is what brings a poem to life, makes it audible even if we're not saying it aloud. It is the opposite of awkward self-consciousness. A poem may succeed in other ways—vivid images, polished craft—but unless it finds its own voice, it will remain a beautiful corpse. Although a poet may find his or her voice in a variety of ways, choice of pronoun is crucial to locating it. As Berryman said, "A pronoun may seem a small matter, but she matters, he matters, it matters, they matter. Without this invention . . . I could not have written either of the two long poems that constitute the bulk of my work so far" (*FP*, 327). A distinctive voice is present in many of Berryman's early poems, in individual lines and passages, and occasionally throughout a poem. It surfaces most often in persona poems, poems with a third-person narrator, poems using first-person plural, and poems in second person, addressed to a specific other. The early poems that use an *I* are among the stiffest and most awkward. "The Statue," for example, never successfully meshes its third-person descriptive distance with the first-person speaker who puts in two brief appearances, one at the beginning of the second stanza: "Where I sit, near the entrance to the Park, / The charming dangerous entrance to their need"; and one at the beginning of the third stanza:

> Fountains I hear behind me on the left,
> See green, see natural life springing in May
> To spend its summer sheltering our lovers,
> Those walks so shortly to be over.
>
> (*CP*, 4)

The first-person here is more intrusive and distracting than unifying or illuminating.

Persona poems provide the valuable focus of first person, but declare themselves to be spoken by someone other than the author and so offer an escape—not from personality, but from self-consciousness. The shy actor can forget himself or herself and at the same time express powerful emotions by assuming a role. In "The Nervous Songs," Berryman assumes a range of identities: a young woman, a priest, a young Hawaiian, a bridegroom, a professor, among others. The most powerful is "The Song of the Tortured Girl," in which Berryman completely submerges himself in the girl's identity. Having summoned up her horrifying captivity in a few understated lines:

> I must have stayed there a long time today:
> My cup of soup was gone when they brought me back.

and:

And then the strange room where the brightest light
Does not shine on the strange men: shines on me.
I feel them stretch my youth and throw a switch.

The girl then escapes to the past:

Through leafless branches the sweet wind blows
Making a mild sound, softer than a moan;
High in a pass once where we put our tent,
Minutes I lay awake to hear my joy.
—I no longer remember what they want.—
Minutes I lay awake to hear my joy. (*CP*, 52)

Apart from persona poems, the poems in which the voice seems
most natural, most compelling, and most fluid are those that include
one or more other people in addition to the speaker—either as part
of a general *we*, a particular *we*, or as a *you*, a specific other the poem
is addressed to. A specific and personal *we* appears in "Parting as
Descent":

The sun rushed up the sky; the taxi flew;
There was a kind of fever on the clock
That morning. We arrived at Waterloo
With time to spare and couldn't find my track.

The bitter coffee in a small café
Gave us our conversation. When the train
Began to move, I saw you turn away
And vanish, and the vessels in my brain

Burst, the train roared, the other travellers
In flames leapt, burning on the tilted air
Che si cruccia, I heard the devils curse
And shriek with joy in the place beyond prayer.

(*CP*, 17–18)

The first two stanzas are wonderfully direct. Only in the third—when
the *we* and the *you* fall away—does the poem stiffen into rhetoric.
    Given these glimpses of some of the elements with which Berry-

man seemed most at ease in the early poems, it isn't surprising that
the sequence of love sonnets written in 1947 should have freed him
into an extended expression of the tone, diction, and syntax that
we've come to recognize as "Berryman's voice." We have the advan-
tage of hindsight: we can read backwards from the Dream Songs,
looking and listening for earlier instances of their distinguishing char-
acteristics, their intimations of what was to come.

Poets don't have that advantage as they are working, of course.
Berryman had been trained and trained himself to use a formal, dis-
tanced speaking voice, one addressed primarily to a faceless audience.
Only gradually did he discover that the voice of his own best poems
was to be a personal, autobiographical singing voice. In the *Sonnets,*
that singing voice is as intimate as possible, addressed to one specific
other. It seems likely that the emergence of that voice was made
possible in part by the fact that the poems weren't written for publica-
tion. I think the guilt that pervades the *Sonnets* may have almost as
much to do with the break Berryman was making with his poetic
models as with the adulterous affair the poems chronicle, and that
this was a break he was able to make only in private. Sonnet number
3, for example, can be read as referring to both when it says:

> We think our rents
> Paid, and we nod. O but ghosts crown, dense,
> Down in the dark shop bare stems with their Should
>
> Not! Should Not sleepwalks where no clocks agree!

> > > > > (*CP*, 72)

References to his literary masters appear throughout: Eliot, Yeats,
and Dylan Thomas in number 5, Cummings, Propertius, and Pound
in number 27, Marvell and Villon in number 32, and so on.

In addition, the sonnet form provides a container for powerful
emotions, and poses demanding technical problems that can offer a
useful distraction from discomfort at revealing those emotions. This
combination of intimacy and formality enabled Berryman to develop
the voice that would, in one form or another, sustain his poetry from
the *Sonnets* on. The language itself, especially in the early *Sonnets,* is
not dramatically different from that in the earlier poems. It's sim-

ply—if only it were ever simple—that the voice here brings the various elements into a slightly—but crucially—different alignment, as if a small turn of the dial had brought a faint, fuzzed station in clearly:

> I wished, all the mild days of middle March
> This special year, your blond good-nature might
> (Lady) admit—kicking abruptly tight
> With will and affection down your breast like starch—
> Me to your story, in Spring, and stretch, and arch.
>
> (CP, 71)

Yet even though the *Sonnets* were written in private, and kept private for almost twenty years, they were formally public from the outset: that is, they are carefully crafted poems in a form that has a long-standing tradition, and they allude frequently to literary history. If the fiction of privacy was crucial to their writing, it is hard to imagine that Berryman believed they would never be read. They are spoken to be heard directly by one person, but also to be overheard by others. It was this voice, and this device of speaking to be overheard, that enabled Berryman to find the right balance between private and public—private dream and public song.

Berryman began *Homage to Mistress Bradstreet* the following year, 1948, and even though it wasn't finished until 1953, it seems in several ways a direct outgrowth of the *Sonnets*. It begins as an address to one other, a woman—but in this case a public and historical figure, the poet Anne Bradstreet:

> The Governor your husband lived so long
> moved you not, restless, waiting for him? Still,
> you were a patient woman.
>
> (CP, 133)

Early on, in the third stanza, the speaker addresses her intimately, as he might any absent lover:

> Out of maize & air
> your body's made and moves. I summon, see,
> from the centuries it.

> I think you won't stay. How do we
> linger, diminished, in our lovers' air,
>
> *(CP, 133)*

And by the last line of stanza number 4 the voice passes from his lips
to hers, Anne begins to speak, the poem becomes a dialogue:

> Pockmarkt & westward staring on a haggard deck
> it seems I find you, young. I come to check,
> I come to stay with you,
> and the Governor, & Father, & Simon, & the huddled men.
>
> *(CP, 133)*

Now the poem incorporates a persona, one of the most successful
techniques from the earlier poems, and combines that with the
wrenched syntax and public intimacy of the *Sonnets,* as in stanza
number 9, for example:

> Winter than summer worse, that first, like a file
> on a quick or the poison suck of a thrilled tooth;
> and still we may unpack.
> Wolves & storms among, uncouth
> board-pieces, boxes, barrels vanish, grow
> houses, rise. Motes that hop in sunlight slow
> indoors, and I am Ruth
> away: open my mouth, my eyes wet: I wóuld smile:
>
> *(CP, 135)*

The first speaker interrupts briefly in stanzas 12–13, to ask Anne if
her poems are written "To please your wintry father? all this bald
/ abstract didactic rime I read appalled" *(CP,* 135) and then returns
again, more intimately, in stanzas 25 and following:

> —I miss you, Anne,
> day or night weak as a child,
> tender & empty, doomed, quick to no tryst.

And she replies:

—I hear you. Be kind, you who leaguer
my image in the mist.

And he:

—Be kind you, to one unchained eager far & wild

and if, O my love, my heart is breaking, please
neglect my cries and I will spare you. Deep
in Time's grave, Love's, you lie still.

(*CP*, 139)

From here on it continues as a dialogue, a duet of seduction and
acquiescence that we as readers are allowed to overhear. It continues
through her life, returning to her voice alone in stanza 9 and
continuing in that until she dies, when the first speaker returns in
stanza 54:

—You are not ready? You áre ready. Pass,
as shadow gathers shadow in the welling night.

(*CP*, 146)

And says, in stanza 56:

I must pretend to leave you. Only you draw off
a benevolent phantom.

(*CP*, 146)

Homage can be read in part as a public version of the *Sonnets*,
drawing on the voice Berryman had developed there and combining
it with what he already knew of writing persona poems. He is able
to sustain the intimacy of the *Sonnet* voice but turn it to a more public
subject. I couldn't disagree more with J. M. Linebarger, who says of
Homage: "The poem risks nothing of the poet's self. . . . Hiding be-
hind the mask of Anne Bradstreet, Berryman tells us almost nothing
about himself. *Homage* represents, in my view, the dead-end of
purely Academic verse for Berryman."[4] I have no idea why Berry-
man *should* tell us anything about himself, or what that has to do with
how good and powerful a poem it is. It seems to me that the voice

that addresses Anne Bradstreet implies a great deal about the passions of Berryman the poet.

This process continues in the *Dream Songs,* where Berryman extends and broadens the *I* he had developed as part of a *we,* and sustains it without addressing himself to a specific other. We can read these as if they're addressed to a wider audience, as a turning outward. Or—which is closer to the way I hear them—as if the speaker is talking to himself, to Henry and Mr. Bones, and we are allowed to overhear that conversation. They are in that sense both more private and lonelier than any of the earlier poems. Perhaps that was more than he could bear: the last poems, those in *Love & Fame* and *Delusions, Etc.* are often addressed directly to the reader.

In his biography of Berryman, Paul Mariani describes the teenage Berryman's efforts to turn himself from the boy nicknamed "Blears" because of his thick glasses into someone "more acceptable to his peers. He smoked Lucky Strikes and collected pictures of movie stars," and taught himself popular songs and how to dance (PM, 22). In the Dream Songs and in the later poems, Berryman was still dancing, but alone, and in the dark.

NOTES

1. John Plotz et al. "An Interview with John Berryman," *Harvard Advocate* 103 (Spring 1969): 5.

2. David Kalstone, *Five Temperaments* (Oxford: Oxford University Press, 1977), 11.

3. David Perkins, *A History of Modern Poetry,* vol. 2. *Modernism and After* (Cambridge: Harvard University Press, 1987), 339.

4. J. M. Linebarger, *John Berryman,* (Boston: G. K. Hall, 1974), 149.

Part 3
Psychological Issues in Berryman's Work

Christopher Benfey

The Woman in the Mirror:
John Berryman and
Randall Jarrell

A man looks at himself in the mirror and sees a woman's face. What are we to make of his surprise? If he has turned into a woman, why does he need a mirror to know it? And if he hasn't, who is the woman? Questions such as these are prompted by a reading of certain American poems of the fifties and early sixties, in which male poets assume a woman's identity. For "confessional" poets like John Berryman and Randall Jarrell, whose primary lyric impulse was autobiographical, this exchange of sexual identities was more than just the creation of "female personae." It involved, as I will argue, a probing of repressed and evaded aspects of the poet's own gender identity. If the resulting texts seem ultimately problematic, it is because a palpable fear of the feminine, and of appearing "effeminate," has disguised itself as empathy for woman's experience. These poets write from within certain culturally restrictive notions of "the feminine," which mark their poems as unmistakably of a definite time and place.

But before turning to the texts, some earlier examples of the same scenario—of a man seeing himself as a woman in the mirror—drawn from a story by Sherwood Anderson and a case study of Freud, should help define an approach to the issues of sexual identity posed in the later poetry of Jarrell and Berryman. Consider a passage from Anderson's extraordinary story "The Man Who Became a Woman" (1923). The narrator is a stable groom with a night off, a sensitive young man who is a bit at sea in the macho world of the racetrack where he works.

The point is that the face I saw in the looking-glass back of that bar, when I looked up from my glass of whisky that evening, wasn't my own face at all but the face of a woman. It was a girl's face, that's what I meant. That's what it was. It was a girl's face, and a lonesome and scared girl too. She was just a kid at that.

When I saw that the glass of whisky came pretty near falling out of my hand but I gulped it down, put a dollar on the bar, and called for another. "I've got to be careful here—I'm up against something new," I said to myself. "If any of these men in here get on to me there's going to be trouble."[1]

Two kinds of glasses figure in this scene: looking glasses for women and whisky glasses for men. To each gender its own glass. For the young man, to drink another glass of whisky is to be more of a man—it is an elixir of virility—while to look in a mirror is to risk turning into a woman, as though the long history of mirrors as props of feminine *vanitas* had become a threat to this man's masculinity.[2] But the groom's very effort to "be a man" seems to invite the opposite: to bring on his repressed "feminine" side, with its "lonesome and scared" girl's face.

Freud was one of Anderson's many passing intellectual fascinations, especially during the twenties, when this story was written; he may well have been familiar with Freud's case study of the distinguished fin-de-siècle jurist, Dr. Daniel Paul Schreber, for whom "the idea of being transformed into a woman was the salient feature and earliest germ of his delusional system."[3] Schreber, as he reported in his *Memoirs,* often stood in front of the mirror "wearing sundry feminine adornments," and was "bold enough to assert that any one who should happen to see me before the mirror with the upper portion of my torso bared . . . would receive an unmistakable impression of a *female bust*."[4] But whether Anderson knew the case study or not, the cross-gender scenarios are remarkably similar, and Freud's analysis provides a starting point for making sense of these mirror scenes.

The Schreber case became the basis for Freud's theories regarding psychosis. Following his pioneering analysis, this case has inspired such a voluminous commentary, both Anglo-American and (after Lacan's work on Schreber during the fifties) French, that its subject has been called "by far the most famous mental patient ever."[5] While much of the commentary centers on the nature of psychosis, for our purposes it is the more recent (and mainly French) work centering on sexual identity that will prove most helpful.

Analyzing Schreber's desire to be a woman, Freud himself arrived at precisely the etiology we would expect: "suppressed homosexual impulses"; "the appearance in [Schreber] of a feminine (that is, passive homosexual) wish-fantasy."[6] But to later critics, the very narrowness of this interpretation—with its quick equation of the feminine with the passive homosexual, and its limited conception of the "normal" Oedipal process—has been responsible for the liveliness of debate in succeeding analyses of the case.

It may seem, in particular, that Freud has put blinders on his insight from *Three Essays on the Theory of Sexuality* that we are all bisexual, that each person is part male and part female.[7] Might the "feminine wish-fantasy" be an attempt, by poet or patient, to explore aspects of the self that our culture shies away from? Some recent contributions to the literature on the Schreber case have in fact taken this direction. The French psychoanalyst Janine Chasseguet-Smirgel argues that a culture that places undue emphasis on virility can unwittingly foster precisely such a return of (repressed) femininity in men. (Her concern is with Germany in the 1890s, but surely a comparable case is the United States during the 1950s, with its war-hero president and its stereotyped versions of acceptable masculine roles.)[8] Similarly, Jean-François Lyotard, in an essay on Schreber's "Vertiginous Sexuality," stresses the bisexual possibilities of Schreber's "psychosis." Thus Schreber imagines an afterlife in which "one [would] be finally delivered from the difference between the sexes" and quotes Mignon's song from *Wilhelm Meister: "Und jene himmlischen Gestalten / Sie fragen nicht nach Mann und Weib"* ("And these celestial figures don't ask whether you are a man or a woman").[9]

That Schreber was a gifted writer (or *Schreiber,* in a much noticed pun) introduces the literary problem into the question of sexual identity. The American male poets of the fifties and early sixties—John Berryman, Randall Jarrell, Robert Lowell—achieved their most conspicuous successes with poems that seemed close, and often insisted on their proximity, to autobiography, hence the popular use of the term *confessional* to describe them.[10] Berryman's Dream Songs (1964, 1968), Lowell's *Life Studies* (1959), and Jarrell's *The Lost World* (1965) were all attempts to retrieve the past of the poets, often with the help of Freud—albeit a rather mechanical, fifties version of Freud.

But a striking and neglected feature of the work of these poets—
neglected, no doubt, because it fits uneasily with a stress on autobiog-
raphy—is their various attempts to assume a woman's voice. Given
their confessional poetics, this practice of speaking as or for the oppo-
site gender is more ambitious than merely the use of female *personae*.
The distinction between the poet and the woman speaker seems, at
critical points in the poems of Jarrell and Berryman, to break down,
or to be put in question. The female speakers in these poems seem
deeply uncanny, as though the primary aim of the poets was less to
create "believable" women characters than to produce a truly bisexual
poetry, a poetry in which male poets allow their femininity to
speak.[11]

I want to consider Randall Jarrell first, in order to contrast his
relatively superficial use of a woman's voice with Berryman's more
ambitious experiments. If *persona* derives from the Latin word for
mask, Jarrell found a perfect subject for a poem with a female speaker:
the woman's face—that is, the mask assumed by the male poet. In
several of Jarrell's most interesting and characteristic poems, a
woman speaker looks into the mirror and sees that her face is getting
old. Here the fantasy described by Sherwood Anderson and by
Freud, of a man seeing himself in the mirror as a woman, has taken
a further turn, as male poets imagine themselves *as women* confront-
ing a mirror.[12] Frances Ferguson has read these poems as memento
mori: "the characters who see themselves mirrored [are forced] to
recognize suddenly that they have changed irreversibly and that
movement toward death is their fixed condition."[13] But equally ar-
resting in these poems is their open confrontation with narcissism—
though *whose* narcissism, the woman speaker's or the male poet's, is
not always clear—and their somewhat less open confrontation with
the male poet's own sexual identity.

Some of Jarrell's mirror poems are among his best known, for
example "Next Day" (1965), in which a woman in a supermarket
moves down the aisle "from Cheer to Joy, from Joy to All." But here
I'd like to focus on an earlier and relatively neglected poem. "The
Face" (1951) is, according to the poet's second wife Mary Jarrell, the
poem in which "the idea of altering the gender of his feelings is first
apparent."[14] The poem carries an epigraph from Jarrell's favorite op-
era, *Der Rosenkavalier: "Die alte Frau, die alte Marschallin!"* In a note
at the beginning of his *Selected Poems* (1955), Jarrell explains that the

Marschallin laments her age while looking in the mirror, but he says nothing about the gender of the speaker in his poem. Critics have always assumed that the speaker is a woman. John Crowe Ransom confidently called the poem "the tragedy of Everywoman as she stares and speaks into a mirror"—as though it isn't tough for a man to get old and lose his looks.[15] The poem begins:

Not good any more, not beautiful—
Not even young.
This isn't mine.
Where is the old one, the old ones?
Those were mine.

It's so: I have pictures,
Not such old ones; people behaved
Differently then. . . . When they meet me they say:
You haven't changed.
I want to say: You haven't looked.

Clearly Jarrell associated this speech with *Der Rosenkavalier* because of the shared lament over lost looks, but something else may have triggered the association. In Richard Strauss's opera, sexual identity is foregrounded and "in play." Sexual ambiguity is achieved by means of a Mozartean "pants role." The Marschallin's young male lover, Octavian, whom she decides to renounce while she is still beautiful (and not yet *die alte Frau*), is played by a female mezzo-soprano. At a crucial point in the drama the character Octavian disguises himself as a girl. The ensuing complication of genders—a female singer playing a man who dresses up as a girl—might well have seemed to Jarrell to correspond to his own lyric self-transformation into an aging woman. Jarrell, then, identifies with the Marschallin's dilemma, but it is the transformations of Octavian, across gender, that provide the analogy for the machinery of Jarrell's poem.[16] Aspects of the composition of the poem bear this out.

Sometimes Jarrell seemed to think that switching gender was simply a matter of switching pronouns, as though sexuality was more an issue of linguistic than of bodily difference. By concentrating on tricks of language, he could evade the deeper issues of gender identity, as well as his own ambiguous fascination with switching gender.

Toward the end of his life, in 1965, Jarrell was preparing to write an essay on Emily Dickinson, and he was particularly fascinated with the way Dickinson switched pronouns in her poems, which to him implied a change in the gender of her speakers. He reminded himself to "notice change in versions" of poem 446 (from "I showed her Hights she never saw" to "He showed me Hights I never saw—") and poem 494 ("Going to Him! Happy letter!" and Going—to—Her! / Happy—Letter!").[17]

Along strikingly similar lines, and with kindred evasiveness, John Berryman once claimed "to know more about the administration of pronouns than any other living poet working in English or American" (*FP*, 327). As Berryman remarked, he had discovered "that a commitment of identity can be 'reserved,' so to speak, with an ambiguous pronoun. The poet himself is both left out and put in." "Without this invention," he added, "I could not have written [*Homage to Mistress Bradstreet*]" (*FP*, 326–27). A certain ambiguity in the "administration of pronouns" is, then, a trick Berryman and Jarrell mastered early.

But what Jarrell switched in "The Face" wasn't a pronoun; it was an adjective. Mary Jarrell recalls:

> In a letter to a former student at the Salzburg Seminar he described ["The Face"] as "a sad poem about the way one's face looks in the mirror when one grows old." In the copy he enclosed with the letter, the first line was, "Not good any more not handsome—" and continues with a man's soliloquy about his face.[18]

The adjective *beautiful,* as well as the epigraph ("*Die alte Frau . . .* ") suggesting that the speaker is Hofmannsthal and Strauss's Marschallin, came later, when the poem was first published.

Jarrell leaves the speaker's gender ambiguous, however: a man's face may be beautiful, too, and an epigraph does not necessarily identify the speaker. I suspect that Jarrell added the epigraph from Hofmannsthal's libretto because it made him uncomfortable—as though he were betraying an "unmanly" emotion—to lament his own lost looks. It probably seemed more fitting to him, more in keeping with societal assumptions about physical vanity, that a woman would worry about such things.

The speaker in Jarrell's "The Face" is profoundly double voiced, with Jarrell's own lament about his appearance merging with, and disguising itself by, the hypothetical woman's voice he identifies with Hofmannsthal's Marschallin. There is an interesting biographical context for this doubling. In 1948 Jarrell wrote a letter to Elisabeth Eisler, whom he'd met and fallen in love with in Salzburg earlier that year.

> Hannah Arendt said something last night that gave me the feeling of being talked about by posterity. . . . She said to her husband about me, "He has affinities with Rilke, you know." Then, she added, "His face is a little like." Her husband looked at me and said quietly, in a surprised way, "Why yes, that is so." I sat, rather awkward and silent, and finally remarked what an odd man Rilke had been. They both laughed, and I did, too.
>
> I evidently was quite successful in writing "The Face" in a style quite different from my usual style for she said she would never have recognized it as mine.[19]

More than contiguity links these two paragraphs. In the second paragraph it almost seems that Jarrell is saying that Hannah Arendt wouldn't have recognized *his face* as his own. He may want reassurance that he hasn't revealed too much of his own male, narcissistic fears in his poem "The Face." To look like Rilke, on the other hand, is to resemble one of the immortals, to be transported beyond fears of mere physical aging by being of the ages. But Rilke, of course, had an extremely peculiar face, one with a distinctly androgynous cast, and one of Rilke's best known "oddities" is that until he was old enough to go to school his mother dressed him as a girl and called him by a girl's name, Renée. Here again, as with the ambiguous role of Octavian in *Der Rosenkavalier,* a certain covert theme of female impersonation seems operative in Jarrell's associations.

Jarrell's stylistic remark about "The Face" implicitly raises the issue of disguise, and specifically of disguised gender. To have a style "different from my usual [male, autobiographical] style," and yet one that is still mine, is, in this case, to aim for a style that is uncannily ambiguous in gender, and perhaps, in Freud's terminology, bisexual. In Jarrell's poetry, aging and the loss of looks are understood as fear of death. And Jarrell allows himself, in the guise of a woman, to express what he thinks are unmanly fears about death and the loss of beauty. Surely only a female impersonator would say, as the speaker of "Next Day" says, "my wish / Is womanish: / That the boy putting groceries in my car / / See me." Do men consider their wishes mannish? But female impersonation is double-edged. To impersonate a woman is to use a female disguise for certain purposes—in Jarrell's case to explore anxieties that threaten a conventional masculinity. The disguise itself can be a threat, for what could be more effeminate than to be a female impersonator?

The reader may leave Jarrell's poems with a certain disappointment with his efforts to let the feminine speak in his poetry. For it is finally a narrow view of the feminine that he gives voice to. His women are obsessed with losing their looks. They peer in the mirror, they primp, they shop, they long for the world's (i.e., men's) attention. His aging speakers confine their sexual longing to being noticed, looked at. Except for the displaced fantasies of sexual violence and violation in "The Woman at the Washington Zoo" and "Gleaning," Jarrell's treatment of women's bodies is superficial—a matter of faces and surfaces.

If Jarrell's female speakers are primarily concerned with appearance, as though sexual difference were superficial, John Berryman explores a deeper level of sexual difference. Jarrell is primarily interested in faces, while Berryman is drawn to bodies. His answer to the question of sexual difference is Dr. Johnson's: "I can't conceive, Madame. Can you?" In his *Homage to Mistress Bradstreet* (1953, 1956), Berryman adopts the guise of a seventeenth-century American woman poet but—and the qualification is crucial—one he does not admire. "The question most put to me about the poem," he wrote in 1965, "is why I chose to write about this boring high-minded Puritan woman who may have been our first American poet but is not a good one" (*FP,* 328). Critics of the poem, more schooled in twentieth- than in seventeenth-century lyric, have tended to share Berryman's low estimation of Bradstreet. Thus Joel Conarroe, in his pioneering book on Berryman's poetry, writes of Bradstreet's "extraordinarily dull work" and her "derivative blandness," while J. M. Linebarger claims that Bradstreet "is remembered as the first poet in America rather than for the quality of her verse."[20] Berryman himself remarked that Anne Bradstreet concerned him "almost from the beginning, as a woman, not much as a poetess" (*FP*, 328). We may translate this misogynist distinction to mean that she interested him as a maker of babies, not as a maker of poems.

Berryman's Bradstreet poem arises from his disappointment with her verse, from his desire to give her what he thinks are better words than she gave herself. Before his voice, as he puts it in a note, "modulates" into hers, he complains in his "own" voice of

> all this bald
> abstract didactic rime I read appalled
> harassed for your fame
> mistress neither of fiery nor velvet verse,
>
> (*CP*, 135)

It is her body he means to appropriate:

> Out of maize & air
> your body's made, and moves. I summon, see,
> from the centuries it.
>
> (*CP*, 133)

The main reason he has summoned this woman's body is to experience vicariously the act of giving birth to a child.

For this ambitious undertaking, Berryman researched the experience of childbirth by questioning all the mothers he knew, including his own, on the nature of labor and delivery. As one friend remembers:

> J.B. called me one afternoon and said he needed some advice: could he come over and ask me some questions: his "mistress was having a baby." I was in some confusion until it became clear that he was referring to his poem.
>
> He came over and I remember answering, to the best of my ability, his very specific and intense questions: how long did the strong labor pains last; what kinds of pains were they; what kinds of thoughts went through my head during labor; how the pains changed as labor progressed; and so on.
>
> He seemed to be trying to understand, as clearly as possible, *exactly* what a woman went through, both physically and psy-

chologically in the course of giving birth—every step of the way. He tried to understand so clearly that he himself almost seemed to be trying to empathize.[21]

In effect, through his poem, Berryman becomes a woman who, after a barren stretch of five years—the time it took Berryman to write the poem—gives birth to a child. The specificity and ambition of the scene make it seem something more than simply a metaphor for male creativity.[22] Here is Berryman's description, through Anne Bradstreet's voice, of the birth of her baby boy:

> So squeezed, wince you I scream? I love you & hate
> off with you. Ages! *Useless.* Below my waist
> he has me in Hell's vise.
> Stalling. He let go. Come back: brace
> me somewhere. No. No. Yes! everything down
> hardens I press with horrible joy down
> my back cracks like a wrist
> shame I am voiding oh behind it is too late
>
> (*CP,* 137)

There is much to say about this scene, for example that Berryman thinks of childbirth as part fucking, part shitting.[23] More provocative than the "believability" of the scene (which I'm in no position to judge) is the gleeful, virtuoso feel of the passage. Berryman, like Joyce in his Molly monologue in *Ulysses* (who is as much a stylistic influence on the passage as the often-cited Hopkins), conceives of the inner life of women as an uninterrupted verbal stream. Elsewhere, the poem is heavily, even obsessively, punctuated; thus, Joel Conarroe mentions "the unusually large number of caesurae," counting "an average of 12.7 punctuation marks in each stanza, which, in crude terms, comes to something between one and two per line."[24] The equation of male punctuation versus female lack is peculiar, to say the least. Could it be that Berryman and his male critics, in the face of the sheer physicality and otherness of childbirth, can bring themselves to focus on nothing more substantial than punctuation marks and their absence? (The word *caesurae,* in this context, is particularly unsettling, and points to what is being repressed.) At the moment of birth, punctuation all but disappears:

hide me forever I work thrust I must free
now I all muscles & bones concentrate
what is living from dying?
Simon I must leave you so untidy
Monster you are killing me Be sure
I'll have you later Women do endure
I can *can* no longer
and it passes the wretched trap whelming and I am
me

drencht & powerful, I did it with my body!

(*CP*, 137–38)

This woman's peculiar mixture of pride and shame during the act of childbirth may have some historical accuracy; maybe women in Puritan America really felt this way. But one senses a certain distance in the scene, as though Berryman is willing to work out the scene rhetorically without committing himself emotionally to it.

Berryman considered the childbirth scene "the poem's supreme triumph" (*FP*, 329), and his critics—male as well as female—have tended to agree. But I would like to see more discussion of the scene that does not take, as its point of departure, amazement that a male poet could have taken upon himself such an ambitious task,[25] and that addressed instead Berryman's ambivalence toward childbearing and the politics of appropriation involved in his speaking for Anne Bradstreet. Berryman's critics have not advanced beyond admiration, however, and even women critics reading *Homage to Mistress Bradstreet* steer clear of a feminist critique. It is not surprising that a male critic like Berryman's biographer John Haffenden should find the representation of childbirth "almost unprecedented in literature," or that Joel Conarroe should praise "the magnificent twentieth stanza, part of a central passage to which everything in the poem is related, describing the moment of giving birth."[26] One is less prepared for the approving reading by Diane Ackerman, who, after quoting the same stanza, remarks:

This is vivid empathy of course; how many male poets have gone so alertly, so keenly, to the core of a female experience?

> Pain, relish, and disgust come together here to make a shocking, though far from sensationalist whole.[27]

Ackerman veers sharply away from the questions of gender raised by the passage: "It's not just a woman, a woman poet, it's a human being in a fit of being tweaked by body chemistry."[28] The pejorative emphasis of "just a woman" is unmistakable. Ackerman's attempt at universalizing the poem's subject in fact diminishes the complexity of Berryman's empathy; if the subject is "[just] a human being," why bother about the crossing of gender in the first place?[29]

When Berryman arrives at what for him must have seemed the less demanding moment of Bradstreet's approaching death, his/her voice sounds precisely like Jarrell's aging women:

> The seasons stream and, somehow, I am become
> an old woman. It's so:
> I look. I bear to look.
>
> My window gives on the graves
>
> (*CP*, 145)

This is the now-familiar voice of the woman in the mirror, saying what mirrors always say (at least in these poems): you aren't the fairest of them all, and you will die.

Assuming the opposite gender in a poem seems to have had a similarly therapeutic value for Berryman and Jarrell. Both poets felt empowered to express certain things in a woman's voice that seemed forbidden to them as men. Jarrell's discomfort with his own male narcissism is matched by Berryman's unease about the profession of poetry for the male writer. In a perceptive and provocative aside, J. M. Linebarger has seized on this issue for Berryman:

> Most importantly, Berryman admired [Bradstreet] for overcoming "the almost insuperable difficulty of writing high verse at all in a land that cared and cares so little for it." Ironically, in Anne Bradstreet's time a woman was considered a domestic creature and insufficiently bright to compose verse; Berryman once complained [to a *Life* magazine interviewer] that in our time poetry

is considered "effeminate." Both poets therefore had to face a culture that accused them of taking inappropriate masculine or feminine roles.[30]

Thus we may speculate that the promotion of masculinity during the 1950s, like the cult of virility that caused Schreber's discomfort during the 1890s, forced Berryman to abandon his habitually autobiographical poetics and find a more disguised means of expression for aspects of himself that he regarded as effeminate. His merging of Bradstreet's poetic voice with his own allowed him to speak lyrically and without anxiety about the writing of poetry.

The biographical contexts of Jarrell's "The Face" and Berryman's "Homage" confirm this analysis. "The Face" was composed at a time of acute mid-life crisis for Jarrell, when he was entering an adulterous affair with a younger woman (the Salzburg student mentioned above) and worrying about his appearance. Berryman's poem also arose in a time of marital crisis, and aspects of the Bradstreet character were modeled on the real-life "mistress" that Berryman referred to as "Lise" in *Berryman's Sonnets.*

During this period, too, Berryman's own ambivalence about fathering a child reached almost psychotic proportions. He reported in a *Paris Review* interview that his first wife, Eileen Simpson, had been admitted to "the hospital in New York for an operation, what they call a woman's operation, a kind of parody of childbirth. Both she and I were feeling very bitter about this since we very much wanted a child and had not had one" (JH, 223). But Simpson had not in fact had a hysterectomy; the myomectomy she had, to remove a benign fibroid growth, was performed in order to *facilitate* pregnancy. Berryman's fears about his own inadequacy as a father came into play—because of his alcoholism and perhaps his sense that poetry was an unsuitable profession for a man. Consequently, he projected his own "unmanly" ambivalence about childbirth onto what he considered were the more suitable subjects of his real wife and fictional "mistress."

While recognizing the undeniable aesthetic achievement of these poets, we must be willing to historicize their confining notions of woman's voice and female desire. Poems that appear at first glance to be sensitive and empathetic attempts to find an androgynous voice for poetry, and to allow a woman's voice to be heard at a time when the most influential and widely published American poetry was written by men, reveal on closer analysis new evasions, new repressions. For, what Jarrell and Berryman have done is to define a supposedly typical range of "feminine" experience: looking into the mirror, shopping, giving birth, etc. The result is the opposite of a sensitive integration toward some ideal bisexuality. In speaking explicitly as a woman, the male poet may in fact be enforcing an even stronger distinction between the sexes.

What, then, is the task of criticism when interpreting men writing the feminine? One may wish that Berryman had chosen to impersonate a woman poet he admired—Emily Dickinson, perhaps?—but then his words for her would have had to compete with her own. One may wish that Jarrell had imagined himself changed into a woman who worried about things other than her looks, who did not see in every object her own approaching death. The work of the critic, however, is not to rewrite poetry but to understand it. The very limits of these poems are instructive, in historicizing a particular moment in American lyric poetry. A poetry beyond sexual difference may be, as Mignon's song suggests, a poetry from beyond the grave. In the meantime, a questioning of the voices of women and men, in male and female poets, will tell us about the limitations of our own engendered selves.

NOTES

Some of the ideas in this essay appeared, in shorter and substantially different form, in "The Woman in the Mirror: Jarrell and Berryman," *Pequod,* 23/24 (Fall, 1988): 24–33.

1. Sherwood Anderson, "The Man Who Became a Woman," in *The Portable Sherwood Anderson,* ed. Horace Gregory, rev. ed. (New York: Penguin, 1972), 381.

2. See, on mirrors and feminine "*vanitas,*" John Berger, *Ways of Seeing* (New York: Penguin, 1973), 45–64. See also Jenijoy La Belle, *Herself Beheld: The Literature of the Looking Glass* (Ithaca: Cornell University Press, 1988).

3. Sigmund Freud, *Three Case Studies* (New York: Collier Books, 1963), 117.

4. Ibid., 130.

5. Introduction to *Psychosis and Sexual Identity: Toward a Post-Analytic View of the Schreber Case,* ed. David B. Allison et al. (Albany: State University of New York Press, 1988), 2.

6. Freud, *Three Case Studies*, 147. Clearly, the Anderson story has homo-erotic aspects: by the end of the story two men do in fact, as the narrator fears, "get on to" him. In the darkness of the stalls, they mistake the sleeping groom for a girl.

7. Freud, *Three Essays on the Theory of Sexuality*, trans. James Strachey (New York: Avon, 1965), 28–31. See also Freud, *Civilization and Its Discontents*, trans. James Strachey (New York: Norton, 1961), 52–53.

8. Janine Chasseguet-Smirgel, "On President Schreber's Transsexual Delu-sion," in Allison et al., *Psychosis and Sexual Identity*, 162. She finds in the Schreber case "the inability to integrate one's femininity because of a lack of narcissistic cathexis of maternal femininity or a reactive countercathexis of it, and the even-tual return, by way of delusion, of this abolished femininity." Documentation of the cult of virility during the fifties goes beyond the boundaries of this essay, but it might involve such episodes as Norman Mailer's rewriting of *The Deer Park* to make its style more "masculine."

9. Jean-François Lyotard, "Vertiginous Sexuality: Schreber's Commerce With God," in Allison et al., *Psychosis and Sexual Identity*, 153.

10. For a critique of the term *confessional*, see Robert von Hallberg, *American Poetry and Culture, 1945–1980* (Cambridge: Harvard University Press, 1985), 93.

11. Lowell, unlike Jarrell and Berryman, has a very literal way with his women speakers: they are often historical women married to famous men—Lady Raleigh, Marie de Medici—and it's the men who matter to Lowell. He often seems to be raiding his correspondence—with Jean Stafford (as Ian Hamilton has pointed out in his biography of Lowell) in *The Mills of the Kavanaughs*, and explicitly with Elizabeth Hardwick in *For Lizzie and Harriet*. When Lowell tries to embody, or be embodied by, a woman, one may feel that he is simply too resolutely and rigidly masculine for the task. As Jarrell remarked of Lowell's *Mills*, "You feel, 'Yes, Robert Lowell would act like this if he were a girl'; but who ever saw a girl like Robert Lowell?"

12. La Belle, in *Herself Beheld*, is concerned primarily with women writers. "I think it is significant that in my search for mirror scenes I have found precious few in which men use the mirror for acts of self-scrutiny" (9). This is precisely the use that men make of mirrors in the scenes that I am concerned with, but with the added complication that they imagine themselves *as women*. Thus they confirm La Belle's ratio: only as women do they use the mirror of self-scrutiny.

13. Frances C. Ferguson, "Randall Jarrell and the Flotations of Voice," *Georgia Review*, 28 (Fall 1974): 433.

14. Mary Jarrell, "Ideas and Poems," *Parnassus* 5, no. 1 (Fall/Winter, 1976): 218. All quoted texts of Jarrell poems are from Randall Jarrell, *The Complete Poems* (New York: Farrar, Straus and Giroux, 1969).

15. Ransom, "The Rugged Way of Genius," in *Randall Jarrell: 1914–1965*, ed. Robert Lowell, Peter Taylor, and Robert Penn Warren (New York: Farrar, Straus and Giroux, 1967), 173.

16. For an interesting discussion of the genesis of *Der Rosenkavalier* see Herbert Lindenberger, *Opera: The Extravagant Art* (Ithaca: Cornell University Press, 1984). One anecdote addresses the complexity of gender in the opera.

Hofmannsthal imagined the famous singer Mary Garden in the (male) role of Octavian. She never sang it and remarked later that "making love to women all night long would have bored me to death" (250).

17. I would like to thank Mary Jarrell for showing me Jarrell's marginalia in his volumes of Emily Dickinson's poems.

18. Mary Jarrell, "Ideas and Poems," 218.

19. Mary Jarrell, ed., *Randall Jarrell's Letters* (Boston: Houghton Mifflin, 1985), 206–7.

20. Joel Conarroe, *John Berryman: An Introduction to the Poetry* (New York: Columbia University Press, 1977), 81–83; J. M. Linebarger, *John Berryman* (New York: Twayne, 1974), 68–69. For a more positive view of Bradstreet's work, placing her in the tradition of women's poetry in America, see Wendy Martin, *An American Triptych: Anne Bradstreet, Emily Dickinson, Adrienne Rich* (Chapel Hill: University of North Carolina Press, 1984), 15–76.

21. John Haffenden, *John Berryman: A Critical Commentary* (New York: New York University Press, 1980), 23–24.

22. See, on the subject of male appropriation of metaphors of childbirth, Susan Gubar, "'The Blank Page' and Female Creativity," in *The New Feminist Criticism: Essays on Women, Literature, and Theory*, ed. Elaine Showalter (New York: Pantheon, 1985), 292–313. Gubar discusses modern women writers who "were involved in the creation of a revisionary theology that allowed them to reappropriate [from male writers] and valorize symbols of uniquely female creativity and primacy" (307–8).

23. Or, as Haffenden says, "Childbirth is related to incontinence, for example, through the non-predicational collocation of 'shame I am voiding oh behind'" (*John Berryman*, 24).

24. Conarroe, *John Berryman*, 72.

25. For an exception see Carol Johnson, "John Berryman and Mistress Bradstreet: A Relation of Reason," *Essays in Criticism*, 14 (October 1964): 390. Haffenden quotes Johnson on Berryman's "mistake" in "the preternaturally speedy and literal parturition recounted in the space of three stanzas (*John Berryman*, 24).

26. Conarroe, *John Berryman*, 72.

27. Diane Ackerman, "Near the Top a Bad Turn Dared," *Parnassus* 7, no. 2 (Spring/Summer 1979): 144.

28. Ibid.

29. See also the appreciation by Sarah Provost, "Erato's Fool and Bitter Sister: Two Aspects of John Berryman," *Twentieth-Century Literature*, 30, no. 1 (Spring 1984): 69–79. "By projecting himself into Anne, he allowed himself to participate vicariously in this experience [of childbirth]. When he suffered couvade with the laboring Anne, he was immersed in this powerful and rewarding event, while giving birth to the only kind of child he really wanted: the poem itself" (78).

30. Linebarger, *John Berryman*, 70. The *Life* article was in the 21 July 1967 issue of the magazine.

Joseph Mancini, Jr.

John Berryman's Couvade Consciousness: An Approach to His Aesthetics

"Couvade was always Henry's favourite custom," proclaims Henry in Dream Song 124. Apparently, Henry's creator shared that preference: according to John Berryman's first wife, Eileen Simpson, Berryman, having just finished the childbirth stanzas in *Homage to Mistress Bradstreet,* exclaimed, "Well, I'm exhausted. . . . I've been going through the couvade. The little monster nearly killed *me!*"[1]

Berryman and his Dream Song persona are referring to an anthropological phenomenon found in many "primitive" societies, past and present. In its classical form, the father of a newborn-to-be simulates the childbirth activities of the mother, including "experiencing" in himself her physical pain. In other versions of couvade, he may also undergo restrictions of food, activities, and mobility to help insure through empathic connection with mother and infant the safety and harmony of the child. In making *metaphorical* the literal, anthropological definition of couvade, Michael Berryhill describes the phenomenon as "a leaving of the self, but at the same time . . . a recognition of the self's need."[2] He suggests that this concept is a way of viewing Berryman's efforts to learn more about himself by imagining *in himself* the pain of his father, dead by suicide; the anguish of those scapegoated for being Jewish; and the suffering of some of his characters, such as the sobbing student in Dream Song 242 ("I am her") and the boy in "The Ball Poem" ("I suffer and move . . . / With all that move me")[3]

In this brief space I want to gloss this concept further with the aid of Nor Hall's archetypal analysis of the couvade phenomenon. I hope to give some sense of what I call Berryman's couvade consciousness, an orientation that he alternately fought and embraced and that helped him, among other things, to conceive and touch a feminine energy and posture, to empathize acutely with and fully enflesh characters like Anne Bradstreet, to use the wound caused by his father's death as a womb for creativity, and to construct an aesthetics that images the poet as hermaphroditic, birthing the poetic egg that he also inseminates.

The urge toward developing couvade consciousness is, according to Jungian Nor Hall, an *archetypal,* that is, an innate need in men. Though there are many variations of the couvade, all of them, says Hall, recognize that the male needs to actualize his wholeness, his feminine as well as his masculine characteristics. The man enveloped by couvade consciousness, and suffering in his own body the simulated labor pains of the mother, finds that "his role in creation, as in procreation, expands vastly under the cover of couvade because he can act as receiver and carrier of the life force rather than solely as progenitor."[4]

In mythology, where archetypal patterns manifest most explicitly, we see, for instance, Zeus's cutting open his thigh to provide a womb for his unborn son, Dionysus; Paposilenus's using his milk-giving breasts to nurture Dionysus during the latter's girlish phase of growing up; and Tiresias's using his man-womanly presence to birth the secrets of the future for those willing to honor his status (*Broodmales,* 16–17). Hall notes that in its anthropological form, the couvade will be found in those cultures, "that give men no other way of being female" (*Broodmales,* 22), not even through subincision or through the acceptance of the *berdache,* or the man-turned-woman. Only very recently has our own culture begun to acknowledge, understand, and validate the feminine capacity in men to be caretakers, nurturers, and brooding father hens. In Berryman's time this recognition was even less forthcoming, even from men themselves.

According to Hall, a man can be and will want to be mother and nurse only if he arrives at a high level of maturity. To do so requires a loosening or blurring of gender boundaries, an "entering and dwelling in the domain of the other . . . an opening to the play of these [feminine] images in the psyche" (*Broodmales,* 40). In fact, while initiation into manhood involves the male's temporary disidentification with the biological mother, initiation into couvade fatherhood or creativity in general requires the opposite: he must locate his own "capacities for conception and containment that belong to mothering"; in short, "he must locate mother in his own body" (*Broodmales*, 38, 22).

To reach this level of maturity is extremely difficult for males who have not succeeded in the prior initiation, who "have not gone through a natural separation from mother. If they haven't distanced themselves from her to link up with their own soul's lineage, then they are likely to feel compelled to go for it by leaving the mothers of their own children" (*Broodmales*, 25). Far from wanting to develop couvade consciousness by finding the mother within their own psyches, they may wish to distance themselves from that energy anywhere they find it—whether in themselves or in their own wives.

Hall might well have been describing Berryman's own dilemma. Given the vast scope of his preoccupations, including Zen, Freud, and the American character, Berryman no doubt always wished to grow beyond any limiting stage of his psychic evolution. In his comments on Anne Frank, he expressed awe at the "conversion of a child into a person," a phenomenon that is "*not* universal, for most people do not grow up, in any degree" (*FP*, 93). In Berryman's case the earliest obstacle to such conversion was his connection to his mother. In Dream Song 124 Berryman presents Henry's wish to have appropriate access to the mothering principle within him, in opposition to the pull on him toward incestuous fusion with the mother, who with her *vagina dentata* macerates his manhood: "Couvade was always Henry's favourite custom, / better than the bride biting off the penises, pal, / remember?" As Berryman's biographers record and as his poetry and prose confirms, he alternately worshiped and hated his biological mother, the primary incarnation of mothering energy in his life. Both her overbearing attention to him and her iced rejection of him, which attached him even more to her, came to characterize the mother archetype for him. In a 1960 letter to her, he sounded a would-be note of separation: "Everyone wants and needs to be heard, not smothered . . . I am long since grown a man, Mother, and must be treated with the forbearance which I myself try to extend to . . . you & others."[5]

His mother's smothering was not counterpointed by a strong fathering principle. John Smith, Berryman's biological father, killed himself when the boy was eleven. This wound, occuring so early in the child's life, prevented a firm identification with the masculine principle. If it occurs during middle age, after separation from the mothering energy through solid contact with the masculine principle, such a wound can have a *positive* effect, weakening gender identification so that a man "becomes suddenly like a maiden—subject to flowing," "opening, softening" (*Broodmales,* 25, 27), and ready to develop couvade consciousness. This wound, a fissure in a mindset, opens the male to a descent to the underworld; his wound then becomes womb, the capacity to be impregnated and give birth to a new way of being in the world.

For much of his life Berryman felt threatened by the *vagina dentata* of the archetypal mother, which he fought by maintaining an often belligerent if not violent, priapic, pseudomasculine posture toward the many mothering women he—ironically—sought out. In 1970 he "suddenly saw that [his] life long attitude towards women— helpless fascination & universal quest—masked RAGE & HATRED" towards his smothering and rejecting mother.[6] In this context it is not hard to see one source for the strong ambivalence, the "spasm of chagrin" (JH, 406; see also 313–14), that Berryman always felt towards his children (see JH, 257–58, 315, 406–7). According to Eileen Simpson, he feared that children would compete with him for the available mothering energy and be "enemies of [his] promise" (*Poets,* 47). Thus he assumed a posture of uninitiated immaturity, remaining a child who longed for yet feared the mothering energy.

Given this predisposition, it is amazing that Berryman could develop any measure of couvade consciousness. Yet his biographers relate occasions in which Berryman took into himself the pain of others to help them birth a new perspective. Such appeared to be the case when he soothed Eileen's fears over the reception of her master's thesis: "His generous praise," she recalls, "told me I had nothing to fear from the committee of professors that would judge it."[7] In another instance of couvade consciousness, he hovered over the dying Bhain Campbell, encouraging the sick man "to keep up his writing, entertaining him with good conversation, gaiety and wit, and bringing him little things for his physical comfort." (JH, 123).

Such bits of couvade consciousness could not be sustained, however, especially with females who were close to him. The first recorded instance of his referring directly to the couvade—when he was composing *Homage*—is a case in point. Eileen Simpson records that, at the moment Berryman had just been through the couvade with Anne Bradstreet, he "handed me this passage and threw himself down on the floor next to the couch where I was stretched out" (*Poets*, 226). He was placing himself in the posture of couvade relative to Eileen, who had suffered many back problems and was recovering from an operation to remove impediments to her conceiving. Yet Berryman was oblivious to Eileen's own pain and later denied her capacity to have children, describing her operation as a kind of hysterectomy.[8] When Berryman's first child was born, couvade was on his mind though not in his heart: in self-pity he told a friend who was commiserating with him about his broken ankle not to give him "any tenth-grade Freud about my having to be in hospital while my wife is there too!" (JH, 312).

In fact, it was not in life, but only through his mature art that he could sustain couvade consciousness. In a few early poems, like "The Ball Poem" and one or two Nervous Songs, he had briefly joined with his character's process, but he had also distanced himself from the comparably cerebral protagonist of the *Sonnets*. He came closer to developing couvade consciousness in the composition of *Stephen Crane*, for he conceived Crane's issues with parents, God, and art as largely his own. It was *Homage*, however, that provided him with the opportunity to connect with mothering energy inside and outside himself without being inundated by it. Despite his fear, Berryman was determined to go through the couvade with Anne Bradstreet—with his fantasy image of her, that is.

"Our first American poet but . . . not a good one" (*FP*, 328) Anne hardly seemed an intimidating figure. This "boring high-minded Puritan woman" (*FP*, 328) who wrote "bald / abstract didactic rime" (*CP*, 135), could hardly engulf his poetic manhood. "I'll make her dance, that poor harmless woman," he wrote in his draft notes. He could feel "relief at her distance (. . . inaccessible): three centuries."[9] Most important, however, to his readiness to approach her was the fact that her feminine energy had not been manifest in motherhood until five years after she married, a rather long wait in those times.

With such defenses against engulfment, he could tackle "the problem [of making] the fantasy believable" ("Poetry XVI," 196), of making Anne come alive enough for him to really experience her emotions. "Before I commenced my readings & study of AB," said Berryman in his draft notes, "she was to me a myth, without form or comeliness, only a name; now she is a living reality, one of my nearest & dearest friends, w. whom I am well acquainted." He therefore could commiserate in a couvadelike way with several of her painful struggles, particularly with God and the "almost insuperable difficulty of writing high verse at all in a land that cared and cares so little for it" (*FP*, 328). Given his own grievous losses, he could sympathize with her being "Dispossessed! of England, of King, of homes here, of friends, by fire, of children, of parents, of *body*" (Notes). Only this combination of great distance from her and connection to her allowed him to celebrate her mothering energy: she was "the Great Goddess—ancestress—first poetess—Mother—Mary" (Notes) of "the artists and intellectuals who would follow her. . . . People like Jefferson, Poe, and me," ("Poetry XVI," 195).

Seeing himself as son of Anne-the-Great-Mother and feeling her pain as his own was not enough, however, to develop fully couvade consciousness, for the latter implies that one becomes, not just sympathetic, but also mothering—that is, able to conceive as well as inseminate. Inseminating is just what he seemed to want to do when he asserted that, along with his intention "to insert . . . *Me* . . . in my own person, John Berryman, *I*, into the poem" ("Poetry XVI," 195), he wanted in the role of poet " 'to seduce her' " (*Poets*, 226).

In the opening stanzas, where Anne is called back into life out of the grave, the poet tries to tempt her away from her beloved Simon by speaking to her sympathetically about the "grand dark" of the New England winter and by appealing to their connection to one another: "We are on each other's hands / who care. Both of our worlds unhanded us" (*CP*, 133). He seems to recreate her body in this process: "Out of maize & air / your body's made, and moves. I summon, see, / from the centuries it" (*CP*, 133). But such creation does not result from couvade consciousness. Hall notes that "the shady side of sympathy is power, and . . . attempts to act sympathetically can tip over into destructive control" (*Broodmales*, 14). Moreover, "Brooding [like a nurturing hen] turns ominous when it hovers without cherishing. . . . Brooding turns morbid when it loses its object [in self-absorption]. Dark brooding establishes distance between people regardless of proximity" (*Broodmales*, 11). It is hardly surprising then that the poet's next words to Anne are "I think you won't stay" (*CP,* 133).

To his delight, she does stay, when he lays aside his priapic, hegemonic intentions. He becomes like the male undergoing couvade, who by choice weakens "the habitual stance of defended manhood" (*Broodmales,* 35), partly by giving up or restricting his usual masculine activities: "He lays his hatchet in the arm of a tree and sticks his hunting spears into the ground" (*Broodmales,* 12). The poet imitates this behavior by ceasing to speak aloud, by backing off, becoming "wombly," and so letting Anne speak alone and in turn give birth to her life's story, almost without interruption, until she is ready to hear him speak. In this process, he restricts himself instead of her and watches how she manages with other restricting, patriarchal males, including "so-much-older Simon" (*CP,* 136), her father, the ministers who "blether, blether" and banish Anne Hutchinson (*CP,* 138), the devil as "Father of lies" (*CP,* 142), and the "wintry father" God with his "crumpling plunge of a pestle" (*CP,* 135, 141). These unyielding male figures show the poet the darkness of his own single-minded nature, the need to soften into couvade consciousness, especially before the childbirth scene.

His merely *hearing* Anne's painful words is not, however, what develops the poet's couvade consciousness fully. To pursue such development, Berryman engages in a brilliant voicing technique: he makes the poem "entirely voiced"—quotation marks implied at both ends—so that he is speaking the entire poem, including Anne's words.[10] He quotes her words just as she quotes those of her children. As Berryman wrote in his draft notes: "It is clear that in the last line of stanza 4, the poet's voice is already modulating into the woman's, and on the other hand that her voice is not fully established until stanza 7, line 3" (Notes). In this switch, Berryman's becomes a background voice, a parallel whispering. As his voice speaks Anne's words along with her, as she in turn utters her children's along with them, he experiences her perceptions and emotions nearly firsthand. The poem becomes an enacting of the couvade in an almost literal sense, especially in the childbirth scenes. Anne screams and moans her anguish and joy:

> everything down
> hardens I press with horrible joy down
> my back cracks like a wrist

shame I am voiding. . . .

and it passes the wretched trapt whelming and I am me
drencht & powerful

                                                                    (*CP*, 137–38)

As she does so, the poet who voices her words also screams joy and
anguish, and the overseeing male God, formerly hegemonic, now
becomes an "unforbidding Majesty" and "sways . . . nearby" (*CP*,
138), not in power over her but in the yielding of the feminine spirit.

It is only after this mutual birthing,[11] which renders the poet
both father and mother, that poet and character are able to speak to
each other, conceiving their love in a way that realizes Anne's carnal-
ity and the poet's spirituality more comprehensively than did their
historical lives. Though they make love in a passionately spiritual
way, the poet restrains much of his lust and allows her to return to
her historical life, to her husband and children, and to her death. As
Eileen Simpson notes, "In the nightmare period when [Anne] is dy-
ing, . . . John behaved, alternately, as if he was dying, and as if he was
killing her off" (*Poets*, 228). He continues the couvade, experiencing
what she is experiencing, speaking once again as an underground
voice parallel to hers.

Her death is also the end of the poem. When Anne says to her
weakening heart, "Wandering pacemaker, unsteadying friend, . . .
beat when you will our end" (*CP*, 145), she also speaks to the poet.
He is her new heart, the often erratic, yet lovingly unsettling pace-
maker of both the poem and her fantasy life. But he is both speaking
her words along with her and saying these words to her as a fellow
poet and creator with whose help he has birthed the poem. As Nor
Hall might say, the poem (her life, their encounter), which both of
them generated, conceived, and brooded over, is like a child "twice-
born . . . once from the mother and once from the father" (*Broodmales*,
16). It is also twice-born into death, once from the mother and once
from the father. Yet this death is also a new birth, a permanent source
of love: "In the rain of pain & departure, still / Love has no body and
presides the sun, / and elfs from silence melody" (*CP*, 147).

Berryman's couvade consciousness, fully birthed in this poem,
helped him create the Dream Songs, wherein he once again used the
voicing technique of speaking along with his character. Henry himself

also engaged in the couvade, his "favourite custom," as he gave birth to and spoke along with personified aspects of himself.[12] As with Anne, feeling Henry's labors to conceive a self was a way for Berryman to birth more of his own self. With the distance, and thus safety from engulfment, provided by the form of his mature art, Berryman could both inseminate the poetic egg and use his mothering energy to hatch it. With such safety he could also say that the wound of his father's death, which opened so many other wounds, had made a poet out of him.[13] That wound, faced directly in the Songs, could now sustain the wombly posture, initiated in *Homage,* by loosening his rigid defenses long enough for him to feel his way into the painful experiences of friends and colleagues and thus into his own.

Despite the creation of a wombly art, Berryman could not sustain couvade consciousness to any comprehensive degree outside his art. Even in *Homage,* he was able to engage in couvade only with the wife of another man. Nevertheless, through his masterpieces, he was able to touch in a real way his masculine and feminine energies. He used them to turn wounds into wombs, to explore a hermaphroditic consciousness, and to have what Nor Hall describes as a "palatial interior life, labyrinthine levels of meaning to explore, red niches to dig souls out of, and deep enclosures for his own not-yet-born" (*Broodmales,* 39). In his late works, *Love & Fame* (1970) and *Delusions, Etc.* (1972), Berryman dropped the voicing technique that helped him sustain couvade consciousness. In doing so, he may also have dropped the defense that allowed him to touch his monumental wounds and to contain the death that finally contained him.

NOTES

1. Eileen Simpson, *Poets in Their Youth: A Memoir* (New York: Random House, 1982), 226, Hereafter cited in the text as *Poets.*

2. Michael Berryhill, "The Epistemology of Loss," in Richard Kelly's *John Berryman: A Checklist* (Metuchen, New Jersey: Scarecrow Press, 1972), xxvii.

3. Berryhill, "Epistemology," xxix–xxx.

4. Nor Hall & W. R. Dawson, *Broodmales* (Dallas, Texas: Spring Publications, 1989), 39. Hereafter cited in the text by title.

5. John Berryman to his mother, dated "Sunday, Berkeley," 1960, JB Papers. This letter may also be found in *DH.*

6. John Berryman, Draft notes for *Recovery,* MS, TS, JB Papers.

7. Eileen Simpson, *Reversals: A Personal Account of Victory Over Dyslexia* (Boston: Houghton, Mifflin, 1979), 196.

8. Peter A. Stitt, "The Art of Poetry XVI," *Paris Review* 14 (Winter 1972): 196–98. Hereafter cited in the text as "Poetry XVI."

9. John Berryman, draft notes for *Homage to Mistress Bradstreet*, MS, TS, JB Papers. Hereafter cited in the text as Notes.

10. For a much more extensive discussion of this very complicated voicing technique, see my book, *The Berryman Gestalt: Therapeutic Strategies in the Poetry of John Berryman* (New York: Garland, 1987), chapter 2 ("'And I Blossom' *Homage to Mistress Bradstreet*"); and, for its use in the Dream Songs, chapter 3 ("'A Living Voice': Dramatic Structures in *The Dream Songs*").

11. For a more thorough discussion of births and deaths in *Homage,* see my *The Berryman Gestalt,* chapter 2.

12. See my *The Berryman Gestalt,* chapter 3.

13. John Berryman, untitled notes, JB Papers.

John Clendenning

Rescue in Berryman's *Crane*

In the final pages of his critical biography of Stephen Crane, John Berryman produced a dazzling, brilliant, though often-disputed explanation of one of Crane's "most puzzling habits": his repetitive structuring of plots based on thwarted rescues ("The Color of This Soul," *SC*, 297–325). Taking a clue from Freud's 1910 essay, "A Special Type of Choice of Object Made by Men,"[1] Berryman claimed that the desire to rescue a love object informs and underlies Crane's art, his art being an effort to represent and heal an ancient wound. In a striking revision of Freud's analysis, Berryman depicted Crane as a failed savior or demonic executioner who avenges his primordial wrong by turning rescue into rape, defacement, dementia, and suicide. As Berryman observed: "Sadism grinds strong in Crane's work, and its counterpart masochism does" (*SC,* 317).

> Torn, miserable and ashamed of my open sorrow,
> I thought of the thunders that lived in my head
> And I wish to be an ogre
> And hale and haul my beloved to a castle
> And there use the happy cruel one cruelly
> And make her mourn with my mourning.[2]

Who else but Berryman, the Berryman of the Dream Songs, was more disposed to extract from and project onto Crane this theme of misbegotten rescues?

> But never did Henry, as he thought he did,
> end anyone and hacks her body up

and hide the pieces, where they may be found.
He knows: he went over everyone, & nobody's missing.
Often he reckons, in the dawn, them up.
Nobody is ever missing.

(*DS*, 29)

Berryman's *Crane*—his critical rescue of Crane and his extrapolation
of rescue in Crane—was a detour that ended twenty-two years later
on the Washington Avenue Bridge. Ostensibly describing Crane,
Berryman wrote: "Death ends the terrible excitement under which
he is bound to live, death resolves panic, death is 'a way out,' a
rescue" (*SC*, 318). In Freud, Berryman sought an understanding of
Crane's mental life, his suicidal behavior, and the theme of suicide
that runs throughout his writings. As Paul Mariani has observed,
psychoanalysis also served Berryman as a source for self-exploration
(PM, 219).

Freud's "A Special Type" does not, however, address the ques-
tion of suicide. Far from it, this first of three "Contributions to the
Psychology of Love" treats the motives underlying certain libidinal
attachments. Freud observed that some of his neurotic male patients
exhibited an obsession, amounting to the exclusion of all other sexual
interests, for a certain type of woman. Such men are ruled by two
"preconditions for loving." The first of these requires that a desired
woman be perceived as belonging to another man, "an injured third
party," against whom the neurotic lover directs his triumphant en-
mity by wresting the chosen object from a prior claim of possession.
More often than not, this woman is also sexually discredited: she may
be an unfaithful wife, a conspicuous flirt, or *une grande amoureuse*. Her
reputation for capricious and promiscuous affairs may alarm the
lover, but it does not deter him. Indeed, this "love for a prostitute"
is his second precondition for loving. Fear of scandal and the vexa-
tions of jealousy actually heighten this lover's passions and become
indispensable components of his fantasies. His behavior is accord-
ingly governed by a compulsion to repeat the scenario. He enters into
a series of replicated liaisons, each one accented by the same degree
of fidelity and intensity, even though these affairs always reduce him
to misery. Freudians will find it easy to understand this behavior as a
regression to the Oedipal stage—especially in men who experience a
strong pre-Oedipal attachment to their mothers throughout child-

hood and well into puberty. In such men the maternal prototype is stamped on all love objects, and every woman who arouses a sexual response will be a mother surrogate.

Freud noted that this neurosis is also accompanied by a startling urge to rescue the woman from some deplorable fate. The seducer clings to the conviction that he alone can be her savior. Having degraded his mother to the level of a harlot, he now seeks to purify her by converting her into a saint. He must show her the way to virtue.[3]

Berryman aligned this frame to Stephen Crane and found it to match at every point. Crane's love affairs with married women (Lily Brandon and others) and his attempted rescues of prostitutes (Dora Clark and others) displayed Freud's thesis "with perfect distinctness" and gave it "decisive confirmation" (*SC*, 300–301). This conclusion, so compelling to Berryman, has not won favor from traditional scholars. Edwin H. Cady, irritated by the "lay-Freudian" approach, chastised Berryman for failing to obey "the rules of evidence."[4] R. W. Stallman condemned the entire effort as "literary pseudo-psychoanalytic conjectures."[5] In fairness to the critics, one must admit that Berryman knew almost nothing about Crane's early childhood, his libidinous attachment to his mother, or his presumed rivalry with his father. In the 1940s the facts known about Crane, limited mainly to his writings and the now-discredited biography by Thomas Beer, provided little basis for depth psychology.

Identifying strongly with Crane, yet lacking crucial information, Berryman delved into his own life in order to fill his subject's interstices. As a result of this transference, the line between the biographer and the biographical subject becomes indistinct, and many readers will feel that *Stephen Crane* tells not one, but two life stories. We know that the Crane project, initiated allegedly by accident, coincided with a crisis—certainly neither the first nor the last—in the poet's life. Addiction, adultery, divorce, psychotherapy—all sinewed into Berryman's *Crane*—produced a work of penetrating brilliance, yet still a maze of mirrors. Searching for Crane, we find Berryman everywhere—especially in their relationships with women, the "objects" that Freud had discerned as "a special type of choice." We are told that Stephen "met his fate" in the person of Cora Taylor, the mistress of the Hotel de Dream, the woman who became "Mrs. Crane" for the remainder of his short life (*SC*, 151). So also John's mistress, Chris, the goddess/tigress/SS Woman, "faithful as a

whore," held Berryman ensnared, enthralled (PM, 195). In Sonnet
99 these identities merge as Crane—like a bird, Tiresian—witnesses
the poet's unholy tryst:

> A murmuration of the shallow, Crane
> Sees us, or so, twittering at nightfall
> About the eaves, coloured and houseless soul
>
> . . . .
>
> He fell in love once, when upon her *arms*
> He concentrated what I call his faith . .
> He died, and dropt into a Jersey hole,
> A generation of our culture's swarms
> Accumulated honey for your wraith—
> Does his wraith watch?—ash-blond and candid soul![6]

In the metapsychology of the early Freud, the repetition compul-
sion is governed by the pleasure/unpleasure principle: a painful expe-
rience will be tolerated and repeated in order to gain a consummate
gratification. When a boy learns that he owes the gift of life to his
parents, he wishes, perhaps even feels an obligation, to repay them
by producing a substitute, a replica of himself made by replacing his
father through a union with his mother. When he eventually suc-
cumbs to the reality principle, the child/adult converts his wish for
"making life" into "saving life," and so his effort to rescue the harlot
compensates for a long-deferred and impossible desire.

With a bold stroke Berryman projected his analysis of rescue
forward ten years to *Beyond the Pleasure Principle*. In this essay, which
most profoundly treats the compulsion to repeat, Freud explored the
possibility of another instinct, biologically primitive and independent
of the libido, that overrules the quest for pleasure, an innate desire for
an ultimate quiescence: death. In the earlier essay the rescue fantasy
is an investment for future pleasure, a debt postponed, a gift ex-
changed but of equal value. In *Beyond,* the expenditure through com-
pulsive repetition leads not to eventual pleasure, but to the restoration
of the original form of things: *"the aim of all life is death."*[7] In the
economic dialectic of life and death instincts, one is profit, the other
waste. *Différance,* says Derrida, is "the economic detour
which . . . always aims at coming back to the pleasure or the presence
. . . deferred." *Différance* is also "expenditure without reserve, . . . the

irreparable loss of presence, the irreversible usage of energy."[8] Not one aim or the other, but both aims simultaneously: ending life in the act or appearance of saving it.

Berryman was the first to notice how inexorably the rescue theme repeats itself in Crane and how insistently his rescues . . . are thwarted. For the Swede in "The Blue Hotel" "the rescue is over . . . "; he is "wild to die . . . even kills himself" (*SC,* 213). In "The Open Boat," the most successful rescue in the major works, the men cannot defy the "old ninny-woman, Fate," who means to drown them. The snarling waves and their sacrificial victim, the oiler, disguise Crane's "passion for retribution . . . his displacements of rage" (*SC,* 281). The same rage sends Maggie Johnson to her "rescue," not "*from* the water but *to* it" (*SC,* 319). In *George's Mother,* the sequel to *Maggie,* Kelsey imagines "scenes in which he rescued the girl." "He reflected that if he could only get a chance to rescue her from something, the whole tragedy would speedily unwind." Except in fantasy, George saves no one; instead, he "drives his mother to her death by drinking" (*SC* 318–19). The young Henry Fleming in *The Red Badge of Courage* wrestles to save the delirious Jim Conklin who dies in a "prolonged uncanny ecstasy" (*SC,* 282), and the old Henry Fleming in "The Veteran" rushes into the fire to save the colts—"Why, it's suicide for a man to go in there!"—and is immolated (*SC,* 325). Most remarkable is Henry Johnson's rescue of Jimmie Trescott in "The Monster." Racing into the doctor's laboratory, Henry is attacked by a flame: "a panther . . . a delicate, trembling sapphire shape like a fairy lady . . . swifter than eagles, and her talons caught him as he plunged past her." He falls to the floor, and a molten jar turns into a snake, coils, hesitates, then flows "directly down into Johnson's upturned face."[9] "A rescue may be a rape," says Berryman, "and it is only in this unsatisfactory way that I can understand the extraordinary events in the father's room during the fire" (*SC,* 323).

The terror aroused by these menacing rescues prompted Berryman to search for the prototype of fear concealed in Crane's childhood. A version of what he identified as Crane's primal scene turned up in Beer's biography. Although Berryman had ample reason to distrust Beer, he accepted the authority of this anecdote without reservation. "Stephen," writes Beer, "was riding the retired circus pony his brother Townley had found for him along a road behind the seaside town in May of 1884 and saw a white girl stabbed by her

Fig. 1. Holograph worksheet, dated 15 January 1949, by Berryman for his *Stephen Crane*. Documents Berryman's discovery of what he refers to as Crane's "Primal Scene," a breakthrough that allowed him to complete his Freudian interpretation of Crane's life and work. (Courtesy of John Berryman Papers, Manuscripts Division, University of Minnesota Libraries.)

negro lover on the edge of a roadmaker's camp. He galloped the pony home and said nothing to Mrs. Crane although he was sweating with fright."[10] Finding these two sentences, Berryman suddenly erupted. He quickly constructed an elaborate chart, *"PRIMAL SCENE: negro killing girl,"* covered it with more than thirty cross-references to Crane's works, and taped it to a cardboard (fig. 1).[11] "I found the Primary Scene in Crane," he wrote in his diary, "just now at noon and with my brain ready to burst with what is in it I climbed out on the terrace in the cold and sat on the edge" (JH, 210). He could have jumped, but checked the impulse. The chart ends with a frenzied note: "all this, suddenly at last, on Sat. noon: 19 Jan 49—and then the terrace-edge, & *my own life* (as *rivalling* father): it is all fated. Freud saw *truth.*" It was nearly four weeks after he had "absolutely prom-ised" to deliver the book to the publisher and only two weeks before he finished the first draft (*DH,* 230).

The most curious feature of this chart is the inclusion of a variant of a familiar nursery rime:

Hi diddle diddle
The cat & the fiddle
The cow jumpt over the moon
The little dog laught to see such sport
& ran away w. the spoon

This rime appears nowhere in Crane, and yet it is clear that Berry-man considered it a cryptogram for the primal scene. His notes tell us that "diddle" means "fuck" and "cheat"; the "cat" and the "cow" both stand for "mother" ("mountains—to *crush man*"); the "fiddle" is the "phallos"; the "moon" is "father" ("father underneath!"); the "little dog" is apparently the son who witnesses the scene, its vio-lence pacified by his laughter and escape. The "dish," usually in-cluded in the last line, is omitted, and as for the "spoon," Berryman noted "???suppressed utterly?" but he probably considered it a vagi-nal or uterine symbol. A series of rapid-fire conclusions following these glosses shows Berryman, almost hysterical, as he reads the primal scene on this, *"the most important day of my life"* (JH, 210). Using the abbreviation for *therefore,* he lists his psychological in-sights: "aggression against women"; "fear of them (every one is a *forbidden* mother)"; "special fondness for elderly women: he didn't have to *fear* them"; "*rescue* of *whores* (i.e, *keeping mother* [no better than a whore, if she does it too] *from it*")"; "insistence on father's hypocrisy"; "father a 'priest' (I wish him not to do it)"; "SC 'fool' & 'donkey'—*to be crushed by mountain* is *to enjoy mother!!*"; "his *jealousy* of father & mother."

Thus decoded and placed in apposition to Beer's anecdote, the rime reveals a new primal scene, quite as violent as the first, but with the sex roles of the parents reversed. In the first scene, the black man uses his knife to stab (rape, kill) a white woman; in the second, the phallic mother is the sexual aggressor, she mounts (fucks, cheats) the father.

Berryman planned to use the rime as the "key" for a separate essay, "Stephen Crane and the Primal Scene," but abandoned the project after two abortive beginnings. We can only hazard a guess concerning the pattern of interpretation he intended to develop. Perhaps he hoped to relate the primal scenes to Crane's rescues; indeed, they seem very close to the rescue scene in "The Monster." Fire, the sapphire lady, armed with claws, talons, and fangs, leaps upon the prostrate Negro, bites deeply into his trousers, lacerates his face. The black man who stabbed the white woman now becomes her victim. He entered the burning house to save the child, but the "old ninny-woman, Fate," has her revenge. The cat has the phallos, the cow jumps over the moon. Freud's patients wished to rescue their mothers; this mother, quite literally *la femme fatale,* is the enemy.

We know that Berryman once cautiously confided to his psychiatrist the suspicion that his mother had murdered his father, or that she had driven him to suicide (JH, 192). The father's corpse "spreadeagled," Johnson's "upturned face," men crushed by mountains, trampled by horses—these converge, variants of primal scenes, menacing rescues, detours on the path toward death. They belong not exclusively to Crane or to Berryman, but rather to both, like shared mental landscapes.

Undeniably, Berryman's biography of Crane was substantially a self-portrait. One might be tempted to say that it was the product of an irresponsible countertransference. Indeed the two lives are so closely intertwined that it is often impossible to separate biography from autobiography. But as most clinicians insist, countertransference is an indispensable tool in analytic technique. When understood and mastered it facilitates vicarious introspection, without which probably no worthwhile biography can be written. Biography is a palimpsest. The author's traces, inscribed in the text, are imperfectly erased, partially covered by a more spectacular image. To some, these traces are flaws; to others, they add depth, a text within a text, a subplot that enhances the main narrative. Berryman's *Crane* is a work of assiduous scholarship and critical insight. It is, of course, also his effort to work through personal torment, to exorcise his "wraith," and to seek his own rescue through Crane. It has flaws, certainly, but these are the flaws attendant to masterpieces.

NOTES

1. Sigmund Freud, *The Standard Edition of the Complete Psychological Works of Sigmund Freud*, ed. James Strachey, 24 vols. (London: Hogarth Press and the Institute of Psycho-Analysis, 1953–74), 11:165–75.

2. Stephen Crane, *The University of Virginia Edition of the Works of Stephen Crane*, ed. Fredson Bowers, 10 vols. (Charlottesville: University Press of Virginia, 1969–76), 10:66. Berryman (*SC*, 318) quotes these lines from "Intrigue IV" using *The Work of Stephen Crane*, ed. Wilson Follett, 12 vols. (New York: Alfred A. Knopf, 1925–26), 6:149.

3. Freud, *Standard Edition*, 11:166–68.

4. Edwin H. Cady, *Stephen Crane*, rev. ed. (New York: Twayne, 1980), 17, 55.

5. R. W. Stallman, "That Crane, That Albatross Around My Neck: A Self-Interview by R. W. Stallman," *Journal of Modern Literature* 7 (1980): 164.

6. John Berryman, *Berryman's Sonnets* (New York: Farrar, Straus and Giroux, 1967). Cf. the variant of this sonnet in *CP*, 120. Charles Thornbury notes (*CP*, 312) that Berryman changed "German" to "Jersey" (line 11) in 1966. Apparently circa 1947 Berryman knew that Crane had died in Germany but had not yet learned that Crane had been buried in New Jersey. In line 12 of *CP* "or" is apparently a misprint for "of."

7. Freud, *Standard Edition*, 18:35–39.

8. Jacques Derrida, *Margins of Philosophy*, trans. Alan Bass (Chicago: University of Chicago Press, 1982), 19.

9. Crane, *Works*, 7:24.

10. Thomas Beer, *Stephen Crane: A Study in American Letters* (New York: Alfred A. Knopf, 1923), 48.

11. SC and the Primal Scene, Stephen Crane, Box I, JB Papers.

Jerold M. Martin

Things Are Going to Pieces: Disintegration Anxiety in *The Dream Songs*

> I don't understand this dream,
> said Henry to himself in slippers: why,
> things are going to pieces.
>
> (Dream Song 137)

If one were to attempt a bold and vulgar distillation of the sprawling body of thought we call structuralism, the idiom that Henry here employs—"going to pieces"—might serve as a crude, but suggestive, one-phrase summary. The central effect of structuralist modes of thought has been to reveal the fragmented and multiplicitous structures—the pieces—underlying our world, the language through which we perceive it, and, especially, the subjects that do the perceiving. The resulting chaos of linguistic and psychological pieces has littered the landscape of twentieth-century literature. Indeed, I suggest a connection between John Berryman and structuralism because it seems to me that the definitive themes of structuralist analyses are also the salient features of the wasteland of twentieth-century poetry from which Henry's lonely and disoriented voice emanates. Henry's enfeebled cry epitomizes a poetic tradition marked by fragmentation, interconnection, lack of closure, loss of meaning, and, most importantly to Henry's Dream Songs, the collapse of a coherent subjectivity.

The form of Berryman's poem, with its 385 fragments linked by an inexhaustible network of meaning, and its lack of plot or beginning or end, is perhaps the ultimate exemplar of these modern poetic tendencies. Moreover, the fragmentation of the poetic structure is conflated here with the fragmentation of the poetic subject, Henry's psyche, and since Berryman's poetic form seems almost deliberately structural in nature, it is wholly appropriate that certain structuralist psychoanalytic theories should provide the most fruitful approaches to Henry's emotional condition. I am thinking primarily of the slightly dissident school of psychoanalysis that was developed by Heinz Kohut during the 1970s and that has come to be called *self psychology;* but I should note at the outset that the work of Kohut and his successors bears close similarity, on several points, to the theories of another great structuralist reinterpreter of Freud, Jacques Lacan.

Structuralist modes of thinking have always had more or less deleterious effects on the concept of the unified and autonomous self. One crucial by-product of such modes, from Marx to Levi-Strauss, has been the annihilation of the individual subject: the subject has existence only insofar as some surrounding system constructs it. In existential phenomenology, for example, the subject or self is reduced to mere objectness—the subject is defined by the others ("the they") who perceive and thus objectify it. In the view of Heidegger and Sartre, the subject's own being has been taken away. George Atwood and Robert Stolorow, two of Kohut's followers who have developed his ideas within a rigorously structuralist theoretical framework, note that, for Sartre, "the subjective being of the individual is perpetually threatened by the objectivating, engulfing power of alien consciousness."[1]

Modern subjectivity—particularly post-Freudian subjectivity—like many of the texts that express it, feels itself fragmenting into a system of components. From a more cultural materialist perspective, one might conceptualize such subjectivity in terms of the multiplicitous voices of culture that construct identity and hence leave it "deconstructable." The self, as conceived in its more postmodern sense, is a mere reflection of the multidimensionality or heteroglossia of culture. Henry, in this sense, is a vessel or field traversed by a plurality of "other" voices and concerns for which he speaks, and his peculiar anxiety stems from his awareness, however vague, that his own unique self is dissipating into those many voices.

However the material base of that self is conceived, it is structuralist psychoanalysis that provides both the clinical background and the vocabulary for elucidating Henry's discomfort. In fact, Freudianism is important to the Dream Songs on several levels. First, a thread of structuralism is foundational to Freudian psychology, as is suggested by its deconstruction of both dreams and the self into composites of instinctual and social elements. Second, Freud consistently suggested that dreaming and creative writing play comparable roles in symbolizing the unconscious (see *Delusion and Dream*). Berryman is obviously playing with this identity of art and dream throughout the Dream Songs, using dream as a trope for both text and life. Finally, Berryman himself underwent psychoanalysis for several years and was fascinated by Freudian psychology throughout his life. His critical study of Stephen Crane is partly psychoanalytic, and he made a habit of writing down his own dreams for self-analysis. Henry comments on this interest in Song 327, noting that he once analyzed a dream "to forty-three structures," and adding that "a dream is a panorama / of the whole mental life." Berryman made it clear that the Dream Songs were an attempt to write the mental life, and these lines point out the identity between text, dream, and life with which he is playing, as well as the structuralistic (that is, fragmentary) nature of all three.

These themes converge in Henry's bewildered lament in Song 137: "I don't understand this dream . . . why, / things are going to pieces." Henry's inability to understand his dream/life is due to his perception of the fragmentation around him; his persistent anxiety is due to the perception that his subjectivity—his self—is likewise going to pieces. Kohutian self psychology as it has developed over the past twenty years stresses precisely this axis of fragmentation and coherence as the heart and soul of psychological illness and health. True to the background of structuralism, the subject is obliterated in the thought of Kohut and his successors in favor of an "intersubjective context" that actually constructs the "self." The self, viewed as a construct of the experiential environment in which it is embedded, becomes more a structure dependent on the organization of that environment for its own stability, and less a self-determining subject or acting agent.[2] This emphasis on intersubjectivity as opposed to the autonomous subject, incidentally, is one area where Kohut's orientation converges with that of Lacan, who formulated a similar critique of subjectivity.[3]

Given this view of an unconsolidated and dislocated self, the motivational principle behind all human behavior becomes "the need to maintain the organization of experience."[4] All problems of psychological health then are based on the stability of the self's structures of experience:

> A theory of personality development centering on the structuralization of experience will seek a conception of psychological health in some formulation of *optimal structuralization*. [The patient's] subjective world, in other words, is not unduly vulnerable to *disintegration or dissolution*.[5]

Of course, we are not interested in the healthy side of optimal structuralization but in the pathological side, that is, the side that applies to Henry. Specifically, Henry's disorder is that of "insufficient or faulty structuralization."[6] Henry suffers from what Kohut calls *disintegration anxiety,* the feeling that the self is breaking apart.[7]

Both Kohut and his successors make it clear that the development of healthy structuralizations, and hence the avoidance of such feelings of fragmentation, are dependent on the presence of appropriate *selfobjects* during the self's formative years.[8] Kohut defines a selfobject as an object that is experienced as incompletely separated from the self and that serves to maintain the sense of self. That is, the self recognizes the selfobject as a separate entity yet also sees in it an image of itself. In normal development, selfobjects are the parental figures who serve as images by which the child develops its own firm structure. Disintegration anxiety is produced when such selfobjects are themselves improperly structured or absent altogether, leaving the developing self without the necessary mirror response.

In the Dream Songs, we find that Henry/Berryman is obsessed with the absence of his father, who "shot his heart out in a Florida dawn" (*DS,* 384) when Berryman was eleven. The shot rent a gaping hole in the fabric of Berryman's developing subjective structure, one which was never mended. "That mad drive wiped out my childhood," Henry cries in Song 143. The anxiety of the entire book revolves around this great absence at its center, and the suicide is bemoaned again and again. Songs 34, 42, 76, 136, 143, 145, 235 and 384 all refer explicitly to the absent father and the catastrophic results for the son. Left without the mirroring selfobject at a critically formative age, Henry's/Berryman's subjective structure became vulnerable to the kind of self-fragmentation analyzed by Kohut.

It is a fragmentation that is everywhere present in the Dream Songs. In Song 195, Henry evokes the very language of the psycho-analytic scheme I have just discussed in relating the absence of his father to his disintegration: "I stalk my mirror down this corridor / my pieces litter. Oklahoma, sore / from my great loss leaves me." Shattered to pieces by the "great loss" of his father (who worked and was buried in Oklahoma), Henry seeks the mirror—the selfobject—he never had. To reiterate the point from Atwood and Stolorow: the child relies "on parental figures as 'selfobjects' whose idealized attri-butes and *mirror* functions provide him with the *self-cohesion* and self-continuity that he cannot yet maintain on his own."[9] Deprived of that "mirror," the self lacks cohesion and is stranded in the immature emotional state of disintegration anxiety.

Again, there is an overlap here with the theoretical assumptions of Lacan, who posited the *mirror stage* as that point when the develop-ing infant, cognizant for the first time of its own image reflected in a mirror or in the shape of other human beings, initiates an illusion or dream of unity and autonomy. Based on this reflected image, forma-tion of the ego begins (modeled on the wholeness of the surface of the body), and an attempt is made to escape the fragmented state of infancy, when the idea of the body as an organized whole was un-known.[10] Lacan, too, was aware of the ever-present encroachment of the infantile state of fragmentation, which made itself known in dreams and anxieties of bodily mutilation. He described something very like disintegration anxiety, though he traced its roots to a stage far earlier in development than did Kohut (the mirror stage occurs at age six to twelve months, while Kohut's structuralization by selfob-jects occurs during the Oedipal years):

> The fragmented body manifests itself regularly in dreams when the movement of the analysis encounters a certain level of aggres-sive disintegration in the individual. It then appears in the form of disjointed limbs, or of those organs . . . growing wings and taking up arms for intestinal persecutions.[11]

The mirror stage, like the quest for the idealized selfobject, is an attempt at unity by a subject in disarray. When the projection of

unity begins to break down and disarray prevails, images of bodily
dismemberment are the commonly observed result. Atwood and
Stolorow, too, basing their conclusions on their own clinical investi-
gations, make it clear that bodily disintegration and mutilation,
particularly in dreams, is a common "concretization" of feelings of
emotional fragmentation.[12]

As a victim of such disunity, Henry repeatedly refers to and
dreams of mental, bodily, and environmental disintegration. Two of
the earliest comprehensive studies of Berryman's poetry, Joel Conar-
roe's and J. M. Linebarger's, noted this aspect of the Dream Songs.
As Linebarger comments, "The Dream Songs became the autobiog-
raphy of a fragmented personality." Henry, he adds, "saw all the
world and saw it fragmented."[13] Henry first describes in Song 8 his
anxiety that his self may consist only of components that might be
peeled away, leaving nothing. Interestingly, it is some indeterminate
"they"—perhaps the surrounding social milieu that is viewed by
structuralists as both constituting and threatening the self—that
threatens him with this disintegration:

> "Underneath,"
> (they called in iron voices) "understand,
> is nothing. So there."
>
> . . . They lifted off
> his covers till he showed, and cringed & pled
> to see himself less.

The horror of subjective fragmentation is intertwined with the body's
progressive deathward decay in the Song, as "they" also take away
Henry's teeth, hair, eyes and "crotch."

Elsewhere, Henry has a nightmare in which his left leg is
"sawed off / at the knee," leaving him to continue life as a "peg-leg"
(*DS,* 319), and Songs 163–66 bemoan a broken arm in particular
and a breaking body in general. In Song 164, Henry agonizes that
"three seasons" have seen three limbs "smashed" and wonders why
"his friends alas went all about their ways / intact. Couldn't William
break at least a collar-bone?" There are also more general references
that complete Berryman's portrayal of Henry's overwhelming anxi-
ety about going to pieces. "Henry is vanishing" in Song 140: "the

poor man is coming to pieces joint by joint." Bodily disintegration as a metaphor for disintegration of the self, moreover, is again conflated with the actual physical deterioration of the body leading toward death. This is true both in the description of the mentally disordered Delmore Schwartz's death ("He flung to pieces and they hit the floor," *DS,* 147) and in the Opus Posthumus Songs, when Henry himself is dead and buried. This series of Songs that makes up book 4 begins with Henry describing portions of his "subject body" (a notable term, given the present discussion; Kohut uses the term *body-self*) being "slowly sheared / off" as he becomes "smaller & smaller" (*DS,* 78). In Song 81, "they" are again at work, removing pieces until Henry has lost his body: "they will take off your hands, / both hands; as well as your both feet, & likewise / both eyes." Finally, with the worms of the grave at hand, Henry seems to be again searching for the missing something that was expected to provide coherence: "I am—I should be held together by— / but I am breaking up" (*DS,* 85).

That Henry represents a textbook case of disintegration anxiety is made abundantly clear by a further study of the types of behavior typically exhibited by such individuals. In general, according to self psychologists, persons who are prone to self-fragmentation "require immersion in archaic ties to selfobjects to sustain the cohesion and continuity of their precarious self-experiences."[14] When such persons undergo psychoanalysis, the analyst serves as the selfobject the patient never had (the Kohutian version of transference), and by so doing hopes to complete the arrested formation of the patient's structural organization.[15] Outside the clinical setting, however, these "archaic ties to selfobjects" may take different forms, several of which are present in the Dream Songs.

One common form is a tendency toward perverse or exaggerated sexual behavior, activities that "may be viewed as sexualized attempts to . . . counteract experiences of inner deadness and self-fragmentation . . . in an effort to find an eroticized replacement for the selfobjects who in [the subject's] formative years were traumatically absent."[16] Henry spends the better part of the Dream Songs struggling with his uncontrollable lust and the everpresent possibility of adultery—what he calls, in Song 163, his "lust-quest." This first surfaces in Song 4 with his lascivious desire for a strange woman in a restaurant and continues throughout the book with his attachments to numerous women (Songs 69, 142, 227, 289, 343) and the recurrent imagery of "tree-climbing," a metaphor for adultery.

Behavioral responses to the lack of structuralization like Henry's obsessive sexuality involve what Atwood and Stolorow call *concrete symbolization,* a process by which fragmented individuals seek to maintain the organization of experience. Other examples of symbolization may involve attachment to physical objects, like the child's tie to a teddy bear in the absence of the mother. Fragmented adults may have similar "childish" ties to "archaic selfobjects," or they may find symbolization through *enactments* (the exaggerated sexual behavior is an example of the latter, as is hypochondria, like Henry's obsession with his bodily pains and infirmities). More significantly, the fragmented individual may find comforting symbolization simply through expression of his or her condition (one form of which is, of course, art). The constant description of various forms of fragmentation and disunity in the Dream Songs, then, is precisely what the Kohutian psychoanalyst would expect from a victim of disintegration anxiety. Concretizing the condition in this way allows the victim to organize his experience or, to put it another way, the concrete expression of the condition serves as a mirror or selfobject. Within the poem, we see Henry carrying out this symbolization; in writing the poem, of course, the symbolization is Berryman's. He has produced a mirror image of himself, an expression of his own condition, which can now serve as selfobject in aiding his organization (structuralization) of experience.

Dream Song 311 stresses both modes of symbolization—the uncontrollable pursuit of archaic selfobjects and the concrete expression of the condition through art—as elements in the battle against fragmentation:

> Hunger was constitutional with him,
> women, cigarettes, liquor, need need need
> until he went to pieces.
> The pieces sat up & wrote. They did not heed
> their piecedom but kept very quietly on
> among the chaos.

Exaggerated sexual behavior, as we saw above, is one manifestation of the abnormal quest for substitute selfobjects, as is drug addiction.

Kohut explains the result of "the traumatic loss of the idealized parent imago (loss of the idealized self object . . .)" during the Oedipal phase as follows:

> The child does not acquire the needed internal structure, his psyche remains fixated on an archaic self-object, and the personality will throughout life be dependent on certain objects in what seems to be an intense form of object *hunger*. The intensity of the search for and of the dependency on these objects is due to the fact that they are striven for as a substitute for the missing segments of the psychic structure.[17]

"Such individuals," Kohut continues, "remain thus fixated on aspects of archaic objects and they find them, for example, in the form of drugs."[18] Henry's "need need need" for "women, cigarettes, [and] liquor" thus might be explained by our psychoanalytic scheme in terms of the intense hungers produced by early selfobject failure. Though not intended to provide any simplistic (and rather irrelevant) explanations for Berryman's problems with smoking and alcoholism, such an assessment does suggest the possible connections between those problems and some of the insistent themes of the poetry. It allows us to make sense, for example, of the correlation here of Henry's "hungers" with his feelings of fragmentation.

Finally, Henry's pieces refuse to "heed their piecedom": rather, they sit up and write. Some organization or unity is attainable for the victim of disintegration anxiety through expression of his or her condition, and Henry's/Berryman's writing achieves that function. Out of his piecedom comes the artistic expression that organizes (by symbolizing) his experience. In Berryman, as in many structuralist analytical approaches, form is inextricably linked with content. In order to express his condition of fragmentation and produce his own mirror object, Berryman needed a writing form as fragmented as his life. And just as Henry's/Berryman's shattered consciousness still achieves optimal structuralization through the concrete symbolization found in writing, the Dream Songs maintain their organization as a whole despite existing in the fragmented and chaotic form of 385 tiny pieces. The pieces of the poem do not heed their piecedom because a tightly coherent long poem is found in the sum of these parts; Berryman did not heed *his* piecedom because to do so would have meant annihilation. To refuse fragmentation by forcing his "pieces" to sit up and create a work of art that maintains wholeness despite its manifest piecedom was his great—almost heroic—act of self-preservation.

I might have substituted the words *dream* and *dreaming* throughout the paragraph above for *write* and *writing,* for the almost indistinguishable counterpart of art in the process of symbolization, as Freud noted, is dream. Berryman's entire work, as evoked by its title, is a way of playing with this identity between poetry and dream. Atwood and Stolorow, too, note that dreams play as crucial a role in maintaining optimal structuralization as any other means available to the self. Dreams, they contend, "are the *guardians of psychological structure,* and they fulfill this vital purpose by means of concrete symbolization."[19] Berryman held an identical view of the dream world as the defender of the waking conscious, conceiving of dream activity as a "combination of Maginot Line and . . . Strategic Air Command" (PM, 292).

As might be expected, then, Henry's Songs are as reminiscent of the disintegration anxiety sufferer's characteristic dream activity (beyond the basic focus on fragmentation) as they are of such a patient's conscious behavior. In a typical recurrent dream, to cite one clinical illustration, a female patient sees herself being burned down to a heap of ashes and isolated body fragments—most significantly the eyeballs—followed by a symbolic effort to reconstitute the parts: the eyeballs roll and quiver together in the ashes, in a surreal gesture of "communication" or reconnection.[20] Henry, too, often figures his self-disintegration as bodily incineration, referring to himself at one point as a burning cigarette being crushed to ashes by God (*DS,* 266). In Song 199, a jeremiad of dissolution and death, Henry calls himself "ashes" and chants "ashes, ashes, all fall down," a phrase that recurs in Song 253. He similarly laments the infirmity and discomfort of his body in Song 134, where dissolution is again related to incineration, and where such anxieties are again nursed by feeding one of his substance hungers:

> One day the whole affair will fall apart
> with a rustle of fire,
> a wrestle of undoing, as of tossed clocks,
> and somewhere not far off a broken heart
> for hire.

He had smoked a pack of cigarettes by 10
& was ready to go. Peace to his ashes then,
poor Henry,

Henry also exhibits a preoccupation with the eyes in his visions of dismemberment and reconstitution that, while puzzling, is nevertheless also intriguingly parallel to the illustrative disintegration-anxiety dream cited above. The eyeballs (or the eyesight) are the conspicuous objects of removal in several Dream Songs (81 and 85, for example), and it is the eyeballs that are a key element in one of Henry's desperate attempts to envision a reconnection. In Song 195 all of Henry's pieces kneel, and they all scream, "History's Two-legs"—the father's corpse—"was a heartless dream."[21] Henry frantically tries to convince himself, that "reality's the growing again of the right arm . . . & the popping back in of eyes." Henry's effort to quiet his screaming pieces, by imagining a restoration of the dislocated eyes, is elucidated by the interpretation Atwood and Stolorow apply to the final eyeball activity in their patient's incineration dream: "The image of the interaction and communication between the eyeballs at the end of the dream symbolized a further restitutive effort to reconnect the broken fragments and restore a measure of coherence to [the] splintered self."[22] Like this clinical case study, Henry's expression of his anxiety centers around incineration, the separation of body parts (often the eyes), and a symbolic effort to reconstitute the parts.[23] It seems worth noting, finally, by way of stressing the reality of this psychological condition, that the patient who had the dream described above also suffered from an anxiety that her body was actually falling apart. In repeated clinical episodes, the patient would hold her fingers up to the light and, noting their separation, respond by literally stitching them into a single unit with needle and thread. This enactment is the more neurotic reaction to a persistent anxiety, like Henry's, that one is quite physically "going to pieces."

I have suggested here that Berryman's creation of the Dream Songs was an instance of concrete symbolization, clearly explicable in psychoanalytic terms, which amounted to a heroic act of self-preservation. Faced with a horrifying anxiety that his self—his very being—was somehow disintegrating into nonexistence, Berryman devoted his creative energies to describing his horror. By thus expressing his condition, and doing so through a poetic form that finds wholeness in fragmentation, the poet was perhaps able to retain some semblance of psychological integrity—of structure—and avoid the impending emotional dissolution. By forcing his pieces to sit up and write, he demanded that they not heed their piecedom. Berryman's leap from the Washington Avenue Bridge, of course, suggests to us that ultimately the effort to allow these "Bones" to heal and knit ran awry. He could no longer maintain the structuralization—could no longer "hold it together," as it were. As Eileen Simpson suggested in *Poets in Their Youth,* however, we might view the Dream Songs most optimistically as the structuralizing agent that allowed Berryman to put off the ever impending repetition of his father's grim fate for an extra seventeen years. Far from being destroyed by poetry, it was through the Dream Songs that Berryman "kept very quietly on among the chaos."

NOTES

1. George E. Atwood and Robert D. Stolorow, *Structures of Subjectivity* (Hillsdale, N.J.: Lawrence Erlbaum Associates, 1984), 29.

2. Ibid., 34.

3. The Kohutian clinician, for example, does not treat a patient per se so much as he or she engages in an ongoing process of analyst/analysand intersubjectivity, in which neither "subject" is wholly distinct from the other. As Jane Gallop's description indicates, Lacan's view was identical: "Through his emphasis on the intersubjective dialogue of the analytic experience as well as his discovery that the ego itself is constituted in an intersubjective relation, Lacan has shifted the object of psychoanalysis from the individual person taken as a separate monad to the intersubjective dialectic." See Jane Gallop, *Reading Lacan* (Ithaca: Cornell University Press, 1977), 117.

4. Atwood and Stolorow, *Structures of Subjectivity,* 35.

5. Ibid., 39 (latter italics added).

6. Ibid., 40.

7. See Heinz Kohut, *The Restoration of the Self* (New York: International Universities Press, 1977), 93–111, for an exemplary discussion of disintegration anxiety, its developmental causes, its clinical treatment, and its manifestation in dreams.

8. Ibid., 137 and 147. See also Heinz Kohut, *The Analysis of the Self* (New York: International Universities Press, 1971), 44. See also Atwood and Stolorow, *Structures of Subjectivity,* 71 and 82–83. Kohut places these crucial formative events during the years of the Oedipal phase, though he largely disregards the psychosexual traumas that made those years so important to Freud.

9. Atwood and Stolorow, *Structures of Subjectivity,* 37 (italics added).

10. Jacques Lacan, "The Mirror Stage," in *Ecrits*, trans. Alan Sheridan (London: Tavistock Publishers, 1977), 1–12.

11. Ibid., 5.

12. Atwood and Stolorow, *Structures of Subjectivity*, 107–13.

13. J. M. Linebarger, *John Berryman* (New York: Twayne, 1974), 80 and 151.

14. Atwood and Stolorow, *Structures of Subjectivity*, 40.

15. Ibid., 61.

16. Ibid., 94.

17. Kohut, *Analysis of the Self*, 45 (italics added).

18. Ibid., 46.

19. Atwood and Stolorow, *Structures of Subjectivity*, 103.

20. Ibid., 107.

21. I have taken the words "History's Two-legs" to be a reference to the image of Berryman's dead father for several reasons. Among them are the obvious contextual indications here and several other references to the suicide which seem to focus on the father's legs, on the "pastness" or historical nature of the event, and on the cruelty (i.e., heartlessness) of the act (see for example Songs 42 and 76).

22. Atwood and Stolorow, *Structures of Subjectivity*, 107.

23. While the preoccupation with eye imagery in the case of both Henry and the clinical example is peculiar, Atwood and Stolorow do provide a possible explanation. "The specific symbol of the eyeballs," they maintain, "captured an essential feature of what became [the patient's] principal mode of relating to her social milieu." That is, "both her self-restorative efforts and what remained of her vanishing self became crystallized in her waking life in the act of looking and in her recurring dreams in the imagery of the eyes" (*Structures of Subjectivity*, 107). This too, I believe, would be agreeable to Lacanian theory, since in his hypothesis it is the act of looking—the apprehension of a reflected image—that initiates ego formation and first creates the illusion of a unified identity on which the individual thereafter bases its structures of experience.

Part 4
Berryman and Alcoholism

Lewis Hyde

Alcohol and Poetry: John Berryman and the Booze Talking

In looking at the relationship between alcohol and poetry I am work-ing out of two of my own experiences. For two years I was a coun-selor with alcoholics in the detoxification ward of a city hospital. I am also a writer and, when I was an undergraduate at the University of Minnesota, I knew John Berryman (briefly, not intimately).

Berryman was alcoholic. It is my belief that his disease is evident in his work, particularly in *The Dream Songs.* His last poems and *Recovery,* his unfinished novel, show that by the time of his suicide in January of 1972 he himself was confronting his illness and had already begun to explore its relationship to the poetry. What I want to do here is to continue that work. I want to try to illuminate what the forces are between poetry and alcohol so we can see them and talk about them.

Alcohol has always played a role in American letters. Those of our writers who have tangled with it include Fitzgerald, Hemingway, Malcolm Lowry, Hart Crane, Jack London and Eugene O'Neill, to name a few. Four of the six Americans who have won the Nobel Prize for literature were alcoholic. About half of our alcoholic writers eventually killed themselves.

This essay begins with a short description of alcoholism and then a longer sketch of the ways in which it is entangled in our culture and spiritual life, the two areas where it bears most heavily on poetry. In the second part of the essay I will turn to Berryman and take a close look at *The Dream Songs.*

I

Most of what we know about alcoholism comes from alcoholics themselves, specifically from Alcoholics Anonymous. It is their experience that an alcoholic is someone who cannot control his drinking once he has started. He cannot pick up just one drink ("one is too many, a thousand's not enough," is the saying). Another way of putting this is to say *if you are alcoholic, you cannot stop drinking on will power.* In this it is like other diseases of the body. It may be hard to believe—and harder for the active alcoholic!—but I have seen enough strongwilled alcoholics to know that good intentions and will power are as useful for recovering from this disease as they are for curing diabetes.

Because of this it seems clear that alcoholism has a biological component. It is common to call this an "allergy," that is: alcoholics' bodies react differently to alcohol. Some people may be born with this "allergy" (it seems to run in families), others may develop it through heavy drinking. Once present in a person, it hooks into his social, mental, and spiritual life, and it is in these areas that most alcoholics first get hurt. Most have trouble in their family life or with their jobs or end up doing things they don't want to, long before alcohol destroys their bodies.

Alcoholism cannot be cured. Once a person becomes alcoholic, he can never again drink in safety. However, there is a way to arrest the disease, and that is the program of Alcoholics Anonymous. AA is the "medicine" and it works. Of those who join a group, get a sponsor, and become active, more than half never drink again, and all enjoy some improvement. Those alcoholics who don't manage to find sobriety end up in jail or in mental institutions or dead from cirrhosis, brain damage, suicide, or something else related to alcohol.

It is commonly believed that AA is a religious group, but it is more correctly described as a spiritual program. It has no creed. The only requirement for membership is a desire to stop drinking. It does have a series of "12 steps to recovery" and these include the concept of a "higher power." The first three steps read:

We admitted that we're powerless over alcohol—that our lives had become unmanageable.
Came to believe that a Power greater than ourselves could restore

us to sanity.
Made a decision to turn our will and lives over to the care of God
as we understood Him.[1]

They say you can get sober on the First Step alone, but certainly not
with the ease of those who find their way to the others. The move
from the First to the Second Step is a problem for many, but logically
it shouldn't be, for every active alcoholic already has a higher power
at work in his life: the booze.

In AA it is common to refer to alcoholism as a threefold disease:
it is physical, mental, and spiritual. This holistic description was first
put together in this country in the 1930s, and it led immediately to
the first recovered alcoholics and the founding of AA. A key in-
sight—that the disease includes the spirit—came indirectly from Carl
Jung. The story is interesting and helps me begin to show how alco-
holism is tied up with creative life.

Many alcoholics try psychotherapy of one sort or another to deal
with their problems. It notoriously fails. They say that alcoholism is
"the siren of the psychiatrists." In 1931 an American alcoholic sought
out Jung for treatment. Whatever analytic progress they made did
not affect his drinking, and Jung told him that his only hope was to
become the subject of a spiritual experience, a true conversion.

It was Jung's belief, as he explained in a letter thirty years later,
that the "craving for alcohol was the equivalent, on a low level, of
the spiritual thirst of our being for wholeness for the union with
God." He included the line from the Forty-second Psalm: "As the
hart panteth after the water brooks, so panteth my soul after thee, O
God." And he concluded his letter: "You see, 'alcohol' in Latin is
spiritus, and one uses the same word for the highest religious experi-
ence as well as for the most depraving poison. The helpful formula
therefore is: *spiritus contra spiritum.*"[2]

What is a "spirit" in this broad sense? There are several things to
say. First, a spirit is something larger than the self, and second, it has
the power to change you. It alters your gestalt, your whole mode of
perception and action. Both alcohol and the Holy Ghost can do this.
But a spirit does more than give you new eyes: it is the mover. This
is the sense of spiritual power when St. Paul says, "I have planted,
Apollos watered, but God gave the increase." A good spirit does not
just change you, it is an agent of growth.

Spiritual thirst is the thirst of the self to feel that it is a part of something larger, and, in its positive aspect, it is the thirst to grow, to ripen. The self delights in that as a fish delights in water. Cut off from it, it seeks again. This is a simple and basic human thirst, comparable to the body's need for salt. It is subtle and cannot be extinguished. Once woken, it is very powerful. An animal who has found salt in the forest will return time and again to the spot. It is the same with a taste of spiritual powers.

The disease of alcoholism includes what they call a *mental obsession* with alcohol and a *physical compulsion* for it. Once we have understood this matter of spiritual thirst, we see that this is like saying that the moon has a "compulsion" to orbit the earth, or a whale has an "obsession" with the ocean. Man is compelled to move with powers greater than himself. The compelling forces may be mysterious, but they are not a problem. The problem is why a person would get hooked up with alcohol—which is a power greater than the ego, but not a benevolent one. I do not know why, though by the end of this essay I will make a few guesses.

All the psychotropic drugs—alcohol, the amphetamines, LSD, mescaline, and so forth—could be called spirits in the sense I am using. But I would prefer to call them spirit-helpers, first because they are material spirits and seem to be limited to that level, and second because it now seems clear that they are not actually agents of maturation. They do have power: they can show the novice in a crude way the possibility of a different life. I call it crude because it is big-footed and able to bust through the novice's walls. I say *show* because a spirit-helper does not give you the new life, it merely points.

The amphetamines, for example, can show you that it is possible for huge amounts of energy to flow through the body and leave you in a state of almost hopeless attentiveness. However, this is not you. It affects you, but you do not own it. Properly used, such a spirit-helper makes a demand: find the path that leads to the place where you can have this experience without the help. Often the path is long and the things the spirit-helper shows you do not actually become yours for five to ten years. The risk, especially in this civilization and without a guide, is that you will get weary, forgo the five-year walk, and stay with the material spirit. And when you stay with the material spirit, you stay at its level, you do not grow. This is why we speak of their effect as *getting stoned* or *intoxicated,* rather than *inspiration.* Inspiration refers to air spirits such as those that come through meditation, or the Holy Ghost, or the power that rises above a group of people. Air spirits are less crude and they abide. They have power over matter.

Few of these spirits are good or evil of themselves. Their value varies by their use. Alcohol has many uses and all of them change depending on a person's drinking patterns. It is a relaxant and social spirit; it has always been used as a ceremonial spirit; it is a medicinal, a sedative hypnotic, and an anaesthetic.

It is also, along with others of the material spirits, a possessing drug: it is addictive. (Withdrawal from alcohol addiction is worse than that from heroin.) As a spirit possesses a person, he more and more becomes the spirit itself. In the phrase of AA's First Step—"powerless over alcohol"—is implied the idea that the alcoholic is no longer running his life, the alcohol is. Booze has become his only experience and it makes all of his decisions for him.

If he senses this at all, it is a numbed recognition that he himself is being wiped out. After several years an alcoholic commonly begins to have apocalyptic fears. He stops going out of the house because he is afraid that buildings will fall on him. He won't drive across a bridge because he fears the car will suddenly leap off of it. This is the self realizing it is being forced out, but so blind with the booze that it can't see the true cause, it can only project its death onto everything in the outer world.

I am saying that as a person becomes alcoholic he turns more and more into the drug and its demands. He is like a fossil leaf that mimics the living but is really stone. For him the drug is no longer a spirit in the sense I have used, or if it is, it's a death spirit, pulling him down into itself. He has an ever-increasing problem knowing what "he" is doing and what the booze is doing. His self-trust collapses. He doesn't even know if his feelings are his own. This state does not require physical addiction. Long after his last drink, the symptoms of the alcoholic's physical addiction linger and recur—sometimes for years—a phenomenon known as the *dry-drunk.* The drinker becomes alcohol in a human skin, a parasite dressed up in the body of its host.

These issues—spiritual powers, possession, growth, inspiration—clearly have to do with the life of a creative person. But here is a further thing to say about alcohol that connects it even more closely with poetry. Alcohol is described medically as a sedative hypnotic or an anaesthetic. It progressively relaxes and numbs the different centers of sensation, coordination, and control, starting with faculties such as judgment and physical grace and progressing (as with other anaesthetics such as ether) down through the voluntary nervous system.

Anaesthetic does not just mean a thing that reduces sensation. The word means "without-aesthetic," that is, without the ability to sense *creatively*. The aesthetic power, which every human has, is the power that forms meaningful configurations out of all we sense and feel. More than that, it makes configurations that are themselves lively and creative, things that, like art, begin to exist separately from their creator and give meaning and energy back to all of us. If this power were not free and active, a human being would die, just as he would die if he lost the power to digest his food.

An anaesthetic is a poet killer. It is true that some poets have found alcohol a spirit-helper; for some it has broken up static and useless interpretations of the world and allowed them to "see through" and move again. Theodore Roethke appears to be an example. But this doesn't happen for alcoholics. An alcoholic cannot control his drinking and cannot selectively anaesthetize. A poet who has become wholly possessed by alcohol is no longer a poet, for these powers are mutually exclusive. The opposition of these forces is a hidden war in our civilization. On one level it is a social war, for ours is a civilization enamored of drugs that deaden the poetry-creature. But for many the fight is personal; it has already entered their bodies and become a corporeal war between the powers of creation and the spirit of alcohol.

To conclude the first part of this essay I want to show some of the ways in which alcohol is involved in our culture and civilization. To look at it from this level I want to turn to some ideas developed by Ivan Illich in his new book about health care, *Medical Nemesis*.[3]

One of Illich's main points is that pain asks a question. Discomfort makes an urgent demand on us to find its cause and resolution. He distinguishes between suffering and feeling pain. The latter is passive but it leads to suffering, which is the active process, the art, of moving from dis-ease to ease. It turns out that the idea of a *pain-*

killer is a modern one. This phrase appeared in this country only a century ago. In the Middle Ages it was the belief of doctors that if you killed the pain you killed the patient. To the ancients, pain was only one sign of disharmony. It was nice if it went away during the healing process, but this did not mean that the patient was whole. The idea is that if you get rid of pain before you have answered its questions, you get rid of the self along with it. Wholeness comes only when you have passed *through* pain.

Illich's thesis is that "health care and my ability to remain responsible for my behavior in suffering correlate." Relief of this ability, through the use of drugs to separate pain from the performance of suffering, is a cornerstone of which Illich calls "medical technocracy." He writes:

> Pain had formerly given rise to a cultural program whereby individuals could deal with reality, precisely in those situations in which reality was experienced as inimical to the unfolding of their lives. Pain is now being turned into a political issue which gives rise to a snowballing demand on the part of anaesthesia consumers for artificially induced insensibility, unawareness, and even unconsciousness.

A culture in the sense being used here is, by nature, a healing system. Illich speaks of "the health-granting wholeness of culture," and of "medicinal cultures." The native American tribes are a good example: they called their whole system of knowledge and teaching "the medicine," not just the things that the shaman might do in an emergency. As a member of the tribe it was your privilege to walk daily inside of the healing air.

A culture faces and interprets pain, deviance, and death. It endows them with meaning; it illuminates how they are a part of the whole and thereby makes them tolerable. We do not become trapped in them because the culture continually leads out of pain and death and back into life. Medical civilization reacts in the opposite way: it tries to attack, remove, and kill these things. With this the citizen becomes separated from his own healing and interpretive powers, and he and the culture begin to pull apart and wither, like plants pulled from the soil until both become dust.

The widespread use of alcohol and other central nervous system anaesthetics is directly linked to a decline in culture. The wider their use, the harder it becomes to preserve, renew, and invigorate the wisdom that a culture should hold. This then doubles back and escalates. Alcoholism spreads when a culture is dying, just as rickets appears when there is no vitamin D. It is a sign that the culture has lost its health-granting cohesion.

The native American tribes would again be an example. Here were cultures rich in spiritual life and healing power. The Indian, cut off from the sources of his own spiritual strength by the European tribes and unwilling to adopt the gods of his oppressors, was left with an empty spiritual space, and too often the spirit of alcohol moved in to fill it. The Europeans were all too happy at this and often shipped the liquor into the dying Indian villages.

Nobody knows what causes alcoholism. It is one of those things, like a war, whose etiology is so complex that attempts to describe it do not yet help us heal. One of the insights of AA was to quit wondering why a person drinks and just work with the situation at hand. In doing this they figured out how to keep an alcoholic sober after he has stopped drinking. Two chapters in the AA "Big Book" describe how the program works. They list typical situations in which alcoholics who have found sobriety begin to drink again. By looking at these, we can do a sort of backwards etiology of the disease. Here are three examples:

"Resentment is the 'number one' offender. It destroys more alcoholics than anything else."

The alcoholic is "driven by a hundred forms of fear, self-delusion, self-seeking, and self-pity."

"The alcoholic is an extreme example of self-will run riot."

In summary, AA has found that the following may lead a sober alcoholic back to drinking: resentment, self-centeredness, managing, trying to do everything yourself, and keeping secret the things that hurt you. There are two categories in this list. An alcoholic will drink again (1) if he sets himself up as self-sufficient and (2) if he gets stuck in the mechanisms that defend this autonomy. *Individualism and its defences support the disease of alcoholism.* Just one more example: in this civilization we take personal credit for change and accomplishment. But it is AA's experience that if an alcoholic begins to feel personally responsible for his sobriety, or if he tries to take control of the group, or if he breaks his anonymity, he will probably drink.

Getting sober goes against the grain of our civilization. This grain consists of money and technology. For more than a century these have been our dominant models for security and liveliness. I want to show quickly how these models feed "individualism" and its false sense of human and higher powers. To begin with we have misperceived the nature of machines. First, we have assumed that they run by themselves, that they can be isolated and self-sustaining. Second, we have thought they were our slaves. But it has turned out that the model of life that includes slavery diminishes humans, regardless of whether those slaves are people or machines. And finally, we have forgotten that mechanical power is only one form of power. It is authentic and important, but limited. In the last fifty years it has become so inflated as to impoverish other forms of power. (These points can also be made about money—we have assumed that money could be left alone to "work" for us, and out of this assumption it has become an autonomous and inflated power.)

But neither money nor machines can create. They shuttle tokens of energy, but they do not transform. A civilization based on them puts people out of touch with their creative powers. There is very little a poet can learn from them. Poems are gifts. The poet works them, but they are not his, either in their source or in their destination. The differences between mechanical and monetary power and creative power are not of themselves a problem, but when the former become inflated and dominant, as they have in this century, they are lethal to poetry.

Hart Crane is an example. He was a poet born into a typically mercantile American family. His father invented the life saver and built up the family candy business. Between the time he left home and the time he killed himself, Crane made endless flesh trips back and forth between his creative energies and his father's designs. There was one horrible hot summer when he ended up in Washington, D.C. trying to sell the family sweets. You cannot be a poet without some connection to others—to your group or family or class or nation . . . —but all that was offered to Crane was this thing that kills poets. It is not an exaggeration to say that these forces divided him from his own life energies and contributed to his alcoholism and his death.

The link between alcoholism and technical civilization—and the reasons they are both antithetical to poetry—is their shared misunderstandings about power and powerlessness. It is a misunderstanding that rises out of the inflation of mechanical power and results in the impoverishment of personal power, the isolation of creative energy, the blindness to high powers, the limitation of desire to material objects, and a perversion of the will.

In a technological civilization one is deprived of authentic expressions of creative energy because contact with the outer world does not lead to real change (transformation). When this happens it becomes impossible to make judgments on the limits and nature of your personal power. You become stupefied, unable to perceive either higher powers or your own. You have a vague longing to feel creative energy, but no wisdom to guide you. Such a person is a sitting duck for alcoholism.

The disease begins and ends with an empty willfulness. The alcoholic fighting his disease has no authentic contact because nothing changes. The revelation that the alcoholic is powerless over his drinking was one of the founding insights of AA. And the admission of this powerlessness is the First Step in arresting the disease. The paradox is that the admission of powerlessness does not lead to slavery or obliteration, but the opposite. It leads to revaluation of personal power that is human, bounded, and authentic.

II

Here is a curious quote from Saul Bellow's introduction to John Berryman's unfinished novel, *Recovery*. It refers to the time when Berryman began *The Dream Songs*[4]:

> John had waited a long time for this poet's happiness. He had suffered agonies of delay. Now came the poems. They were killing him. . . . Inspiration contained a death threat. He would, as he wrote the things he had waited and prayed for, fall apart. Drink was a stabilizer. It somewhat reduced the fatal intensity. (*R*, xii)

What does this mean, "Inspiration contained a death threat"? Bellow is hot on the trail of a half-truth. When one is in-spired, filled with the breath of some other power, many things die. The conscious ego dies, or at least falls back, when the inspiring powers speak. But is this a *threat*? Certainly it is a risk, like any change, but religions and artists have long held that this inspiration is joyful and enlivening, not threatening.

There seem to be two kinds of death: the "greatful death" that opens outward with release and joy, and the bitter or stone death that tightens down on the self. An alcoholic death is of the second kind. The self collapses; it does not rise. Bellow is right, there was a relationship between this poet's drinking and his inspiration, but he has the structure of it wrong. For an alcoholic, imbibing itself is fatal to inspiration. The poems weren't killing Berryman. Drink was not the "stabilizer" that "reduced the fatal intensity." Alcohol was itself the "death threat."

It is my thesis here that this war, between alcohol and Berryman's creative powers, is at the root of the Dream Songs. I will show how their mood, tone, structure, style, and content can be explicated in terms of alcoholism. Further, that Berryman himself (at the time he wrote the poems) was blind to this. His tactics, aesthetics, and epistemology were all wrong, and by the end of the book booze had almost wholly taken over. He lost the war. The bulk of the Dream Songs were written by the spirit of alcohol, not John Berryman.

Before I unfold a particular example, I want to say a few words related to the tone of the Dream Songs. As I outlined above, in the course of getting sober an alcoholic must deal daily with his own anger, self-pity, willfulness, and so on. If he doesn't face these, the booze will latch onto them and keep him drinking. As the "Big Book" says, they "may be the dubious luxury of normal men, but for alcoholics these things are poison."

Self-pity is one of the dominant tones in the Dream Songs. To understand it we must first look at pity. William Blake wrote that "Pity divides the soul." Apparently a part of the soul goes out to a person we pity. A corollary to this is that one cannot grow or change and feel pity at the same time, for growth comes when the soul is whole and in motion. This is old wisdom, common in ancient tales. For example in Apuleius's story "Amor and Psyche" (lately revived by Erich Neumann)[5] Psyche, when she has to journey into the underworld, is warned by a tower that pity is not lawful down there. "As thou crossest the sluggish river, a dead man that is floating on the surface will pray thee, raising his rotting hands, to take him into the boat. But be thou not moved with pity for him, for it is not lawful." Another example: among the Zuni Indians, a gravedigger is supposed to be immune to pity, for if he pities the newly dead he will be vulnerable to their cries and they will carry him off.

In pity, when a part of the self goes out to the sufferer, the self is not free to move until the sufferer has been relieved of his hurt. So there are two situations in which pity is dangerous. One is that in which the self is in need of all its faculties to survive, as in Psyche's passage through the underworld. The other is the case in which the sufferer cannot be made whole again, as with the truly dead. It seems that death-energy is so strong that if a person identifies with the dying, he will be hopelessly sucked in.

This is why Jesus says, "Let the dead bury their dead." When Jesus himself took pity on Mary and her tears over Lazarus, his own soul was torn. (St. John says that he "groaned in the spirit.") The interesting thing is that he could not raise the dead in this condition. Before he could act, he had to first address the Father in order to regain his wholeness. You cannot raise the dead if you have pity on them. It is only done with love and love's wholeness. Pity is directed to the past and present, love is directed toward the future. So Nietzche says, "All great love is above pity: for it wants to create what is loved!" It wants the future, and pity is a stony place in the present.

Self-pity has the same structure, only it works entirely inside a person; he needs no outer object. His own soul is divided, to use Blake's image, and self-pity is the mechanism through which the division and its stasis are enforced and solidified. The self casts off its hurt part, sets it up as an object, and broods over it. Resentments work the same way and to a similar end, the maintenance of the status quo. In alcoholism they call it "the poor-me's" and its metaphysics is "Poor me, poor me, pour me a drink."

In the end, all the dividing emotions—self-pity, pride, resentments, and so on—become servants of the disease of alcoholism. Like political palliatives, they siphon off healing energy and allow the sickening agent to stay in power. Their tone and mood are part of the voice of booze.

Let us look at a poem, one of the early, solid Dream Songs. When Robert Lowell reviewed the first book of Songs in 1964 he chose to print Song 29 in full as "one of the best and most unified."[6] It reads:

There sat down, once, a thing on Henry's heart
só heavy, if he had a hundred years
& more, & weeping, sleepless, in all them time
Henry could not make good.
Starts again always in Henry's ears
the little cough somewhere, an odour, a chime.

And there is another thing he has in mind
like a grave Sienese face a thousand years
would fail to blur the still profiled reproach of. Ghastly,
with open eyes, he attends, blind.
All the bells say: too late, This is not for tears;
thinking.

But never did Henry, as he thought he did,
end anyone and hacks her body up
and hide the pieces, where they may be found.
He knows: he went over everyone, & nobody's missing.
Often he reckons, in the dawn, them up.
Nobody is ever missing.

Though not apparent at first, this poem is deeply connected to alcohol. The last stanza describes what is known as a *blackout,* a phenomenon of heavy drinking in which the drinker goes through periods of unremembered activity. In a blackout one is not *passed* out; he goes to parties, drives home, has conversations, and so forth, but afterwards he has no memory of what he has done. The next day he may meet someone on the street who thanks him for the loan and returns money, or he may find himself in an airport and call home only to discover he has inexplicably taken a plane halfway across the continent. Berryman gives an example in the novel. The main character is a teacher (so close to Berryman that we needn't maintain the fiction) who reports, "My chairman told me one day I had telephoned a girl student at midnight threatening to kill her—no recollection, blacked out." This incident may be the actual basis of the last stanza here. (The misogyny of the Dream Songs would take another essay to unravel. Suffice it to say here that sexual anger and alcoholism are connected through similar misconceptions of human power. As it has been men who "get into power," men have traditionally outnumbered women alcoholics. This will change to the degree that women mistake feminism for a route to centralized power.)

This poem has one other personal allusion in it. When he was an eleven-year-old boy, Berryman's father killed himself. (It is implied in the novel that his father may also have been alcoholic.) His suicide is the subject of several of the Dream Songs, especially numbers 76 and 384. In fact it lurks throughout the book. William Meredith reports that Berryman once said of the Dream Songs that "the first 384 are about the death of his father . . . and number 385 is about the illegitimate pregnancy of his daughter."[7] This remark is as much truth as wit. I have no doubt Berryman believed it, certainly when he wrote the Songs and perhaps even when he was writing the novel. Though it is intentionally vague in this poem, if you had asked him what the "thing" was that sat down on Henry's heart, he would have said his father's suicide.

Let us return to Song 29. I take this poem to be about anxiety, and I should say a few words about this to make it clear why it is not just the mood of the poem, but the subject. Anxiety differs from fear in that it has no object. This means there is no *action* that will resolve the feeling. The sufferer who does not realize this will search his world for problems to attend in hopes of relieving his anxiety, only to find that nothing will fill its empty stomach. For example, anxiety is a major symptom of withdrawal from alcohol addiction, in which case it has a cause—the sudden absence of the addicting drug—but still no object. There is still nothing to do to resolve the feeling. If the alcoholic in withdrawal begins to drink again, his anxiety may be relieved but not resolved; it is merely postponed with an anaesthetic glow.

Anxiety is a symptom not just of withdrawal, but of active alcoholism, and it even plagues sober alcoholics long after their last drink. The mood in this poem is typical of alcoholic anxiety; it is intense, mysterious, and desperate. This is not grief and this is not suffering. It is important to make this clear because both Berryman and his critics have seen the mood here as grief or suffering. But both of these differ from anxiety in that they are active and directed toward an end. The grief we feel when someone dies moves toward its own boundary. The mourning song usually last three days, and its biological point, as it were, is that it leads out of itself. Grief that lasts much longer than a year does so because it has been blocked in some way. It is then pathological, just as a blockage in the blood system is pathological. In fairy tales the person who weeps and cannot stop finally turns into a snake, for unabated grief is not human.

Suffering, like grief, is an activity, a labor, and it ends. There are healthy ways to suffer—that is, ways that move with grace from pain to ease. This is not what happens either in *The Dream Songs* as a whole or in this poem.

Now let us look more closely at the content of Song 29. It is one of the strongest of the Dream Songs precisely because its vagueness is true to anxiety. Throughout the Songs the character Henry is bothered and doesn't know why. The cause of his pain is always abstract, "a thing" here; elsewhere "a departure" (*DS,* 1), "something black somewhere" (*DS,* 92), and so on. Typically an anxious person does not realize this lack of content but projects his mood onto the outer world. Everyone else knows something is being projected because the proportions are all off, as when a dying man begins to worry about his cat. A strength of this poem is that Berryman does not unload his mood directly. However, behind the vagueness there are ghosts.

The first stanza I sense as a description of the recurrent and inescapable memory of his father's suicide. The anxiety is projected backwards. The second stanza has as its main image the "grave Sienese face." The reference is obscure to me, but I associate it with art, religion, and death ("grave"). It carries Berryman's sense of the future. His hope is that spiritual life and poetry will be the path out of his misery, but he fears he won't make it. (That this was in fact the form of his activity can be shown from other poems. In Songs 73 and 99, for example, he approaches temples but is unable to make any contact. Song 66 has spiritual wisdom as its background but at the end, "Henry grew hot, got laid, felt bad" and is reproached as he is by the Sienese face here.) The middle stanza of Song 29 is future directed and hopeless. It has in it a premonition, certainly the fear, of his own suicide.

Therefore the structure of the poem is the structure of his anxiety: it is felt as inescapable, it is projected backward (onto the father's suicide) and forward (onto his own), and he senses himself, in the blackout stanza, as an alienated field of violence between these two deaths.

We can now return to self-pity that I judge to be the final tone of this song and of the book as a whole. The Dream Songs do not move to a resolution. Berryman told Richard Kostelanetz in 1969: "Henry is so troubled and bothered by his many problems that he never actually comes up with solutions, and from that point of view the poem is a failure."[8] The core mood in the poems is anxiety and dread, and when they leave that, they do rise out of it but slide sideways into intellectualizing, pride, boredom, talk, obfuscation, self-pity, and resentment. This happens so often that these are the dominant tones of the Dream Songs. Here are a few examples of resentment and self-pity:

God's Henry's enemy. (*DS,* 13)

Life, friends, is boring. (*DS,* 24)

Henry hates the world. What the world to Henry
did will not bear thought.
Feeling no pain,
Henry stabbed his arm and wrote a letter
explaining how bad it had been
in this world.

(*DS,* 74)

All this is being scrutinized in the critical literature about Berryman under the fancy handle of "the epistemology of loss." But it's really just an alcoholic poet on his pity-pot. Not having decided if he wants to get well, he is reinforcing his disease with a moan. The poems articulate the moods and methods of the alcoholic ego. But as the "Big Book" says, "When harboring such feelings we shut ourselves off from the sunlight of the Spirit. The insanity of alcohol returns and we drink again. And with us, to drink is to die." This means that when approached by an alcoholic with a magnificent problem, all years a-drip with complication and sorrow, one's response has to be "Yes, but do you want to get sober?" To become involved in the pain before the disease has been arrested is to help the man or woman stay sick.

Berryman's father killed himself more than forty years before these poems were written. It is a hard judgment, but inescapable, that the use of the father's death here and elsewhere in the Dream Songs amounts to self-pity. Certainly there is grief and anger, but in the end the memory of that death is used as a device in a holding action of the alcoholic ego. I think Berryman himself saw this before he died. I presume he is referring to the two books of Dream Songs (1964 and 1968) when he writes in the novel of "self-pity, rage, resentments—a load so great I've spent two well-known volumes on it" (R, 34).

When making judgments like these the question arises whether or not Berryman was trapped. If he couldn't resolve his pain for reasons beyond his control, then his expressions of it are not self-pity. This is important because this was Berryman's sense of himself. He identified with the trapped and oppressed: Anne Frank, Bessie Smith, Victoria Spivey, Job, Jeremiah in the Lamentations, and so on. Can an alcoholic be classified in this group? In one sense yes, he is trapped: once the booze has possessed him, it also baffles his healing powers, so that demanding he simply quit drinking is a bit like asking a catatonic to snap out of it.

And yet people get sober. AA guarantees a day of sobriety to any who follow their suggestions. So once the alcoholic, like the early Christian, has heard the Word, he is no longer trapped; it comes down to whether or not he wants sobriety. And then the real war begins. It is when the active alcoholic is presented with the option of sobering up that he starts to defend his right to drink, to deny he is having any trouble with alcohol, to attack AA, and to hoard his resentments and pain.

In the end Berryman's tone leads me to judge he was not trapped. The blues don't have that tone. They are not songs of self-pity. Leadbelly or Billie Holiday have more resonance than the Dream Songs precisely because they were not divided against themselves by their oppressor (as an alcoholic is) and because the enemy is identified (not vague as in Berryman) and the self is in motion. Likewise the

strength of Anne Frank is that her diary is direct, not whiny. Berry-
man was lost and in pain, but not trapped.

> and something can (has) been said for sobriety
> but very little. (*DS*, 57)

> Why drink so, two days running?
> two months, O seasons, years, two decades running?
> I answer (smiles) my questions on the cuff:
> Man, I been thirsty. (*DS*, 96)

This voice is to alcohol what the Uncle Tom is to the racist.

I want to turn now to the structural innovations, the emotional
plot, of the Dream Songs. As a person becomes alcoholic he becomes
divided inside and typically turns into a con man. The booze hustler
in him will command all of the self's true virtues to maintain its hold.
He has a double voice then: sincerity with a motive. Berryman's
device of having his central figure, Henry, be a white man in black
face is an accurate imitation of this. Henry has become a con man and
can't figure out why. His mood is accurate to alcoholism: he is anx-
ious, guilt-ridden, secretly proud, baffled, and driven. "Huffy Henry
hid the day / unappeasable Henry sulked" (*DS*, 1).

As Berryman wrote, Henry has "suffered an irreversible loss."
He knows somewhere that he is not responsible for it, and yet he
can't escape it either. His sidekick in the poems, a black man who
calls him Mr. Bones, is exactly like the alcoholic spouse who keeps
saying, "You're suffering, you must be guilty." They conspire in
keeping each other unhappy.

When Berryman says that the book is a "failure" in terms of
finding a solution to Henry's problems, it seems clear that he would
have preferred to work with Henry, to exorcise him or at least objec-
tify him and his loss. But this is a disease and not susceptible to such
powers. "Will power is nothing. Morale is nothing. Lord, this is
illness," (*R*, 50) he wrote in the novel. That is, when confronted by
the will and the ego, alcohol always wins. James Dickey noticed that
when a Dream Song gets off the ground, Berryman gets it there
"through sheer will and guts." Some of the poems do not work this
way, through will power, like Song 29. But they are oddly empty,
like screams.

The will is a power and a necessary one, but by itself it is neither creative nor healing. But it is Berryman's tool, and this is why I said earlier that he loses his fight with alcohol because his tactics and epistemology are all wrong. Of course it did not help him that these misunderstandings about power and willfulness are everywhere imitated in our civilization.

The original design of the Dream Songs has a resonant tension that is lost as the spirit of alcohol (Henry) takes over. This begins in book 3. Berryman's inspiration in book 4 was to kill Henry off. The poems are written from the grave. My guess is that he hoped to cleanse him through a night journey. It fails. Henry leaves the grave in Song 91, and it is the resurrection of a material spirit: the media invoke Henry to rise; he does and immediately calls for a double rum. The last stanza I judge to be Berryman's horror at this, caught in the gut assumption that if the spirit of alcohol won't die, he'll have to:

A fortnight later, sense a single man
upon the trampled scene at 2 a.m.
insomnia-plagued, with a shovel
digging like mad. Lazarus with a plan
to get his own back, a plan, a stratagem
no newsman will unravel.

Berryman always insisted that Henry was "an imaginary character, not the poet, not me." Everyone has disregarded this as a poet's whim, for the two are so clearly connected. When Berryman goes to Ireland, Henry goes; when Berryman is visited by the BBC, Henry is visited, and so forth. So we have said that Henry is only a thin disguise for Berryman. But the opposite is more accurate: during those years, Henry came out of the book and possessed his creator. Berryman was reduced to a shadow. He hardly appears in book 7 at all. Its flatness and silly pride are nothing but booze talking. Nowhere can you find the passion, insight, erudition, and music that mark Berryman's earlier poetry. "He went to pieces. / The pieces sat up & wrote" (DS, 331).

As a final part of this look at the Dream Songs I want to say a few words about their style. The innovations are fairly well represented by the last stanza of Song 29. They are mostly syntactical oddities:

mixed tenses ("never did Henry . . . hacks") and reordered phrases ("he reckons, in the dawn, them up"). It is a deliberately broken speech that is striking when it fills with music and alternates with direct statement. Songs 29 and 1 are both good examples. The voice is reminiscent of and drawn from several sources: black blues and dialect, baby talk, drunk talk, and the broken syntax of extreme anxiety.

Why was Berryman drawn to these sources? The connections are in power relationships. In a power structure, dialect is the verbal equivalent of the slave's shuffle. It is an assertion of self in an otherwise oppressive situation. It says: "I'll speak your language, but on my own terms." Baby talk works the same way. It is the speech equivalent of the child's pout. Both are signs that there is a distance between real personal power and desired personal power. And yet neither of them is a true confrontation of that distance. They reveal that the imbalance has been neither accepted *nor* rejected, for such would lead to direct speech. When the child pouts, he doesn't want his parents to leave. When the slave shuffles, he has been baffled into the myth that he has no internal power and his only hope is to cajole a piece of the action out of the master. The cloying voice depends on the audience it hates. It is divided, identifying with a power not its own and hoping to control that power through verbal finesse. This is the style of the con man.

In a case of real and inescapable oppression, stylized speech might be an assertion of self. But this would be short term; when it becomes a way of life, it is something different. In these poems, written by a grown white male, the voice is a whine. When the child whines, he doesn't want the grown-ups to go away, and when Berryman writes like this, he doesn't want to give up the booze.

The question arises: who is the mean parent/slave driver? At times Berryman thought it must be God himself. He commonly equated Henry with Job, announcing that "God's Henry's enemy" (13). But this won't wash. As before, the tone is the tip-off. Job is neither cynical nor ironic. What successfully imitates anxiety in Song 29 deflates into weary irony as it is spread over 385 songs. Irony has only emergency use. Carried over time it is the voice of the trapped who have come to enjoy their cage. This is why it is so tiresome. People who have found a route to power based on their misery—who don't want to give it up though it would free them—become ironic. This sustained complaint is the tone of active alcoholism.

The stylistic innovations in the Dream Songs are epistemologically wrong—an alcoholic is not a slave—and this is why they are so unsatisfying. The style obscures and mystifies, it does not reveal. Berryman himself knew there was a growing distance between his style and his self. The question is honesty. The more developed the style became, the more he was conning himself, reinforcing the walls of his cage. So in *Recovery* when he tries to write out some self-criticism, he reads it over and comments to himself: "No style: good" (*R, 86*). This is a remarkable sentence for a poet to write.

His last poems, written at the same time as the novel, move away from the old style. They were written in a drying-out place where Berryman had gone for help. Judging from the novel, many of his old ploys were falling away as he attended to his disease and, more importantly, as he attended to other people and received their attention. Through other people he began to feel a "personal sense of God's love," which he had not had since his father's suicide. The poems from this period still have syntactic twists, now more like an old nerve tic, but on the whole they are direct and clear, descriptive and loving:

> Jack went it was, on Friday, against the word
> of the staff & our word . . . violent relief
> when Sunday night he & his son, absurd
> in ties & jackets, for a visit brief
> looked back in, looking *good*.[9]

I have shown that the Dream Songs can be explicated in terms of the disease of alcoholism. We can hear the booze talking. Its moods are anxiety, guilt, and fear. Its tone is a moan that doesn't revolve. Its themes are unjust pain, resentment, self-pity, pride, and a desperate desire to run the world. It has the con man's style and the con game's plot. It depends for its survival on an arrogance of will, ascendant and dissociated from the whole. These poems are not a contribution to culture. They are artifacts of a dying civilization, like one of those loaves of bread turned to lava at Pompeii.

The way out of self-pity and its related moods is to attend to something other than the self. This can be either the inner or the outer world, either dreams and visions that do not come from the self, or other people and nature. The point is that the self begins to heal automatically when it attends to the nonself. Pablo Neruda is a good example of a poet who did this. He had great trust of the interior world and turned to it automatically when he was otherwise isolated. And when I asked him once what made the melancholy of his early work disappear, he spoke immediately of politics. The Spanish Civil War made him change. "That was my great experience," he said. "It was a defeat but I never considered life a defeat after that. I had faith in human things and in human people."

Berryman found neither of these things. I think his trust was broken early in both the inner and the outer worlds and he was never able to regain it despite his desire. He had no politics except patriotism and nostalgia. He refused to read at the first antiwar readings in Minneapolis. He wrote the only monarchist poem (Song 105) to come out of the sixties. And there is no spiritual energy or dream consciousness at all in the Dream Songs.

This leads us to the question of how Berryman was handled by the rest of us. We did not handle him well. Few of his critics faced the death in these poems. Most were snowed, as he was himself, by Berryman's style and brains, as if they thought rhetoric, intellectualizing, and references to famous friends were what poetry is all about. At the end Berryman began to see that his fame was built on his sickness. The character in his novel "really thought, off and on for twenty years, that it was his duty to drink, namely to sacrifice himself. He saw the products as worth it." Berryman felt that "the delusion that . . . my art depended on my drinking . . . could not be attacked directly. Too far down" (*R, 96*).

This is not true. He could have attacked it. But it would not have been easy. He would have had to leave behind a lot of his own work. He would have had to leave his friends who had helped him live off his pain for twenty years. And the civilization itself, which supported all of that, weighs a great deal. *Life* magazine unerringly made the connection between our civilization and disease and went straight to Berryman as their example of the poet from the sixties. They called the piece "Whisky and Ink, Whisky and Ink," and there are the typical photographs of the poet with the wind in his beard and a glass in his hand. Berryman bought into the whole thing. Like

Hemingway, they got him to play the fool and the salesman the last
ten years of his life.

I am not saying that the critics could have cured Berryman of his
disease. But we could have provided a less sickening atmosphere. In
the future it would be nice if it were a little harder for the poet to
come to town drunk and have everyone think that it's great fun. You
can't control an alcoholic's drinking any more than he can, but the
fewer parasites he has to support the better. No one knows why
some alcoholics get sober and others don't. They say in AA that it
takes a desire to stop drinking and, after that, the grace of God. Here
are Berryman's words on this, with which I will close.

> Is escape . . . too difficult? Evidently, for (1) the walls are strong
> and I am weak, and (2) *I love my walls*. . . . Yet some *have es-
> caped*. . . . With an effort we lift our gaze from the walls upward
> and ask God *to take the walls away*. We look back down and they
> have disappeared. . . . We turn back upward at once with love to
> the Person who has made us so happy, and *desire to serve Him*.
> Our state of mind is that of a bridegroom, that of a bride. We are
> married, who have been so lonely heretofore. (*R*, 232)

1975

NOTES

1. The AA "Big Book" is properly referred to as *Alcoholics Anonymous* (The
General Service Board of Alcoholics Anonymous, New York: 1955). This is
available at any AA meeting or by mail from Box 459 Grand Central Station,
New York, N.Y. 10017. It is the best place to start reading about alcoholism.

2. Jung's letter is printed in the AA monthly magazine, *AA Grapevine*, No-
vember 1974, 30–31.

3. Ivan Illich, *Medical Nemesis* (London: Calder & Boyars, 1975).

4. The Dream Songs were originally published as two volumes: 77 *Dream
Songs* (New York: Farrar, Straus and Giroux, 1964) and *His Toy, His Dream,
His Rest* (New York: Farrar, Straus and Giroux, 1968).

5. Erich Newmann, *Amor and Psyche, The Psychic Development of the Feminine,
A Commentary on the Tale of Apuleius,* (New York: Princeton University Press,
1971), 48.

6. Robert Lowell's review was in the *New York Review of Books*, 28 May 1964,
2–3. James Dickey's was in *The American Scholar* 34 (Autumn 1965): 646f.

7. The William Meredith quotation is taken from *John Berryman: A Checklist,*

compiled by Richard J. Kelly, with a foreword by William Meredith (Metuchen, N.J.: Scarecrow Press, 1972), xviii.

8. Berryman's remark to Richard Kostelanetz was made in an interview published in *The Massachusetts Review* 2, no. 2 (Spring 1970): 340–47.

9. Berryman's "From the Hospital" poems were published in *The American Poetry Review* 4, no. 1 (January 1975). The stanza I use is from "5th Tuesday."

George F. Wedge

The Case of the Talking Brews: Mr. Berryman and Dr. Hyde

Lewis Hyde's "Alcohol and Poetry: John Berryman and the Booze Talking" is an early and important text for the study of the literature of intoxication.[1] Wide reading in works by authors known to have been alcohol dependent confirms Hyde's central point: that alcoholics drink in a vain search for spiritual insights otherwise denied them and that Berryman, like other alcoholic writers, is thus engaged in a spiritual quest. It is harder to accept the argument that *The Dream Songs* is irreparably flawed because during its composition Berryman was an active alcoholic with the result that his "tactics, aesthetics, and epistemology were all wrong, [so that] by the end of the book booze had almost wholly taken over" (215). As Thomas Gilmore has observed:

> Although Hyde announces elaborate plans to examine Berryman's *Dream Songs* as the locus of a "war, between alcohol and Berryman's creative powers" [215], his analyses of individual poems are not nearly numerous or detailed enough (nor, to be frank, sound enough) to carry out such an ambitious plan.[2]

In fact, Hyde's only full analysis of a poem is of Song 29, and this analysis depends on a reading too loose to be convincing. These problems in Hyde's essay spring from his use of the AA model of recovery as his analytical base. Models of therapy, though they may provide insights for critics, are not by themselves adequate to critical reading of the life and works of active alcoholics.

When I first read Hyde's essay, I was deeply impressed. As a recovering alcoholic myself, I know that Hyde's discussion of alcohol dependency is accurate; its application to the Dream Songs seems plausible—it even has some supporting evidence from Berryman's late works. Like Hyde, I had experience as an alcoholism counselor dealing with recidivist clients like Henry House. And, like Hyde, I had observed Berryman's monstrous ego from a close distance while studying at the University of Minnesota. Still, the Dream Songs offered moving descriptions of emotions I had felt and some that I avoided only because I found recovery when I did. Gradually, I concluded that neither the poet nor the critic, the good Dr. Jekyll nor the menacing Mr. Hyde, was unqualifiedly good or monstrous—hence the reversal of honorifics, "*Mr.* Berryman and *Dr.* Hyde," in the subtitle of my paper. I will start with what is especially hard for a recovering alcoholic to accept—the inapplicability of some features of the AA program to the discussion of the lives and works of alcoholic writers.

That recovery includes a spiritual component is a central principle of Alcoholics Anonymous and a premise adopted in many free-standing treatment centers. Observation of the spiritual growth of *recovering* writers provides helpful insight to a change in the character of their works, but is of little help in discussing the works of active alcoholics. Not many writers have a conversion experience of the kind reported by some recovering alcoholics; those who have not include nonalcoholic writers of good reputation as well as both active and recovering alcoholics. Their works may or may not exhibit the spiritual tension that characterizes the Dream Songs. All one can appropriately say in a case like Berryman's is that the spiritual struggle laid bare in the Dream Songs accurately reflects his troubled spirit. The same can be said of St. Augustine's *Confessions,* which has other points of similarity in content with the Dream Songs, for example, a very convincing "war" against sexual appetite and a lifelong struggle to learn humility.

Secondly, good alcoholism therapy, as in AA, does not deal in any specific way with the wide variation in past productivity and accomplishment among alcoholics who seek recovery. Millionaires or paupers, highly acclaimed poets or failed garbage collectors, at the moment of crisis, they are all the same: spiritually bankrupt. Much is made of this commonality, as well it should be. That all men are brothers, all women sisters, is an insight necessary for recovery from many of the ills that affect our society, not just addiction. Individuals work out the application of principles of recovery to their personal situations. Nearly all who recover report that life is better than before; some with dramatic improvements in productivity and "success," others without. AA fosters personal recovery by encouraging specific action in the present. "One day at a time" is the slogan.

Thus, in principle, AA discourages dwelling on the past and minimizes members' past accomplishments. It properly observes that alcoholics are egocentric and that recovery requires curbing of the ego, the development of healthy humility. Because acquiring these qualities is highly prized, it is easy in the early stages to mistake for humility an exaggerated rejection of everything accomplished prior to recovery. Yet, one of the "promises" of the AA program is "we will not regret the past nor wish to shut the door on it."[3] The inventory taken at step 4 of the program results in a realistic rejection of past behavior and helps lay a foundation for a new life without alcohol. Most gradually relearn the functional parts of the life they lived before. A businessman continues his successful business tactics; a scholar-drunk the habits of scholarship, minus the alcohol. The poet-drunk writes poetry again, maybe better, maybe not, but from a base that is more healthy—and perhaps more personally satisfying. Members are happy for one another's successes because they still have something in common: they have moved on from defeat to a normal life in their chosen field and learned to respect one another's differences while confronting their common failure. They have learned to rely on a program of rigorous self-honesty.

AA's strength is in the principles of personal recovery, not its explanations of why some individuals do not, or cannot, or have not recovered. "There are such unfortunates," *Alcoholics Anonymous* says. "They are not at fault; they seem to have been born that way. They are naturally incapable of grasping and developing a manner of living which demands rigorous honesty."[4] The honesty demanded is self-honesty and refers, essentially, to abandoning denial. Some very tricky inner conflicts arise when rigorous self-honesty goes one-on-one with extreme rejection of the past. Is it honesty or denial of a past accomplishment for Dr. Severance to say, "self-pity, rage, resentments—a load so great I've spent two well-known volumes on it"? (*R*, 34). His recovery is still at an early stage when self-honesty and exaggerated self-blame are especially difficult to separate. Were the volumes valuable or worthless? Some might think that if writing them led to recovery they were worth something.

That Berryman died before he could experience fully the rebirth of personality and renewed creative energy recovery can bring creates problems for the critic. Assuming that Severance refers to volumes written before recovery, Hyde says that the reference is to *77 Dream Songs* and *His Toy, His Dream, His Rest* (221), a conclusion that fits Hyde's thesis. But Berryman could be thinking of the collected *Dream Songs* and *Love & Fame*. The early reviews certainly took *Love & Fame* for a notable excursion in self-pity, rage, and resentment, and Berryman's strong self-pity, rage, and resentment over those reviews must have created a conflict in him at AA meetings. There he was obliged to see resentment as the cardinal emotion related to recidivism and humility as requiring him to accept the critics' judgment.

Paul Mariani describes this conflict between ego and realistic self-appraisal in his essay on *Love & Fame* in *A Usable Past:*

> Berryman had an enormous ego, as his poetry and criticism alone will show. . . . But there is in the poetry, in among the verbal evasions and aggressions, a vulnerability, an ability on Berryman's part to laugh at all his ego-flaunting peacock struts. And it is to this eye of self-assessment, this relatively calm eye at the middle of this Lear-like moving storm that dominated Berryman's life, that I would like now to turn my attention . . . the fourth section, the marvelous close, of *Love & Fame*.[5]

Mariani sees the "Eleven Addresses to the Lord" that close the volume "as an honest deflation of the speaker's ego." The first three sections of the book can well be characterized as full of self-pity, rage, resentment, full of a false appraisal of the nature of love, the nature of fame. But the resolution of the volume comes from the same place as Severance's remark about spending two well-known volumes on these emotions. That the ironic intent of the first three sections was lost on the early critics gave Berryman reason to feel again emotions dangerous to his sobriety.[6]

While the "searching and fearless moral inventory" of AA's fourth step leads at the fifth step to admitting the "exact nature" of "wrongs" one has committed, the point of this exercise is that one recognize the sum of the past and not dwell on its parts.[7] Berryman went farther, faster than was safe, in trying to deal explicitly with the present in *The Dream Songs* and with the past in both *The Dream Songs* and *Love & Fame*. We do not and cannot know which volumes Dr. Severance meant. Was writing *The Dream Songs* something to lament because they were tokens of drunken desperation or something to be grateful for because they led to discovery of his spiritual crisis? Were the critical success of *The Dream Songs* and failure of *Love & Fame* true evaluations or equal and opposite misreadings, something to be proud of or something to be ashamed of?

Reliance on principles of therapy for biographical or critical insight leads to the conclusion that writers who do not recover or recover without a conversion experience are dishonest and write from that dishonesty in dishonest ways. If Berryman believed that spending two volumes on self-pity, rage, and resentment was wasteful, as Hyde does, Berryman was wrong. The works speak for themselves as portrayals of the struggle to achieve sobriety and humility, frustrated as the antagonist may be by his continuing dependency and his fear of humiliation.

No matter how true a study written from the vantage of AA may be—and Hyde certainly speaks truly on many of the topics covered—the resulting picture is distorted by a built-in prejudice against the possibility that an active alcoholic can write truthfully. Even ignoring nonaddicted authors who wrote works based in self-pity, rage, and resentment, we may shudder at the cost of this prejudice in whole canons of much loved and highly honored authors. London, Fitzgerald, Faulkner, and Lowry spring to mind, plus O'Neill, Carver, and Cheever prior to their recoveries. The list can readily be expanded. An objective look at what active alcoholic writers have been able to accomplish despite addiction does not support some of Hyde's assertions about Berryman and the Dream Songs. It is too late to doctor the man, and there are many reasons to believe that poems written from the center of active alcoholism are both open to critical interpretation and useful to readers.

My test case is Dream Song 29, Hyde's principal example of how denial of his alcoholism undermined the whole of Berryman's *The Dream Songs*. Hyde sees the subject as alcoholic anxiety, a vague and objectless dread erected out of Berryman's inability to stop brooding over his father's suicide, his fearful presentiment of his own suicide, and his alcoholic blackouts. He observes that "the mood in this poem is not grief," a point "it is important to make . . . clear because both Berryman and his critics have seen the mood here as grief or suffering." Drawing from models of therapy for grief as contrasted to anxiety, Hyde states that grief is "active and directed toward an end." If it lasts much longer than a year, it is pathological (219). All this may be true; yet, Tennyson's *In Memoriam* began with a handful of lyrics mourning the loss of Arthur Hallam, just as the Dream Songs began with a handful of lyrics mourning the suicide of Berryman's father. Tennyson's prolonged grief may have been pathological, but it cannot be said to have sprung from alcoholic anxiety. Nor is *In Memoriam* commonly viewed as having "tactics, aesthetics, and epistemology [that are] all wrong." Thinking of the grief and guilt we all carry, Marianne Moore observes in the poem "In Distrust of Merits" that "the world's an orphan's home," a world of universal loss.[8] Since the traits Hyde thinks set Berryman apart from other people and other writers are not the exclusive property of alcoholics, they cannot be ascribed to his alcohol dependency.

Berryman himself chose to discuss this Song in the essay "One Answer to a Question: Changes." Berryman says that Song 29 illustrates what he means when he says that the Dream Songs involved "problems of decorum most poets happily do not have to face." He observes that "neither of the American poets [Robert Lowell and Adrienne Rich] who as reviewers have quoted it admiringly" would commit to "whether [its] diction . . . is consistent with blackface talk, hell-spinning puns, or both," and declines to commit himself. He is unwilling to say whether the end of the poem is "funny or frightening" (*FP*, 330–31). One may assume that decorum, since it was a problem in composing the poem, is also a reason for not explicating it. Berryman shows no decorous restraint elsewhere about suicides or blackouts. There must be something more here.

As J. M. Linebarger observes, "The tone [is] intentionally mixed, confused, ambiguous." He makes little more commitment to analysis of the poem than had Lowell or Rich, saying only, "The Song is about Henry's response to the death of the father, the funeral itself (the 'cough,' 'odor,' and 'chime'), and Henry's hallucinations about killing others."[9] But he quotes only the first and last stanzas and has avoided, even in this paraphrase, the second. Robert Pinsky offers an "imaginary revision" that does include the second stanza, but only to straighten out the syntax, not to explicate the images.[10] Hyde, too, leaves the stanza to speak for itself, yet finds in it Henry's presentiment of the future and his own suicide. The third stanza, as Hyde states, is clearly about an alcoholic blackout; Henry knows that he remained functional during his drinking of the preceding night, but he is unable to remember what he did or to distinguish real from imagined action. While the substance of this passage is a recurrent nightmare reported by Mariani (PM, 210), the poetic use of an actual dream or nightmare as waking hallucination or alcoholic blackout is common in works by alcoholic writers. That seems to be what has occurred here.

But what *is* Henry talking about in the second stanza?

In the first stanza, Henry is unable to lift from his heart the heavy weight of his father's suicide, which he takes as a betrayal. In the second, he has "another thing in mind," which is "like" a reproachful, "grave Sienese face." In Purgatorio, canto 5 of the *Divine Comedy,* there is a woman from Siena, known as "La Pia de' Tolomei." She is in the company of those who died without absolution because their death was sudden, offering opportunity for repentance only at the last moment. Her husband, Nello della Pietra, had confined her at Maremma, where she died either of malaria or of poison. She says to Dante, "Remember me. Siena gave me birth and Maremma undid me. He who with this ring espoused me caused my death." In D. G. Rosetti's painting of Jane Morris as "La Pia," her face is in three-quarter profile. The final paragraph of W. D. Paden's article on this painting suggests several other points parallel to the content of the second stanza of Dream Song 29:

> In 1880 Rosetti took up again the canvas of *La Pia,* long ago put aside. When he had first designed the picture in 1868 the image of La Pia, sent by her husband to a quiet death, had been relevant to his own (perhaps then unadmitted) jealousy of Morris. Jane had remained for him the symbol of love and life, the emblem of desire and beauty; having possessed her, having lost her, he saw her now shadowed by his own guilt and agony and remorse. Now, when as La Pia she meditated gravely upon her wedding ring, she suggested larger meanings. These are of a kind which words seldom convey with as much effect as images:—

Beauty is bound to sorrow, love to pain and despair: death, which delivers man from all of these, may come to be desired.[11]

It is hard not to think that Berryman had read these very words, so close is the phrasing of "grave Sienese face" to "meditated gravely," so close to a situation in his own life the details of Rosetti's.

Additional support of this identification of the "Sienese face" was called to my attention, after I had read this paper in Minneapolis, by John Clendenning. He cites Eliot's footnote to line 293 of *The Waste Land,* which quotes the passage from Dante—"Ricorditi di me, che son la Pia / Siena mi fe', disfecemi Maremma." Clendenning observes, "Isn't it clear that Berryman was remembering both Eliot and Dante in this stanza?" I, of course, concur.

Noting Berryman's comment about "hell-spinning puns," this identification of the Sienese face is the more plausible because the pun on *grave* is a doubly apt allusion—to La Pia's fate and to Mercutio's pun on the word *grave* in Shakespeare. To the weight of his father's suicide, the second stanza adds the weight of Henry's betrayal of some woman whom he "possessed" and "lost" and whom he sees now as "shadowed by his own guilt and agony and remorse." Decorum suggests we leave identification to awful, huffy Henry and let John's torment speak only to John.

Borne down by these twin betrayals, one as much by self as of self, Henry "ghastly, / with open eyes, . . . attends, blind." A rich, frightening, and pun-full line. Henry is *blind drunk,* staring into the past (not the future, as Hyde believes). He is blind with open eyes, like Oedipus, another note in the betrayal motif connected with his father's suicide, including as well the motif of the mother's betrayal of the father in marrying so soon after the father's death. And "All the bells say: too late." Too late for his dead father, too late for the betrayed woman. It is also too late in life to mend the past, too late into the drinking night to escape the tormenting visions, and absolutely too late because he is himself already dead—*dead drunk,* a grave condition indeed. "This is not for tears; thinking," Henry says. Self-pity will get him nowhere; though he feels the tears, he must think it through. As Pinsky says, "The dry hard sense of circumstance and limit, which seems to rule out tears as well as atrocity, condemns the poet to insomniac meditation."[12]

In the real world, thinking it through is a losing game; it only

Fig. 2. Painting by Dante Gabriel Rossetti entitled *La Pia de' Tolemei*. (Courtesy of Spencer Museum of Art, University of Kansas.)

perpetuates drinking. One cannot think one's way out of a depression. Yet, Henry is thinking, up to the moment of the blackout, thoughts he will remember only as jumbled images. Little wonder, then, that the next morning Henry fears he has been violent toward some woman, the ambiguity being part of Henry's confusion and necessary to Berryman's sense of decorum. His guilt-ridden thoughts of the past night have become haunting violent images from Dante, Shakespeare, and Sophocles, terrifying bits and pieces. Expressing them in an ironic, distanced tone makes them "funny," that is, both ridiculous and peculiar, as well as "frightening."

In the Dream Songs, all pronouns have become ambiguous, and one may reasonably repeat, with one slight change, Berryman's comment on "The Ball Poem" to account for the effect and for critics' difficulty disentangling the life of the poem from the biography:

> The discovery here was that a commitment of identity can be "reserved," so to speak, with an ambiguous pronoun. The poet himself is both left out and put in; [Henry] does and does not become him and we are confronted with a process which is at once a process of life and a process of art. (*FP*, 326–27)

Song 29 is an excellent example of the technique and one of the most successful songs of the work. Rather than rising, as Hyde says, from Berryman's alcoholic anxiety, the song seems to lack only a detail or two of being a clinical description of such anxiety in Henry. I cannot believe Berryman was ignorant of what the poem said when he wrote it, published it, and offered reticent comments in the essay. The subject of the Dream Songs, the plight of the poet in the modern world, was Berryman's poetic subject from the beginning of his career. But in this poem, alcohol and its debilitating effects are also the subject, making ever more personal and more isolated the view of the poet he presents. Hyde, I believe, errs in seeing the poems as "the booze talking":

> It is my thesis here that this war, between alcohol and Berryman's creative powers, is at the root of the Dream Songs. I will show how their mood, tone, structure, style, and content can be explicated in terms of alcoholism. Further, that Berryman himself (at the time he wrote the poems) was blind to this. His tactics, aesthetics, and epistemology were all wrong, and by the end of the book booze had almost wholly taken over. He lost the war. The bulk of the Dream Songs were written by the spirit of alcohol, not John Berryman. (215)

The poems do depict, as Hyde demonstrates, alcoholic anger, resentment, self-pity, willfulness, and anxiety. But the poems are not, as Berryman had plaintively to insist again and again to those who read them as straight autobiography, about Berryman—they are about a man named Henry, who bears specific resemblances to Berryman, and whose very name was chosen because Berryman and his second wife, Ann, called one another "Henry" and "Mabel," having agreed that "these were the most awful names anyone could be called."[13] Henry, like John, is an alcoholic. Henry does not know he is, but John, distancing himself behind the mask of Henry, knows what he is looking at and describes the alcoholic in him with remorseless accuracy.

If Henry were only and simply Berryman there would be no escape from Hyde's conclusion. To grant this argument is to deny the conscious art of *The Dream Songs* as surely as it would deny the art of Malcolm Lowry to see Geoffrey Firmin in *Under the Volcano* as always and only Lowry. Using such a procedure, we might, if Donald Goodwin's estimate of the number of alcoholic authors is correct, eliminate a third to a half of modern literature from serious criticism.[14] Of course, in an alcohol-drenched society, booze does a lot of talking—as from time to time have opium, coke, pot, what have you. When we tell someone to ignore what a drunk said, that it was "only the booze talking," we distract attention from an equally valid bromide: *in vino veritas*. Drunks themselves use "It was the booze talking" in an attempt to obscure the fact that they have unintentionally and ill-advisedly told their true thoughts.

The voice of the poems did not suddenly appear out of nowhere when Berryman turned alcoholic. There are many precedents in the early poems for features found in the Dream Songs. When Hyde sees the very late poems, written in recovery as "still hav[ing] syntactic twists, now more like an old nerve tic, but on the whole... direct and clear, descriptive and loving" (225), he ignores the fact that the voice was developing syntactic twists and vague pronouns and all as early as "The Ball Poem" and "Song of the Tortured Girl," that is, before Berryman drank alcoholically.[15] From the start he was searching for a voice for the speakers of his poems. We may safely assume that Berryman identified with the emotions of the boy in "The Ball Poem" and of the tortured girl, with both the poet-narrator and Anne Bradstreet in *Homage to Mistress Bradstreet* and with Henry, whom many readers confuse with Berryman at some risk both to the poetry and to their biographic subject.

He experienced the pain of the speakers and comprehended the

disconnected thoughts engendered by their pain. That was part of his
"discovery" in creating the style, part of his talent, part of the cross
he had to bear, part of what drove him to use alcohol to relieve (and
uncover) his pain. Hyde views the syntactic devices Berryman uses
to achieve these effects as mannerisms: one may read them as indices
of the degree of psychic pain Berryman portrays.

Because Henry is an alcoholic, his psychic pain is more obviously
similar to Berryman's than is the pain of the tortured girl, a victim
of the Gestapo. The reader can hardly deny Berryman a claim to
distancing in one case and grant it in the other. Through much of his
work, he both is and is not the protagonist, is inside the experience
and outside it, is engaged in "a process which is at once a process of
life and a process of art." On this point depends the difference be-
tween Lewis Hyde's opinion that the Dream Songs represent "the
booze talking" and my view that the poet remains in control—even
when drunk—and portrays the psychic pain of Henry (Pussycat)
House, hero of an alcoholic epic.

If these traits are indeed part of a steady development throughout
the corpus of Berryman's poetry, one would expect them to appear
with gradually increasing density. They do, up to the point at which
he began to undertake "the care and feeding of long poems." Then,
with the composition of *Homage to Mistress Bradstreet,* there is a sharp
increase in the density, the convolution of syntax. That this dramatic
shift in style coincides with the onset of Berryman's alcoholic drink-
ing is probably no accident, but it is as reasonable to suppose that loss
of some inhibitions freed him to write the way he wanted to and
about the subjects he wanted to treat as it is to assume that he lost
control of his poetry. What he had been seeking, after all, was a
highly flexible vehicle for long connected narratives developed in
brief lyrical stanzas. Scott Fitzgerald found that a fifth of whiskey and
a short story were compatible, but that a novel could not be managed
on alcohol. Berryman sought the best of both worlds, a form that
was long—he proposed *epics*—but that could be written in stanzas of
manageable length, compatible with drinking. That the price was
addiction is largely a biographical consideration.

Hyde does note a cost to literature that must be admitted.
Fitzgerald is correct about the incompatibility of drinking and com-
plex writing projects. Individual Dream Songs, like individual stories
in a Fitzgerald collection, are beautifully realized and testify, as do

some of Fitzgerald's stories, to the state of mind and emotion characteristic of a drinker who has gone "one toke over the line" or more. The problems of organization of a long work are confronted even less well in *The Dream Songs* than in Fitzgerald's *Tender Is the Night*. Passages in both works can be set beside some of the best writing either man did before alcohol had done him in, but neither work shows the attention to the story arc a long work demands, the kind of attention we praise in *Homage to Mistress Bradstreet* and *The Great Gatsby*. Both later works provide a whole that is less than the sum of its parts. Both men lived far enough into recovery to produce fragments that show they had not lost their powers; they had for too long a time allowed something destructive to come between them and their talent. In Berryman's case, Henry came close to taking over the controls. Had he done so, it is unlikely that Berryman would have come to a period of recovery, for Henry, as portrayed in *The Dream Songs* is a much weaker candidate than Berryman himself, and he could hardly take control of the poems without taking control of the poet for once and for all.

Henry is as "awful" as his name, a bad boy, a wild man, filled with lust, alcohol, and sometimes pills or marijuana smoke, self-conscious, self-centered, and self-pitying. Another speaker in the poems, Tambo, sometimes eggs him on to further outrageous speech and sometimes cuts him down. Tambo knows Henry's life so well, in fact, that he appears to inhabit the same space as Henry, a fictive space on the page, of course, and in the poet mind of John Berryman. Berryman, it is my thesis, came to recognize as he composed these poems that his alcoholic self, named Henry, was increasingly out of control and helpless. Sentient within his alcoholism, he acted as scribe for this "awful" part of himself, using his wit and his enormous talent to establish the reality of their painful bondage. Distancing his alcoholic personality as a third-person "other," Henry, frequently mentioned with a pejorative descriptive adjective before his name—huffy, criminal, willful, ridiculous—allowed Berryman to continue the one activity that mattered to him: to write poems. He could not stop drinking; there was and would continue to be, even in recovery, "Fear as a companion." Torn apart by two imperatives—"You *must* have another drink!"—"You *must* write another poem!"—he distanced the drinker and wrote poems about him, even while drunk. The effort involved was surely gargantuan; Saul Bellow has put it as well as it can be put: "He drew [his poetry] out of his vital organs, out of his very skin. At last there was no more" (*R,* xiv).

NOTES

I wish to thank Larry Bradfield, John Clendenning, and James Hartman for thoughtful suggestions incorporated in this paper.

   1. Lewis Hyde, *Alcohol and Poetry: John Berryman and the Booze Talking* (Dallas, Texas: The Dallas Institute Publications, 1986). Originally published in *American Poetry Review* 4 (July-August, 1975):7–12. Subsequent references are to the essay as reprinted in the present volume and are incorporated in the text.

   2. Thomas B. Gilmore, *Equivocal Spirits: Alcoholism and Drinking in Twentieth-Century Literature* (Chapel Hill: University of North Carolina Press, 1987), 121.

   3. *Alcoholics Anonymous: The Story of How Many Thousands of Men and Women Have Recovered from Alcoholism,* 3d ed. (New York: AA World Series, 1976), 83.

   4. Ibid., 58.

   5. Paul Mariani, *A Usable Past* (Amherst: University of Massachusetts Press, 1984), 216.

   6. See the account in Bellow's "introduction" to *Recovery:* "John sat at my table . . . coughing softly and muttering that he couldn't understand—these were some of his best things. Then he snatched up the copy of *Love & Fame* which he had brought me and struck out certain poems, scribbling in the margins, 'Crap' 'Disgusting!'" (*R,* xiii). In a footnote Bellow adds that Berryman deleted six poems from the second edition.

   7. The twelve steps and an explanation of the "housecleaning" fourth and fifth steps appear in "How It Works," chapter 5 of *Alcoholics Anonymous,* 57–71.

   8. Marianne Moore, *The Complete Poems of Marianne Moore* (New York: Viking Press, 1981), 136.

   9. J. M. Linebarger, *John Berryman* (New York: Twayne, 1974), 124.

   10. Robert Pinsky, "Berryman," *The Situation of Poetry* (Princeton: Princeton University Press, 1976). Also in Harry Thomas, ed., *Berryman's Understanding: Reflections on the Poetry of John Berryman* (Boston: Northeastern University Press, 1988), 190.

   11. William D. Paden, "La Pia de' Tolemei by Dante Gabriel Rosetti," *Register of the Museum of Art,* Lawrence, Kansas: University of Kansas, 2:1, (November, 1958):20.

   12. Pinsky, "Berryman," 1991.

   13. Joel Connaroe, *John Berryman: An Introduction to the Poetry:* (New York: Columbia University Press, 1977), 92. See also John Plotz et al., "An Interview with John Berryman," in Thomas, *Berryman's Understanding,* 7, for this account of the origin of the name.

   14. Donald W. Goodwin, *Alcohol and the Writer* (Kansas City, Missouri: Andrews and McMeel, 1988), 2–6.

15. Plotz et al., "Interview," 12. In the interview, Berryman does not reject the interviewer's association of the stanza form of "The Nervous Songs" with the Dream Song stanza. Not only the linguistic quirk but also the formal means of narrative development were taking shape before Berryman's heavy drinking.

Roger Forseth

Spirits and Spirituality: Notes on the Art of John Berryman's *Recovery*

If alcoholism is a disease, how come we make them confess it like any other sin? We don't make them confess cancer.
            —Father Tim, in Ed Fitzgerald, *That Place in Minnesota*

O down a many few, old friend, and
down a many few.
            —John Berryman, *In Memoriam* (1914–1953)

My first real exposure to John Berryman was the unfinished novel *Recovery*. I had, over the years, heard a great deal about him, of course, and had read some of his poems, but not until a friend recommended the poet's last creative effort did I personally feel his power. Surely one reason for the book's impact on me was the fact that, fifteen years ago, I went through chemical dependency treatment in an institution similar to Hazelden and St. Mary's alcohol rehabilitation centers. Another was the discovery that the poet was a fellow alcoholic and, furthermore, one who was able to articulate and refine an experience not infrequently obscured by jargon and platitudes.

These were, for me, reasons enough to treasure *Recovery* as a medical or moral testament, a wayward pilgrim's progress on the road to promised serenity. But the book is also the creation of an artist; it is therefore not unreasonable to ask, is it art? Are we to take it to be a contribution to literature? I believe that it is art, and further that it is possible to reasonably evaluate the author's achievement, in spite of the book's fragmentary state, keeping firmly in mind that Berryman, like many Romantic authors, as well as many alcoholics, was an exploiter, a dramatizer, of his personality, a merchandiser of the self. This combination presents the critic with an additional analytical challenge: to take account of the effect of alcohol use and abuse on the biographer or critic or memoirist who is judging the artist. Hemingway's mordant commentary, for instance, on Fitzgerald's drunkenness in *A Moveable Feast* strikes one as somewhat less clever, not to say less honest, and therefore less critically useful, when one discovers that Hemingway was himself a drunk, if a drunk at an earlier state of disintegration than Fitzgerald.

Unlike Scott Fitzgerald's *The Last Tycoon,* that other fascinating unfinished novel, *Recovery* has not so far received anything like the critical attention it deserves independent of its apparently accepted status as a refined diary. There are, to be sure, powerful autobiographical elements in it, so strong that Berryman's first wife was able to state flatly: "On our return from Europe . . . I had told John that I was leaving him. In *Recovery* he gives as *my* reasons his 'drinking and bad sex'" (italics added).[1] Alan Severance, of course, the protagonist of the novel, made that statement, not the author, and one of the burdens of my argument is that this distinction is not a mere semantic technicality. Berryman *is* a profoundly personal writer, as I have said, and therefore the reader expects to find, and does find, throughout his work, autobiographically based incidents and allusions. But if he had intended to write a memoir of his inpatient experience at St. Mary's Intensive Alcohol Treatment Center, he surely would have done so. He was scarcely a literary naïf. The critic, then, has some obligation to respect the *distance* between the novelist and "Alan Severance, M. D., Litt. D, formerly Professor of Immunology and Molecular Biology, now the University Professor, Pulitzer Prize winner, etc.—twice-invited guest on the Dick Cavett Show" (*R,* 7).

I have no objection to the reading of *Recovery* as a biographical document for the purpose of reconstructing the life of the poet. Both John Haffenden and Paul Mariani make discrete and intelligent use of it (JH; PM). But I do object to Joseph Mancini's flat statement: "Though *Recovery* is cast as fiction, there is absolutely no doubt that it is primarily an autobiographical document. . . . [T]herefore, I will frequently use Severance's statements as though they were Berryman's."[2] The book is more than a private journal reformatted into chapters with the names changed to protect the innocent.

Berryman's own attitude toward biographical interpretations is discriminating. With regard to *The Dream Songs* he emphatically urges that

> opinions and errors in the Songs are to be referred not to the character Henry still less to the author, but to the title of the work. . . . The poem, then, whatever its wide cast of characters, is essentially about an imaginary character (not the poet, not me) named Henry. (*DS*, vi)

In an introductory note to *Recovery,* however, he appears to encourage a documentary interpretation of his text:

> I don't write as a member of the American and international society, Alcoholics Anonymous . . . , but as an author merely who has experienced certain things, witnessed things, heard things, imagined some. The materials of the book, however, especially where hallucinatory, are historical; all facts are real: ladies and gentlemen, it's true. (vii)

The thrust of the first statement is disassociation; of the second, association, indeed intimately so, with the references to AA, to witnessing, and to hallucinations. But one should hesitate to take either claim literally. To say that "it's true" is to say, perhaps, no more than it's sincere. And the disclaimer about AA is necessary and proper. Berryman is simply affirming that anonymity in that fellowship is not a convention but an article of faith.

It is, then, vital to "place" *Recovery,* since judgments of its homiletic, biographical, or aesthetic merit are impossible otherwise. The reason that the judgments of the novel as contained in the original reviews as well as subsequent commentary are all over the map is owing to confusion concerning the work's proper genre. How otherwise can one account for the wildly divergent assessments, for example, by Arthur Oberg and David Perkins? "*Recovery,*" says Oberg,

> descends to A. A. group therapy, which makes the possibility of recovery seem one more delusion along the way. The titles of the two posthumous books are almost beyond irony. *Delusions, Etc.* suggests in its second word the will toward some movement counter to delusion as much as it suggests pure physi-

cal, psychological, and artistic exhaustion and spiritual despair.
And *Recovery* gives the lie to the emergence of recovery on every
page of the book.[3]

Perkins, in contrast, urges that it is an

account, fictionalized and unfinished, of his final struggle to
overcome alcoholism and of his deep ambivalence in that strug-
gle. The book is so insightful and articulate that it is appalling,
wringing the heart with pity for the psychological trap he was
in.[4]

It strikes me that when we find these extremes of judgment between
thoughtful scholars, our critical work is cut out for us.

Part of the problem of interpretation is that *Recovery* is not a
roman à clef, as conventional opinion largely has it, but rather a
bildungsroman. Alcoholics are, among other things, cases of arrested
development, of unwillingness or inability to grow up. An essential
part of the treatment for alcoholism, therefore, is the training of the
prospective recovering alcoholic in the responsibilities of adulthood.
Alcoholics Anonymous, the bible of AA familiarly called "The Big
Book," with its "creed" called the Twelve Steps, is not only a guide
to spiritual healing: it also embodies a code of behavior, a species of
courtesy book.

The literary antecedent of Berryman's novel is, in sensibility, not
such classics of the genre as *Buddenbrooks* or *A Portrait of the Artist as
a Young Man,* but rather Wordsworth's *The Prelude.* Objecting to the
classification of "philosophical poet," Wordsworth said that he was
not a philosopher, that what *The Prelude* is about is what it *feels to
think.*[5] The "Growth of a Poet's Mind" is a history of the disciplining
of feelings into maturity, parables of spiritual exercises. Similarly, the
incessant hammering at feelings in *Recovery* that may strike readers
as both oppressive and tedious is in reality the education—drill, as it
were—for the recovery of sanity and health, for the restoration of the
normal, for the acceptance of matter-of-factness that must be
achieved before the alcoholic is truly in a state of recovery.

To define *Recovery* as a work about the education of the feelings
is not to classify it as a didactic temperance tract or a self-help manual.

Nor is it a narcissistic exploitation of the author's lurid past. In his *Paris Review* interview, Berryman is queried:

> You . . . have been called a confessional poet. How do you react to that label? . . . With rage and contempt! [Berryman shot back] . . . The word doesn't mean anything. I understand confessional to be a place where you go and talk with a priest.[6]

What I take it Berryman is objecting to here is the illegitimate exploitation of incident and emotion, of publicly formalizing the exclusively private. And while what is said and heard in a chemical-dependency treatment center is at times bizarre, as well as trivial and dull, the purpose of the exploration is one not of exhibitionism but of healing. Berryman's artistic problem in *Recovery,* then, is not to contribute to our clinical knowledge, but to cause an aesthetic transformation of the therapeutic: in short, to structure his narrative around the deceptively simple declaration of Alcoholics Anonymous that the "only requirement for membership [in AA] is an honest desire to stop drinking."[7]

Among the Berryman Papers at the University of Minnesota Libraries is a four-page signed typescript (dated 27 December 1970) titled *Third Alcoholic Treatment.* The preamble to it states: "This summary & deluded account of the beginning of my recovery is devoted to the men & women responsible for it . . . and to its primary divine Author." It consists of two brief chapters setting out clearly and intelligently what appears to be the beginning of an expository work on alcoholism. "The disease," he wrote,

> is more grave than even the worst cancers, where spontaneous remission can occur, and where, also, the personality of the sufferer is not attacked. In alcoholism it is. Alcoholism . . . produces inevitably what are known as "sincere delusions." A sincere delusion is a lie—an affective deformation of reality—which the liar does not know to be a lie. . . . A chilling feature of the disease is that even in an advanced stage even its most sophisticated victim does not know he has it. Until last fall, I thought I was just a "heavy social drinker"—even though I had seen three of my oldest friends die of alcoholism. . . . A blindness or stupidity so

dangerous undoubtedly requires some explanation. Partly it must be delusional. The "problem drinker" (this is a euphemism) does not want to believe that he is "an alcoholic," because that belief might actually interfere with his drinking, and would certainly disturb his comfort in his drinking. . . . His delusion is shared in some degree by that part of his society which is concerned with his welfare.[8]

One notices Berryman's fascination with the term *delusion*. It occurs like a liturgical refrain here, as it also does in his last volume of poems, in his annotations to his *Paris Review* interview, and in dozens of places throughout *Recovery*. It is the Gloria Patri of the drunk in treatment.

The "sincere delusion" of Alan Severance is to remain forever seduced into thinking that his wit and wisdom will guide him to recovery from his affliction. Early in *Recovery,*

Severance hoped everyone else was as well prepared as he was. He looked around the room eagerly. Maybe they could pop through this in fifteen minutes at the outside—it wasn't likely that anybody else would have a list of disciplines as long as his, after all—and get down to business at last. He burned to level and confront, be confronted, learn, suffer, and break through. (50–51)

This "sincere delusion" is embarrassingly and ironically lifelike—and pathetically naive. Severance enters this, his third treatment center, not in his own mind as a failure, but as though he were a graduate student returning to complete his degree after a problematic Fulbright. He is, at this point, a treatment veteran, scarred and embattled, but unbroken, who joins the veteran's therapy group. It doesn't occur to him that he is more deserter than hero. In short, Alan Severance reminds one here of Berryman's own experience with group therapy when he was undergoing psychiatric treatment in New York in 1952 (as described by Paul Mariani):

At first [he] was uncomfortable, but soon he was using the sessions as raw material for a novel he planned to write called *The Group*. . . . But he soon grew tired of trying to work with people he considered his intellectual inferiors. . . . [He] lasted only two months in group before he lost his temper with the others and stormed out, refusing to return. By then he decided he could do better on his own, analyzing himself through his poems.[9]

Try as he might, Severance too cannot entirely forego the temptation to exploit his treatment experience professionally.

Yet Berryman was able to objectify this experience and authentically render it in *Recovery* through the establishment of ironical distance between himself and his fictional protagonist. One notices, in addition, that the other characters in the book seem to be there essentially to be played off against Alan Severance, to bring out the profound if temporary "selfishness" that is a necessary element of recovery if not a sufficient condition of sobriety. This is not to diminish the function or substantive importance or integrity of the minor characters in the novel; but it is a clinical fact that in the alcoholic rehabilitation process, only one patient's "story" can be told at a time. And as we follow Severance through this process it strikes the reader that he does not come across as a pleasant fellow. He is vain, unreliable, uncompromisingly self-centered, and above all excruciatingly analytical. The celebrated AA admonition, "Keep it simple, stupid," has not touched him. Alan utters the right words, has command of the correct ideas for recovery, is authoritative about AA: but there is more verbal compliance than real acceptance of his affliction, and the result approaches a spiritual vacuum. In one of his early poems, "Epilogue," Berryman wrote:

> He must descend
> Somewhere, vague and cold, the spirit and seal,
> The gift descend, and all that insight fail
> Somewhere. Imagination one's one friend
> Cannot see there. Both of us at the end.
> Nouns, verbs do not exist for what I feel.
>
> (*CP*, 282)

For the nominalist, intellectual Severance nouns and verbs do indeed replace the reality of the pain of genuine, spontaneously expressed feelings.

But in spite of or because of his confusions and pain, Severance is *learning*. In a fascinating essay, "Transformation and the Labor of Gratitude," Lewis Hyde observes,

> AA's teachings are free, a literal gift. Someone who comes to the group will hear it said, "If you do such and such you will stay sober for a day." His pain is heavy or his desire strong, so he tries it. Suppose it works. Now he is in an odd state. He has received the teaching and he's seen it has some power. . . . The Twelfth Step [of AA] is an act of gratitude: recovered alcoholics help other alcoholics when called upon to do so. It is a Step in which the gift is passed along, so it is right it should be the final one . . . . [There are] people who take Step One (accepting they are an alcoholic) and then jump directly to Step Twelve (helping others) without the in-between steps where the labor lies. They try to pass along something they themselves have not yet received.[10]

This characterization fits Severance precisely, save that he has accepted only the first part of the first step: that he's an alcoholic; the second half, the unmanageability of his life, is inadmissible. He would, it seems, rather forfeit his life than, so he believes, his brilliant career. Scientists, like artists, must bear the wound of Philoctetes, must sacrifice their lives on the altar of creativity.[11] In fact, he is convinced, his "creativity" *derives from* his "unmanageability."

Yet the character of Alan Severance develops through the book. Slowly, haltingly, but perceptively, he moves through the process of spiritual detoxification, groping his way toward that dim, distant goal of "serenity."

The main body of *Recovery* is, in fact, a painful, at times hesitant, but always determined dialectic of Severance's quest for sanity and spiritual peace, for what the suffering alcoholic takes to be the normal condition of ordinary people. Against all the contrary messages that his ego, his pride, his pretensions, and his fame bombard him with, he yearns for simple contentment, for (quoting from William Blake) "the secrets of the land unknown" (*R,* 99). This process closely parallels Berryman's own progress as described in his treatment, AA, and *Recovery* documents. For example, his *Twenty-Four Hours a Day* book, dated 1970–71, is literally crammed with annotations in his clear, minute hand.[12] But the focus of these materials and that in the novel are strikingly different. The struggle of Berryman himself appears to have been to live through compliance with, if not necessarily acceptance of, a program he was just beginning to "internalize." The struggle of Severance is to give up as little as possible while adding to his techniques of survival. Severance is, in his own mind, an imaginary alcoholic becoming an imaginary Jew consecrating an imaginary Eucharist. No wonder his counselors and fellow patients are often wary of the confusions he presents as insights!

One of the delusions Berryman develops through the character of Severance is the fantasy of the alcoholic as hero. There are powerful libertarian pretensions in this model: Mill's exalter of self-regarding acts, Camus's moralist of suicide. But by slowly, and not always painfully, drinking himself to death, the eternally adolescent alcoholic is rather like Huck and Tom attending their own funerals, returning to society to enjoy the consternation they have caused. For in the end, the alcoholic, regardless of what he may claim, is not demanding his right to be left alone, to be allowed to go to hell in his own way: rather, in Scott Fitzgerald's chilling words, he is going to "make them pay and pay and pay and pay." This, perhaps, is the ultimate rationalization, and I think Berryman's central objective in *Recovery* was to dramatize the achievement of spirituality through ordeal. That objective, of course, was not realized, but my impression is that Berryman stopped trying because, as Matthew Arnold observed of the Romantic poets, he did not know enough at that point in his life. After his stunning success writing about Christ's Nativity, the young Milton determined to tackle Christ's Passion. He didn't make it, and concluded the unfinished poem by saying: "This subject the author finding to be above the years he had when he wrote it, and nothing satisfied with what was begun, left it unfinished." Worthy enough to publish, not destroy. Similarly, *Recovery* as it stands is a work of integrity, and I believe we may speculate that, were its author granted enough "years" (that is, "enough" sobriety), he would have produced a major work of art.

In one of his last poems, "Compline," Berryman writes, "If He for me as I feel for my daughter, / being His son, I'll sweat no more tonight / but happy snore & drouse" (*CP*, 234–35). That last service of the liturgical day, from which the title of the poem comes, begins: "The Lord Almighty grant us a peaceful night and a perfect end. Amen."[13] *That* is where the book is headed, to a condition of serenity, of that spirituality that is called peace with God, that the author himself was never to experience. *Recovery,* then, is an elegy, unfinished but headed in the right direction, the direction of the discovery that alcohol all along was not the handmaiden of the imaginative spirit, but the destroyer of it.

NOTES

I wish to thank Kate Donahue for permission to consult the Berryman papers; and Vivian Newbold and Alan Lathrop, of the Manuscripts Division of the University of Minnesota Libraries, for their assistance.

1. Eileen Simpson, *Poets in Their Youth: A Memoir* (New York: Random House, 1982), 245.

2. Joseph Mancini, Jr. *The Berryman Gestalt: Therapeutic Strategies in the Poetry of John Berryman* (New York: Garland, 1987), 34n. Also, e.g.: "[*Recovery*] is an almost consistently readable (if painfully repetitious) amalgam of conversations, confrontations, anecdotes, flashbacks, and broodings on alcoholism. The latter provide a good deal of information about Berryman's life, provided one assumes—and all the evidence points to a total identification—that 'Severance' is unambiguously the poet, that the minor and not altogether convincing disguise is merely a narrative device" (Joel Conarroe, *John Berryman: An Introduction to the Poetry* [New York: Columbia University Press, 1977], 187); "[Berryman] chooses Severance as the name of the protagonist of his nakedly autobiographical 'novel' [*Recovery*]" (Kathe Davis, "The Freedom of John Berryman," *Modern Language Studies* 18, no. 4 [Fall 1988]: 34); "Except for the first-person passages of Severance's journal, the novel is narrated in third-person point of view. Apparently Berryman was attempting to place some aesthetic distance between himself and his protagonist by the use of the more objective point of view. The attempt fails, for Alan Severance is simply John Berryman by another name" (J. M. Linebarger, *John Berryman* [New York: Twayne, 1974], 145); "Alan Severance, MD (Berryman thinly disguised)" (Sonya L. Jones, "A Mile to Avalon: The Role of Alcoholism in the Life and Work of John Berryman" [Ph.D. diss., Emory University, 1983], 12, 19). Jones similarly reads Eileen Simpson's novel *The Maze:* "*The Maze* . . . reveals Berryman's obsession with finding his own poetic voice" (81). Such comments make one long for the old strictures of the New Critics regarding the biographical fallacy.

3. Arthur Oberg, *Modern American Lyric: Lowell, Berryman, Creeley, and Plath* (New Brunswick: Rutgers University Press, 1978), 87.

4. David Perkins, *A History of Modern Poetry,* vol. 2, *Modernism and After* (Cambridge: Harvard University Press, 1987), 403. Also, e.g.: "The unprejudiced reader who picks up *Recovery* will see that the book is unreadable. The ideas that produced this novel were mistaken in life and mistaken in art" (Louis Simpson, "On Berryman's *Recovery,*" *Ohio Review* 15 [1974]: 114); "*Recovery* is

too deep for tears. It is part, with *Love & Fame* and *Delusions, Etc.*, of a final trilogy that makes apparent what a rare man John Berryman was and how much we have lost. He seemed, near the end, so close to finding the God that would save him. Maybe the next time" (William Heyen, "Delusion and Her Daughters: John Berryman's *Recovery*," *Southern Review* 7 [1975]: 724); "Berryman's respectable reputation as a writer of fiction was harmed by the publication in 1973 of *Recovery*. . . . Even if Berryman had lived to polish the manuscript, *Recovery* seems to be unsalvageable as a work of art" (Linebarger, *John Berryman*, 126); "Rough and incomplete as [*Recovery*] is, however, it is a strong and moving work, one of the most important things the poet did, both for its own intrinsic merit and for the light it throws on Berryman and on his poetry, particularly on *The Dream Songs*" (Conarroe, *John Berryman*, 183–84).

5. For an excellent analysis of the relation of thought to feeling, see Melvin Rader, *Wordsworth: A Philosophical Approach* (Oxford: Oxford University Press, 1967), chap. 6.

6. Peter A. Stitt, "John Berryman," *Writers at Work: The "Paris Review" Interviews*, 4th series, ed. George Plimpton (New York: Viking, 1976), 299.

7. *Alcoholics Anonymous*, 3d ed. (New York: AA World Services, 1976), xiv.

8. John Berryman, MSS 43, Box 1, "Loose File," "*Recovery* Notes, Drafts, Reviews," JB Papers.

9. PM, 248–49. Berryman, at least in the beginning of his experience in treatment, appears to have taken a similarly misguided approach to recovery: "Afraid of the programme—which I caught on to very quickly from the lecturing and am talking to the other men on the unit—it seemed hard & ridiculous to expect to reform one's character, morally & spiritually, in just 3 weeks' time. . . . But on the fifth day . . . I began to improve: . . . and by the end of the end of the [*sic*] second week I was feeling better in every way than I'd felt for many years, and continued so" (*DH*, 282).

10. Lewis Hyde, "Transformation & the Labor of Gratitude," *Kenyon Review* NS 2 (1980): 108.

11. The locus classicus on the subject of suffering and creativity is Edmund Wilson's "Philoctetes: The Wound and the Bow," *The Wound and the Bow* (New York: Oxford University Press, 1941). For a recent analysis, see George Wedge et al., "Under the Influence," *Areté* (Summer 1990): 26–57. The relation of creativity and sacrifice in Berryman is a frequent subject for himself and his critics. See, e.g., Richard Kostelanetz, "Conversation with Berryman," *Massachusetts Review* 11 (1970): 34–47; Kathe Davis, "The Li(v)es of the Poet," *Twentieth Century Literature* 30 (1984): 46–68; Alan Shapiro, "'A living to fail': The Case of John Berryman," *TriQuarterly* 58 (1983): 114–25. Thomas Gilmore comments thoughtfully on the specific relation of alcohol to creativity: "To an important extent, . . . attitudes toward or treatments of drinking . . . are manifestations of literary modernism. . . . The whole modernist ethic and aesthetic, including the desirability of a constant search for ways of altering or destroying traditional modes of perception, may be under increasingly severe critical examination. . . . [I]n the end [one] may question whether any work of art is worth the sacrificial destruction of the artist" (*Equivocal Spirits: Alcoholism and Drinking*

in Twentieth-Century Literature [Chapel Hill: University of North Carolina Press, 1987], 170–71).

12. John Berryman, MSS 43, "Diary 1965–1972 Notes & Undated," File #4, JB Papers. Sample annotation in the *Twenty-Four Hour* book on December 31: "Courbet d. alcoholic in Swiss exile 1877."

13. *The Book of Common Prayer* (1979): 127.

Alan J. Altimont

The End of *Recovery* and the End of Self-Representation

As my title suggests, I believe we can see two writing processes coming to a halt in John Berryman's novel *Recovery,* and I also believe these processes are worth distinguishing from each other. The distinction reveals not only the novel's remarkable differences from Berryman's earlier works but also clarifies its relationship to the author's suicide.

If we attend only to the more obvious of the two writing processes—the drafting and abandonment of this individual narrative—then we are constrained to view *Recovery* as, at best, a useful supplement to the two Berryman biographies by John Haffenden and Paul Mariani (JH, PM). That is, it portrays in much greater detail than the biographers can Berryman's last extended treatment for alcoholism in October and November of 1970. As a novel, though, *Recovery* is so far from completion that it affords the reader only meager pleasures. Judging from one of Berryman's last outlines (dated 16 September 1971), composition was abandoned with less than half of the planned novel drafted out (*R,* 230). True, certain sections are engaging, even moving, and the hero, Alan Severance, is well drawn; but the supporting cast of characters, with perhaps one exception, remains a shadowy lot. Most of us would probably agree that *Recovery,* whatever its strengths, is the least satisfying of Berryman's longer published works.

Recovery, moreover, is diminished by its relationship to the author's suicide. We tend to romanticize last, unfinished novels like James Agee's *A Death in the Family* and F. Scott Fitzgerald's *The Last Tycoon* because the novelists died fighting the good fight, against considerable odds. Berryman's case is tragically different. A little more than a year after he had undergone the events he was trying to portray, he abandoned *Recovery,* in less than a month temporarily abandoned his hard-won sobriety, and permanently abandoned family, friends, life itself, on 7 January 1972. The text of the novel ends with two pages, each blank except for the name of an unwritten chapter (*R* 225, 227). We read, reluctantly, from these white spaces a grim tale of the author's despair, failure, and suicide.

Another writing process, however, comes to an end with the end of this individual narrative, and that is Berryman's long career of self-representation, which began with his short stories of the mid-1940s—first and foremost "The Lovers"—and continued with *Berryman's Sonnets, The Dream Songs,* and *Love & Fame.* Considered as the closing movement of this the most powerful current of his art, *Recovery,* even in its concluding fragments, represents a partial though remarkable achievement, a literary pyrrhic victory. There are two reasons why this is so. First, in the novel Berryman confronts personal issues he had only skirted previously and portrays himself more candidly than he ever had before. One of the most important of these issues—the one upon which I will focus—is writing itself: problematic assumptions about the therapeutic efficacy of writing, the relationship of writing to fame, and the role the writing process plays in the writer's life. In fact, writing is so often at issue in this novel that the hero seems to be in treatment for a *writing* problem as much as for a drinking problem, a parallel which should come as no surprise given how often Berryman mixed the two in life.

The second reason (a consequence of the first) will appear, I fear, rather outlandish, in part because so many of us, being writers of one stripe or another ourselves, quite naturally have a high opinion of what we do; but I offer it in all seriousness. It is that the abandonment of *Recovery,* of this latest of Berryman's arduous autobiographical projects, was not the result of flagging powers, not a Hemingway-esque collapse, as both Haffenden and Mariani would seem to have it. Rather, the abandonment of *Recovery* is the result of the author's terrible insight that the process of composing such works had become over the years more and more enmeshed with hostile and self-destructive behavior. It is no accident that the insight came during the composition of a sustained prose narrative. The intense but intermittent bursts of activity that produced his poetic sequences allowed

Berryman to manage, to some extent, the darker aspects of his writing process. Sustaining a lengthy prose narrative, however, would not. It is also no accident, then, that he was able to complete only one such work, *Stephen Crane,* despite attempts at several others. The last of these, *Recovery,* obviously does not end as its author had intended it to; nor does it, on the other hand, end haphazardly, cut short by the unforeseen death of the author; rather, it ends when the process of and materials for composing this self-representation—indeed, *all* self-representation—became too painful for the author to endure. The composition of *Recovery* forced Berryman to take a long, hard look at the "bad powers"—not only of alcohol, but of writing—he had had an inkling of for years but never before faced. Putting an end to *Recovery,* and then to his life, were Berryman's responses to the devastating differences that emerged between the writer and the self-portrait, differences aggravated, and to some extent created, by the writing process itself.

Contrary to the thesis put forward a number of years ago by Lewis Hyde (in "Alcohol and Poetry: John Berryman and the Booze Talking"),[1] I am suggesting that drinking and writing, far from being "at war" over a presumably inert John Berryman, were often enlisted under the same banner and collaborating in much more sinister and profound ways than Hyde's analysis of style and subject matter had led us to believe. A more useful paradigm than Hyde's for understanding the relationship between Berryman's writing and his drinking is offered by Dr. Donald W. Goodwin in his *Alcohol and the Writer.* Using a suggestion by the historian Gilman Ostrander, Goodwin attempts to explain why so many American writers have tended to be alcoholics. Goodwin and Ostrander believe that writers and alcoholics are loners, and that the activities of writing and drinking "are two forms of companionship" that allow "the individual to be tremendously convivial all by himself."[2] In the case of Berryman, I would say that solitary writing and solitary drinking came to serve much the same purpose of isolating and insulating him from the increasing demands of his intimate personal relationships.

After two biographies, two memoirs, and a collection of letters,[3] we know, or should know, that Berryman's alcoholism, though detrimental to his work and unquestionably life-threatening, was subsidiary to a longstanding psychological problem. This problem was the source of Berryman's anger and self-destructiveness, which in turn found in his writing practices a vehicle for escape and alienation more subtle and even more potent than alcohol. The influence of the problem is pervasive: it motivates his urge to commence a self-portrait, insinuates itself into his habits of composition, and determines the self he consistently portrays, whether sober or not—especially the story he tells about this self.

I believe contemporary psychotherapists and the literature of self-help would call Berryman's problem "fear of intimacy with women," but since he formulates the problem himself both at the beginning and end of his career as a tension between two opposing forces, let us use his terminology. In Berryman's 1944 story "The Lovers," the young protagonist's mysterious mentor—known only as "the visitor" (but, as I read the story, a representation both of his dead father and of himself as an adult)—announces his ambition to find himself "a wife, and work!" We can recognize in the visitor's agenda, by the way, a nuts-and-bolts version of the two prerequisites posited by modern psychoanalysis for mature and healthy adulthood. As events turn out, the visitor fails to attain his first objective when the protagonist's beautiful mother subtly rejects his improper advances, but we learn that he has apparently done quite well with his second objective, work, because he has become famous enough for the narrator (the grown-up protagonist) to see occasional photographs of him, presumably in newspapers or magazines.[4]

The outcome of "The Lovers," which Berryman composed early in his first marriage, pessimistically suggests that it is impossible to attain normalcy as psychoanalysis defines it, to have both a personal life and also make a significant contribution, in the form of literary work, to society. Twenty-six years later, Berryman would substitute more abstract, Platonic terms for "a wife, and work" in the title of his 1970 sequence of lyrics, *Love & Fame.* In this book Berryman represents his whole life as a struggle for these two objectives—or, more precisely, as two conflicting struggles for these two opposed objectives. Within this framework an advance toward one goal causes a setback in the other struggle, and the frustrations mount until both goals are finally rejected as empty and illusory.[5]

A similar tension, equally frustrating, informs Berryman's 1947 sonnet sequence: the sonneteer fails to woo his beloved away from her husband, and writes first in praise of but increasingly in compensation for what he cannot have; in the end his literary labors cannot bring him fame because he cannot publish them (although Berryman eventually solved this problem two decades later).[6] Only with Henry in *The Dream Songs* does Berryman achieve a precarious and tentative double resolution in that Henry, like his creator, has become a husband and father, as well as a famous poet.

The selves engaged in these struggles are typically portrayed as victims, sometimes passive, often naive. Generally Berryman's narratives and lyric sequences begin by depicting a self ignoring obligations and struggling for a love that is somehow inappropriate—a precocious adolescent crush, an adulterous affair, collegiate sexual experimentation, even love of Jews and, in *Recovery*, addiction to alcohol. The self is persecuted, often figuratively put on trial, and then undergoes a conversion to an older, wiser self who works in penitential isolation, usually writing and earning recognition. Henry, for example, goes through this pattern, which superficially resembles Saint Augustine's conversion narrative, several times during the course of *The Dream Songs;* and the self portrayed in the fourth part of *Love & Fame* prays for the energy to devote himself solely to writing for God even as he fantasizes being disencumbered of wife and family by his own death. Sadly, there is a good deal of accuracy to the isolated writer portrayed at the end of most of these autobiographical projects, because Berryman's writing habits, often accompanied by drinking, were guaranteed to alienate him from those who loved and needed him most, his wives and children. Even as he wrote of himself as a victim, his writing practices victimized those nearest to him. Fame—and the literary work required to earn that public identity—is Berryman's refuge from and substitute for love—which can only be attained by maintaining identity-threatening intimacy with a woman, a wife, and (by extension) a family.

I have already hinted how *Recovery,* the last of Berryman's self-representations, participates in some of these patterns. But what is most impressive about this novel is how it participates in the old patterns in order to dismantle them. In effect, the novel begins at precisely the moment when most of Berryman's earlier narratives conclude, and it does so, at least in part, in order to examine what writing means to the main character and how his writing affects him. Alan Severance, Berryman's self-representation, arrives at his doorstep after a binge and fling with another woman and is promptly carted off to the hospital. Despite his ungovernable behavior, Severance is not the naïve young man of the earlier works. He is, in fact, almost impossibly well educated and broad-minded, an M.D., molecular biologist, and widely published scholar who dabbles in art, literature, and biblical studies. Alcoholic delusion now supplants the naïveté of the earlier self-portraits.

We primarily experience Severance as a writer, though: the narrative is regularly broken by excerpts from the journal he keeps, and we often see him writing and thinking about his writing. One out of every seven or eight pages of the text (30 out of 224 pages) is represented as Severance's own writing. Much of this writing is, of course, in direct response to the text of "The Twelve Steps" of the AA program, as Severance rereads his earlier responses to the steps from his previous treatment, revises his approach, and composes new responses. Eminent scholar that he is, Severance is so confident in his reading and writing abilities he believes at the beginning of his treatment that he is "indomitable" and that he can "create as he did in the lab with ballpoint and paper, create sobriety" (*R,* 17). By the end of his first week in treatment, however, his pride and confidence in his writing are severely shaken. The patients are given an assignment in group therapy "to think and write out whatever things [they think they] ought to do every day," and are cautioned not to "take on too much, but take on anything [they] think is necessary to create a chance for . . . sobriety" (*R,* 43). When Severance is criticized for composing an absurdly long and grandiose list, he does not give up writing, but thoroughly revises his view of what his writing can accomplish:

> Friday afternoon found him writing laboriously. "*Comment:* If this statement has literary merit, that I think is not a con, only the product of the fact that a lifelong effort to put things shortly and forcibly is unbreakable, and harmless, except insofar as it may persuade others to share the patient's delusion and so support his illness (any writer's, or even scientist's permanent message perhaps is really just this: *come and share my delusion,* and we will be happy or miserable *together*) THIS ATTEMPT *is right here. Otherwise* I have made no conscious effort to impress you. . . ." He stopped there, . . . and it was twenty-four hours before, looking at it again with a view to going on, he was horrified to

find that it was *crap*—mere evasion—delusion. . . . Atrociously
written too, and that mattered. (*R*, 54–55)

Regardless, that is, of his conscious intentions, Severance's writing
is essentially an exercise in the propagation of self-deceptions. Style
matters, but it is secondary to "evasion—delusion," those disguised
assumptions and aims of the writing process that perpetuate Sever-
ance's more acute dis-ease.

In chapter 3, "Contract One," which covers the second week of
Severance's treatment, Berryman continues to examine writing prob-
lems, but shifts the focus from Severance's writing to one of his own
earlier works. The climax of this section is, for all intents and pur-
poses, a surreptitious critique of the Dream Songs and of John Berry-
man as he was when he composed them. The only other truly inter-
esting character in the novel is Jasper Stone, author of a book of
poems called *The Screams,* and a man with whom Severance feels
himself "suddenly locked in a death-grip of amity"—no wonder since
the two characters are portraits of the same author at different times
in his life. When Stone asks him if he found *The Screams* interesting,
Severance replies,

"Yes. . . . You sound better aloud. Good deal of authentic ma-
nia there, black and blue wit, pain—the fellow going on to fresh
defeats, flappable, flappable. Surviving however. I bought a lot
of the little I could understand. Do you write when you're
drunk?"
"Not necessarily." (*R*, 84)

Stone goes on to confess he is a "raging egotist" and to identify with
a story about Bertrand Russell, who once refused to be interrupted
when he was reading about himself (*R*, 84–85). Severance inadver-
tently reveals in his next journal excerpt that he is just as much of an
egotist as Stone and Russell, so wrapped up in an interview with a
young journalist (Peter Stitt in the episode from Berryman's life) that
he ignores his wife when she comes to visit (*R*, 87–88). Yet he has
moved past Stone in at least one way: immediately after commenting
on Stone's obscure lyrics, Severance evaluates the straightforward-

ness of his own writing—"No Style: good. Still, it didn't sound too good, exactly"—and finally tears up what he has composed (*R,* 86).

The critique of the Dream Songs is completed when Severance reads one of his own dreams to the group. Severance's dream image for himself is an amphitheater, and immediately after he has discussed the image with the group he relates it to fame: "I have *not* come to easy terms with my fame etc" (*R,* 92). As an amphitheater he is a space for grand performances—perhaps not unlike the minstrel performances of the Dream Songs—but a space so large that Alan Severance, the man, is lost in it. The group counselor asks Severance if he would change anything about the dream, and Severance responds with a drastic revision, amounting to a rejection of his dehumanizing dream imagery: "We need an entirely new dream" (*R,* 95). A recovered self, honest and sober, and a direct style would seem to constitute the "new dream" he wishes to substitute for the old dream of the evasive, incoherent Henry of the Dream Songs.

In section 17, appropriately entitled "Confrontation," Severance reaches a dramatic turning point in his treatment. The confrontation occurs not only between counselors and patient, but more importantly between love and fame, those competing priorities in Severance's life. And Severance discovers, to his horror, that his work, particularly his writing, both finished and unfinished, has crowded out his personal life, embodied in his neglected son:

> "I've done an incredible amount of work in spite of my drinking. *Sober work.*"
> "Exactly: 'incredible.' "
> "It's true," [Severance] shouted.
> "Say it is. What kind of a *life* do you have? You go East how often—three times a year—and you can't remember when you saw your son last? You don't know how many *years* it is."
> Severance felt tears coming. He couldn't deny it. What kind of a father was he? He stared at his boots. He wished with all his heart that he could feel sorry for himself, but that was out of the question. It was simple: he was an utter bastard. . . .
> "Your life-style," Harley said gently, "seems to leave something to be desired. Do all these great accomplishments of yours give you any great pleasure, Alan? You're proud of them?"

"No," he heard his voice weary and low. "No, I'm not. I'm ashamed of them."

"Why are you ashamed of them?" Keg asked robustly. "You ought to be proud of them. Why not?"

"It's not my doing, except the work. I do work some times. But all my priorities are wrong. I see that."

"You see it's not just drinking?"

This was hard, very hard. He couldn't think, he just felt. "I see it. My whole goddamned life is a fucking mess even apart from the drinking." (*R*, 166–67)

I think we can say that what applies to Severance here also applied to John Berryman himself. From this point on Severance, the self-representation, is newly energized, leveling with himself and others, and casting off delusions and personal myths. In the last section Berryman was to complete, "Dry-Drunk," Severance finally considers that part of the AA program he had neglected in his previous treatment, those Steps that force the alcoholic to view himself not as a victim and martyr—crucial characteristics of all of Berryman's previous self-portraits—but as a victimizer:

[Severance] smoked and read, quietly, until he came to a sharp sentence about "obligation." Feeling brought up short, he realized it was high time he did something about the "amends" Steps—got on, altogether, with his Programme. . . . Step Eight was, "Made a list of all persons we had harmed, and became willing to make amends to them all." Well, he had done that at Howarden [i.e., Hazelden] a year ago, a gratifyingly short list, too. He was almost never violent, drinking. It wasn't until last Spring at Northeast [St. Mary's?] that he noticed the Step said nothing about "while drinking" or "by drinking" and the shock of this so lengthened his list that when he went on to Step Nine he quailed. He read it again: "Made direct amends to such people wherever possible, except when to do so would injure them or others." He had *not* done so, except, some, to Ruth [Kate Donahue, Berryman's wife] and their daughter. (*R*, 218)

Finally a Berryman self-portrait is beginning to drop the mask of the helpless victim and own up to his responsibility. The new view raised a new and apparently insurmountable difficulty, however, because writing could no longer be used to make amends. This very novel was exploring how counterproductive the author's writing practices could be.

Yet John Berryman, the autobiographical author, was still writing, still giving top priority to the sort of work that would garner fame but cut himself off from his family. Long uncomfortable in his mother's presence and threatened by the births of his own children, he had first conceived of writing something about his recovery at about the same time he learned of his wife's second pregnancy and also at about the time he decided he would have to begin caring for his ailing mother. He began intensive work on the novel exactly one week before his mother's arrival in Minneapolis and the birth of his second daughter. The work made him irritable, frantic, and as it progressed his marriage suffered further strain. He removed for a short time to Berkeley, California, so that he could be free of domestic and marital pressures to make progress on a narrative about a man who was beginning to get his priorities right. The disparity between the recovered self he wished to represent and the angry, isolated writer he had once again become must surely have been too painfully obvious to have escaped the notice of so ruthless a self-assessor.

As he came to see the extent to which he was not a victim and to see how his writing projects were themselves part of his arsenal deployed against those who loved him, Berryman must also have realized that even this supremely candid self-representation was being used to drive a wedge between himself and his family. While the narrative carries Severance toward sobriety and personal growth, the creation of the narrative carried Berryman toward anger and alienation. In any case, it was clearly not enough that the drinking had stopped. The writing had to stop too. And when the writing must stop, what is left for the writer to do? Berryman's discovery during the composition of *Recovery* was that obsessive, self-destructive writing would not work. His fatal mistake was to succumb to the writer's old delusion, reinforced by his "lifelong effort to put things shortly and forcibly," that nothing less than his all would do.

NOTES

1. Lewis Hyde, "Alcohol and Poetry: John Berryman and the Booze Talking," *American Poetry Review* 4 (January 1975): 7–12. Reprinted in *The Pushcart Prize: Best of the Small Presses,* ed. Bill Henderson (New York: Avon, 1976), 71–94. With its reprinting in the present collection, Hyde's essay is certainly the most frequently reproduced work on Berryman to date. Subsequent references, to the essay as reprinted in the present volume, are incorporated in the text.

2. Donald W. Goodwin, M.D., *Alcohol and the Writer* (New York: Penguin, 1990), 191.

3. E. M. Halliday, *John Berryman and the Thirties: A Memoir* (Amherst: University of Massachusetts Press, 1986); Eileen Simpson, *Poets in Their Youth: A Memoir* (New York: Random House, 1982); *DH.*

4. John Berryman, "The Lovers," *Kenyon Review* 7 (1945): 1–11. Reprinted in *FP,* 344–52.

5. John Berryman, *Love & Fame* (New York: Farrar, Straus and Giroux, 1970).

6. John Berryman, *Berryman's Sonnets* (New York: Farrar, Straus and Giroux, 1969).

Lewis Hyde

Berryman Revisited:
A Response

My essay on alcohol and poetry was written seventeen years ago at a time when almost no one spoke publicly about the topic. That is no longer the case, of course, but it is worth remembering that it once was lest we forget that a gathering of essays such as we have here is in itself an achievement to be valued. Not only that, but these essays illustrate how far we've come. The discussion has marvelous complexity now, and each of these papers has something new to teach us.

I will come back to what seems to me new and valuable in a moment, but let me begin my response by marking the few places where I have reservations about my colleagues' remarks.

To begin with, we have a perplexing problem in this business of honesty and delusion. Addressing my 1975 essay on Berryman, George Wedge speaks of a "prejudice against the possibility that an active alcoholic can write truthfully" (233). I'm not sure that formulation catches the full flavor of my remarks; I think Berryman was witheringly truthful much of the time. But I certainly do claim that he is often divided against himself, and that we often hear the voice of active alcoholism, a voice that willingly sacrifices the truth for other ends.

Wedge's claim, in any event, is not just that we find truth telling in *The Dream Songs* but that Berryman, the writer, was in control of his art as he wrote those poems. "John, distancing himself behind the mask of Henry, knows what he is looking at," Wedge tells us. "My view," he says, "[is] that the poet remains in control—even when drunk" (239, 240).

Against this view let us pose the unsettling description of "delusions" that Roger Forseth found in one of Berryman's manuscripts: "Alcoholism . . . ," Berryman wrote, "produces inevitably what are known as 'sincere delusions.' A sincere delusion is a lie . . . which the liar does not know to be a lie" (249).

The puzzle, of course, is to figure out how we know when we are telling the truth and when we are sincerely deluded. How do we know when we are in control and when we are out of control? These questions smack of old philosophy-class conundrums such as, How do we know if we are awake or asleep and dreaming?

I don't know how to solve such problems. Suffice it to say, first, that I think Wedge is right to find more truth telling in *The Dream Songs* than I allowed for in my old essay; but, second, that I dissent from the idea that "the poet remains in control—even when drunk." The stories I have heard recovering alcoholics tell of their drinking days belie that conceit.

All of which brings me to a second topic. Having addressed the "prejudice against the possibility that an active alcoholic can write truthfully," Wedge "shudder[s] at the cost of this prejudice in whole canons of much loved and highly honored authors" (233), mentioning London, Fitzgerald, Faulkner, Carver, Cheever, and so on.

I must admit that the canon so listed is one I am glad to see revalued. One's attitude here hinges, I suppose, on what one takes to be the uses of literature. Why do we read these books in the first place? Again, the question is not one we can settle quickly, but at some level, in discussing these writers, we are moving toward our answers. For myself, I look to literature for enchantment, beauty, and wisdom, but also for solace and hope. Those works matter to me which have given me courage for living, which have helped me bear suffering and the knowledge of death. In those terms a writer such as John Cheever, while I have admired and learned from his craft, does not appear in the canon inscribed on my heart. In contrast to Wedge, I shudder to think of a culture that would canonize these voices without marking where they fail us.

All this said, let me turn to what I find fruitful in these essays. In addition to his remarks about "delusions," I like very much Roger Forseth's formulation that *Recovery* is "a work about the education of the feelings" (248), and I am grateful to George Wedge for his news about the "grave Sienese face," a line that has puzzled me for decades.

More, both of these essays seem to me to offer a looser and therefore better way to speak of intoxication and literature than the one represented in my old essay.

I share George Wedge's reservations about working from "the AA model." Perhaps because alcoholism is a deadly disease, and perhaps because for recovering alcoholics there is no "in-between" (you're either drinking or you're not), the AA model tends to be categorical. Both of these essays open up possible in-between's and therefore make the discussion less programmatic, less moralizing. In particular, both essays urge us to seek in the struggles of the active alcoholic—half deluded as they may be—seeds and signs of potential recovery. With their wider middle ground, their readings of Berryman are more generous than my own, and I welcome that.[1]

In closing, though, let me place the categorical tone of my old essay in its history. It is useful to remember how far we have come with this topic, how much has changed in the years since Berryman's suicide. Is there anyone now who does not know about Twelve Step groups? We know so much about them, in fact, that one longs for a thirteenth step whose text might begin, "Having awakened a sense of irony as a result of this program . . . "

Seriously, though, in the late 1960s, when I was a student of John Berryman's, there was virtually nothing "in the air" about alcoholism and sobriety. At the college where I now teach, all incoming freshmen receive a lecture on alcoholism; in five years at the University of Minnesota in the 1960s I never once heard the topic discussed. Berryman used to teach while drunk, but no one ever spoke about this remarkable fact within earshot of his students. The whole place was like one of those alcoholic families where no one is allowed to talk about the old man's problem. Part of the categorical tone of my essay drives from this air of denial; I was speaking against a large silence, and felt I had to speak emphatically.

For a second point about the tone of that essay, let me back off and offer a remark that James Baldwin makes in his memoir about his father, in "Notes of a Native Son." In that essay, Baldwin's father, with whom he had fought bitterly, has recently died. For a moment at the father's funeral the son finds himself released from his bitterness and anger; he sees the old man with fresh eyes, and, I think, forgives him. "It was better not to judge the man who had gone down under an impossible burden," Baldwin writes. "It was better to remember: *Thou knowest this man's fall; but thou knowest not his wrassling.*"

I say all this because another part of the tone of my 1975 essay is anger. It is the anger of the young who want much from their elders and are necessarily betrayed. It is the anger of anyone who has been close to an active alcoholic and gotten hurt. It is anger toward an intellectual community that seemed unable to respond to the wounded one in its midst.

Both the silence and the anger feel like history to me now. It is fitting from this distance in time that greater generosity and nuance should mark our readings of Berryman's work. And, for those of us who knew him, acceptance is in order. Looking back on John Berryman these many years after his death, let us say, as Baldwin says, *Thou knowest this man's fall; but thou knowest not his wrassling.*

NOTES

1. I did not have a chance to read Alan Altimont's essay before the conference at which the essays in this volume were presented, but I have read it since. As with Wedge and Forseth, Altimont seems to me to offer a valuable widening of how we might read the links between Berryman and alcoholism. My one reservation has to do with making alcoholism "subsidiary" to the psychological (259). What Altimont sees as an opposition between our approaches I take to be more a matter of point of departure. Berryman surely had "fear of intimacy with a woman" (260) and he surely had alcoholism; to say both is to complicate our reading, as it should be complicated, rather than narrow it as I once did and as Altimont does when he cleaves too fully to the psychological.

Part 5
A Play by John Berryman

Charles Thornbury

An Introduction to
"Cleopatra: A Meditation"

"Cleopatra: A Meditation," written in 1937, is a significant achieve-
ment in Berryman's early writing. It marks the conclusion of his
apprenticeship, which began in 1934, and confirms several directions
he would take in his poetry, most prominently the dramatic mode
of *Homage* and the Dream Songs. Two months before he started
work on "Cleopatra," he discovered that his plan to write his first
play—*The Architect,* a three-act tragedy—was beyond his reach. He
did, nevertheless, learn something about how character, action, and
poetry work together in a dramatic context. In "Cleopatra," he
learned that he handled best a limited number of characters. As he had
said of Yeats's dance plays the previous spring, "frequently, the more
restricted the imagination, the more splendid its activity" ("The Rit-
ual of W. B. Yeats," *FP,* 251). Berryman confirmed as well that he
was most at home in alternating forms of speech, the lightning shifts
and delicate nuances of his later poetry. That he completed the play
is worth noting, for he could see it whole, which he could not in *The
Architect.* The subtleties of characterization in a particular time and
place were now more accessible to him.

On Sunday, 25 April, Berryman began work on "Cleopatra."
"Spent hours today in the library among the authorities," he wrote
to his mother. It would be short and stylized "from the most unfamil-
iar and historically accurate angle."[1] He wanted Brian Boydell, a
pianist, composer, and a fellow student with a fine tenor voice, to be
the Narrator and compose the music. Several months earlier, he had
met Beryl Eeman, a student at Newnham College, "lovely and very
able," and one of the best players in the Cambridge Amateur Dra-

matic Company (A.D.C.). He was writing the play for her, "her all unwitting," and hoped she would take the role of Cleopatra: "It helps unbelievably," he wrote, "to set a part *for* someone."[2] If all went well, the A.D.C. would produce it the next autumn.

He finished the play, except for some final polishing of the second half, the next October. In the main action, Caesar and Cleopatra meet briefly in Rome at Cleopatra's villa in 45 B.C. (a year before Caesar was assassinated). Caesar describes, with a jealousy that "Rots at the heart of the known world's emblem," his recent Spanish campaign, "in which he hunted down and left to die in a cave Cneus Pompey, [Cleopatra's] first lover, with whom she once spent two months at Alexandria."[3] Politic, ambitious, single-minded, sensuous, loving and hating Caesar, Cleopatra prays after his departure for a curse upon him. She dances to the Sun, "a dance of love and death." The Narrator concludes with a song about how Cleopatra's "Resentment got continual strife," and reflects upon "What symbol of degraded death / Will now sustain what she has been?"

Cleopatra is twenty-four and Caesar fifty-two at the moment of Berryman's play. He suffers less from epilepsy since his return from the Spanish campaign, but he is still, Berryman wrote in his planning notes, "physically weak, delicate, hollow cheeks, bad teeth, thin hair combed forward."[4] His present condition does not eclipse his striking presence: "tall, well-made, & melancholy black eyes arresting; elegant in toga, courteous, eloquent—*loose*—conqueror of Gauls, victor of Pharsalia, Master of Rome." Berryman noted Cleopatra's ancestral heritage of incest and murder, and how later accounts, according to Gaston Delayen, one of his sources, gave a distorted view of her: "Cicero, Horace, & Lucan ('meretrix regine') abuse her ('female monstrum')." Cleopatra had given birth to Caesarion, one of her "amours," in June 47 B.C. (In Berryman's play, Caesar is the father and Cleopatra "was with child by hatred"; the son gives her a "power / Unlimited, if odd, upon this man / Who juggles nations.") Two years after the birth of Caesarion, Caesar, "jealous, sent for her & brother to come to Rome." She came in 46 B.C. with Caesarion and stayed nearly three years.

"Cleopatra is not so vapid as she has come to sound, nor Shakespearian either," Berryman declared as he began.[5] The themes—"Ambition, Love, Pride"—would be unmistakable in the Roman "Dictator Perpetual" Julius Caesar and the Egyptian Queen

Cleopatra. Cleopatra herself would manifest a "culture divided be-
tween formal old-Egyptian & naturalistic Greek." The Egyptians,
who spoke little Latin, considered the Romans as "coarse, brutal,
barbarous." The Narrator would set, conclude, and meditate upon
the action, and his sympathies would be with Cleopatra: "To medi-
tate upon the Queen," he says near the end of the play, "Has been
my strict desire." Early in his planning, Berryman anticipated alter-
nating the forms of his characters' speech; the Narrator would speak
in song and Cleopatra and Caesar in blank verse. Song and dance,
particularly near the end of the play, would frame and heighten the
situation and action. He also planned to observe the unities of time,
action, and place, as he had in his first attempt at writing a play.

Berryman's two primary authorities, his notes indicate, were
Gaston Delayen's *Cleopatra* (London: Dent, 1934) and the *Encyclope-
dia Britannica*. He also made notes on Caesar's encounters with
Cleopatra from Thomas North's late sixteenth-century translation
of Plutarch's *The Lives of the Noble Grecians and Romans,* which was
Shakespeare's source for his Roman plays. Berryman especially liked
North's translation of Cleopatra's first meeting with Caesar on a
"flockbed, or mattress."[6] From Delayen's work, he summarized an
image of Cleopatra at age twenty: "large eyes, aquiline nose, pro-
nounced chin—small, graceful, lovely voice & wit, charm—wore
always amethyst ring." She also had "intellectual qualities" and was
a "superb linguist"; she was cruel, proud, willful, "changeable, agi-
tated, ambitious, impetuous, sensual." The *Britannica* described her
as having an "imperious will, masculine boldness, relentless ambi-
tion." From other sources he learned that the "Egyptian family lacked
Roman severity." Egyptian women showed "tenderness" and "occu-
pied high position"; "clitorism & cuckoldry & nymphomania" were
also ascribed to them. Cleopatra was the embodiment of feminine
beauty: "slim waist, full firm breasts, black hair—tattooing on fore-
head & chin & breasts, powder, rouge, mascara." Her historical im-
age suited very well the stylized gestures and masks that Berryman
admired in Yeats's dance plays.

"*Cleopatra* is finished and I'm working over it," he wrote to his
mother on 19 October: "about 400 lines; better than I hoped; there is
an excellent chance of its production at the A.D.C. Theatre next
month."[7] He had begun "Cleopatra" with Beryl in mind as the lead.
During the time he worked on the play between late April and Octo-

ber, they had made plans to marry, and his image of her became
linked with Cleopatra's. She is "a brilliant actress," he had written to
his friend E. M. Halliday in July, "hard, powerful mind, absolute
honesty, *no* sentimentality, very complex wit and great physical
beauty & grace."[8] The A.D.C. decided to produce instead Eliot's
Sweeney Agonistes on 10 November. He was distressed that he had
not revised "Cleopatra" to his satisfaction in time. The sense of the
immediacy of performance had vanished and with it his motivation
to revise the play further. The day after the *Sweeney* production, he
read several of his poems and his confidence resurfaced. He
reaffirmed his commitment to being a poet rather than a dramatist:
"Given life and tenacity in discipline," he vowed, "I shall be a great
poet."[9]

     After Berryman returned to America in June 1938, he worked
briefly on a radio version of "Cleopatra." He thought about doing
something with it again a year later, but nothing came of his plan.
After "Cleopatra," he completed one other play, *Dictator,* a tragedy
written in late 1938 and early 1939 about the takeover of a fascist
regime. Neither "Cleopatra" nor *Dictator* were produced during his
lifetime. During the next twenty years, he made notes for six more
plays. His subjects were mostly historical—Katherine Niarn, the 1916
Irish Easter Rebellion, and Mirabeau.

     While Berryman's *Sonnets to Chris* (1947) has seemed for some
time a sort of rehearsal for *Homage to Mistress Bradstreet* (1953),
"Cleopatra" is more plainly in a direct line of genealogy. It is his first
successful attempt at creating a strong female character. In both
works, as he said of *Homage,* he was concerned with his primary
character "almost from the beginning, as a woman" ("One Answer
to a Question: Changes," *FP,* 328). His portrayal of both Cleopatra
and Anne Bradstreet as actual figures in history gave him a sense of
achievement. He did not wish to appropriate them; he wanted them
to be and speak for themselves. As he began "Cleopatra," he chose
to see his subject "from the most unfamiliar and historically accurate
angle."[10] Where Shakespeare was wrong about her, he remarked, he
hoped to be right. Some thirteen years after completing *Homage,* he
commented that "few critics have seen that it *is* a historical poem";
he was pleased that Robert Lowell pronounced *Homage* "the most
resourceful historical poem in our literature" ("One Answer to a
Question: Changes," *FP,* 329). Both Cleopatra and Bradstreet are

strong-willed and yet vulnerable. Both are ambitious and yet rebellious. Their rebellions, in the play as in the poem, force them into submission, although, as Berryman said of *Homage*, "even in the moment of . . . supreme triumph . . . rebellion survives" (*FP*, 329). In both women, sexual passion is apparent at an early age (Cleopatra delights in her power; Bradstreet at fourteen found her "heart more carnal and sitting loose from God" [*Homage to Mistress Bradstreet*, *CP*, 136]). Both are paired with powerful men who are nearly twice their age, and both are admired more than the men. Both see their children as sources of personal power, though in very different ways.

"Cleopatra," being 449 lines, and *Homage*, 456, are correspondingly parallel in dramatic construction. Each work has five parts and is set in motion by "a series of rebellions" of the main character. The rebellions make up three large sections and are preceded by an exordium and followed by a coda.[11] In "Cleopatra," the Narrator has the exordium, though he does not summon up the body of his subject as the twentieth-century poet does in *Homage*. He prepares the audience for the Queen's entrance. The first section begins when Cleopatra enters the stage alone and prays to the Sun:

> To study lust and war, the goddess
> Taught me to mask the lioness and present at will
> Imperial aspect or the tricks of the bed.

She discloses her cunning rebellion against Caesar, whose son she had borne two years before. As a result of their alliance, "Egypt prospers," which was her ambition. Section 2, the longest, begins with the entrance of Caesar and ends with his exit. Her rebellion against him in this section becomes so outright that he responds fiercely. She is powerless in Italy, he reminds her: "I have sent men / To hell for less." She submits, but on her own terms: "Yet are we not so weak as we do seem," she replies; twenty armed slaves stand ready to "throng the chamber." And yet their union, Caesar says, "will never / Pass from complexity." The section ends with Caesar saying, "I will come to you tonight." Cleopatra replies ambiguously, "To both your Empires, welcome, and farewell."

The third section begins with the Narrator's meditation, "Once a Queen bedded her fixed enemy" and ends with Cleopatra's dance to the Sun. Dramatically, this section is the most interesting and effective of the three: the Narrator and Cleopatra alternately speak, but not between themselves, in song, soliloquy, and prayer. Cleopatra's rebellion, ambition, love, and pride seem at once a curse and a cause for satisfaction: "I beg but a mild thought," she says before her dance of love and death,

> Memory of my son and of this love.
> The rest I consecrate to Egypt and
> An immaculate dream of her white peace.

The Narrator sings the coda and ponders what symbol will "sustain what she has been?"

> Not a Tanagra figurine
> From out the tumult and the wrath.
> Perhaps the sensual eye, the pride
> That spent itself before her breath.

Two months before he started writing "Cleopatra," Berryman was determined to form a style that would have "tone and shift and subtlety, and honesty, and a solid, I hope, individual texture."[12] As he wrote "Cleopatra," he accelerated towards realizing his resolve. The play does not contend for a place in Berryman's mature writing, but it is his most effect and sustained early work, especially the last ninety lines or so, beginning with Caesar's saying, "One life is one life only, though it be mine, / And when it's gone, it's gone forever— once." "Cleopatra" still has a distinctive power in performance. Philip Levine said to me the night it was first produced at the Berryman Conference, "How old was Berryman when he wrote that play?" "Twenty-two," I said. "Amazing," he said.

NOTES

1. Berryman to mother, 27 April 1937. All references to Berryman's letters to his mother, Jill Berryman, are from the originals in the JB Papers.
2. Berryman to mother, 29 April 1937, JB Papers.
3. Berryman to mother, 15 February 1938, JB Papers. Although this description of the plot was written nearly a year after he began the play, Berryman was fairly certain in his early planning that Caesar would tell Cleopatra of how he killed Cneus Pompey.

4. The quotations in this paragraph and the next two are taken from Berryman's notes, unless otherwise indicated, in Plays, "Cleopatra" file, JB Papers.

5. Berryman to mother, 29 April 1937, JB Papers.

6. Cleopatra was "first taken to Caesar by stealth, in a flockbed on the back of a slave," Berryman wrote to his mother, 15 February 1938, JB Papers. When the *Southern Review* accepted one of the songs from "Cleopatra," Berryman wrote to Robert Penn Warren: "You remember she [Cleopatra] was carried to Caesar first by stealth, in a flockbed (North's word and Pope uses it)." Berryman to Warren, 12 February 1938, Beinecke Rare Book and Manuscript Library, Yale University.

7. Berryman to mother, 19 October 1937, JB Papers.

8. Berryman to Halliday, 2 July 1937, JB Papers.

9. Diary, 11 November 1937, JB Papers.

10. Berryman to mother, 27 April 1937, JB Papers.

11. I am using here Berryman's description of the dramatic structure of *Homage*. See "One Answer to a Question: Changes," *FP*, 328.

12. Berryman to mother, 14 February 1937, JB Papers.

John Berryman

Cleopatra: A Meditation

Scene: Rome, Cleopatra's Villa
Time: 45 B.C.

Narrator
Cleopatra
Julius Caesar

The Narrator Enters; stage lightens as he speaks: Sunlight R.

Narrator: The Queen will soon be here. I must be brief.
   And yet I must grieve to think that in Spain
   Last night lay Cneus Pompey in a cave
   Alone, and somewhat less than when a man.
   The wolves went weeks ago, having fed well
   But not fully: they have not taste for bone
   And found the brain protected, where the worms are.
   Not personal grief; Pompey was as crass
   As any Roman and I never liked him.
   But this was the admiration of the Queen
   And all her tenderness; she cherishes
   Two months in Alexandria with him
   As I do these my eyes, the dearest faculty
   Of man, which I'd give only in her service—
   And so I all but do, in a kind, to think
   Caesar returns today and will confirm
   What she now but fears. Neither his respect
   Nor a consideration of their son

283

Cesarion will save his cruelty.
Only she, who in this villa that he gave her
In Rome fences each day the unfriendly Senate,
Will turn the wound a weapon—let him beware
What he inflicts. We were amazed at her
During those months, for twenty saw her wise
Beyond the pitch of any Ptolemy,
All her endeavour a task of government;
Not until then did vigilance relax
In her, the careful midnight plans for Egypt.
His rank (her object) she did quite forget
Wandering with him in a silken maze,
An obdurate and delicate confusion
Intention could not pierce. It is four years:
Ambition has not slept in her since then
And will not sleep again; the sensual
Drive has been set apart as an appetite
Indifferent to empire, is fed with slaves
Or serves her purpose with the conqueror.
I think it is not love that will offend
Her in Pompey's death, but the gall of Caesar
Together with the knowledge that all instance
Of her uncomplicated joy is dust
And cannot speak or stand.

*Cleopatra enters L; as she crosses to the light, the Narrator comes down L,
saying:*

She comes to pray.

Cleopatra: Thou, come again to temper brittle morning,
  Bright sun of the sacred blue, grant my fears
  Unprofitable as the wind against
  White marble is, and issueless. Report
  Stifles my ear with Roman victory,
  Complete perdition of the rebel army,
  The bare escape of Sextus Pompey, while
  Of Cneus nothing. Not for love let him
  Return, or have got free—for I am clear,

By thy fierce ministration, of all aim
That is not Ptolemaic—but as a symbol
Grant him deliverance, merely the sign
And tangible dignity of a time when
My life was mine alone. Nothing simple
Since. To study lust and war, the goddess
Taught me to mask the lioness and present at will
Imperial aspect or the tricks of the bed.
And Egypt prospers: sunlight. But I tire
Nearly to madness with this crafty goat,
A monster of unscrupulous courtesy,
This orator of the legions. Cesarion
I hold, and he is mine—only Caesar's
If Caesar cheat his enemies and rule:
Then he is Rome as well and I have done.
Those weeks, against these years. My palace and
This tedious villa the Senate hates and fears
Across the river. A desperate exchange.
Yet this to secure that; and I have power
Unlimited, if odd, upon this man
Who juggles nations: it is his will
(A thing he will not know nor can admit)
To dominate a subtler than himself;
And he is subtle as lascivious,
Which copes as far as matrons. He loves me,
I'll go so far—a grotesque of affection,
But it can produce jealousy, and does,
And wild as gulls, control down. Bestial fox!
I was with child by hatred: it was policy
Opened my limbs and pressed Cesarion
Into me writhing. The discipline of Thebes
Only will keep me mild. Policy, policy.
Now will he come and wait for me to ask;
Probe my anxiety with deft cold steel,
Leap from his rhetoric to irony
That stabs and waits and poises, waits and waits,
Talk of disease—an experiment in torture—
I will ask nothing.

Caesar enters and approaches her; She halts him:

Welcome. So.

Caesar: No more?

Cleopatra: More at the ninth hour? You forget me thus.

Caesar: You restrain admirably, Cleopatra,
   Your infinite devotion.

Cleopatra: I am not well.
   How is your old complaint?

Caesar: Unspeakable:
   Always in Spain, continually, where it began.
   I think the rain and heat trouble my blood.
   Here it is less; but never once with you,
   Even in the wars, in Alexandria.
   I should have stayed there.

Cleopatra: The Egyptian sun
   Permits no epilepsy nor decay.
   But you have a task here.

Caesar: I am grateful for
   "Decay"; it seasons flattery; for again
   The people crammed the ways to see me pass.

Cleopatra: You are victorious?

Caesar: Roughly. At Grenada
   Our horse broke through immediately and split
   Their loose ranks to confusion. I'd not seen
   For three years such indiscriminate slaughter,
   Great heaps of rebel dead. Not enough men
   Were alive by dusk to gather the slain,
   But the dazzled Pompeys made each survivor

Responsible for his company—in pure mercy
We let them stagger off, one bearing ten.
Next morning they fled westward to recoup,
A shattered mob. Fresh thousands in array,
We followed.—A wretched fit took me the night
Of Munda, foam and foam, I never remember.—
They foamed blood when I recovered and set
The legions to them. A mere butchery.
With twenty or so, Sextus Pompey ran
North like a hare. A few others escaped;
Most we left for the crows, and brought the rest
For the triumph here. A very brisk campaign.

Cleopatra: How difficult for the enemy.

Caesar: You are dry.
   To speak soberly, the right wing crumpling
   Cost me a thousand excellent men; but
   Each of them took thirty rebels with him.
   I've no regret: the devils were tenacious.

Cleopatra: I understand you faint at the sight of blood.

Caesar: An interesting legend: it began—
   Have you no interest in this particular
   Shambles?

Cleopatra: Some; but centuries have taught us
   Patience that is not known in Italy.

Caesar: Well. What difficulties with the Senate?

Cleopatra: A Queen among the greybeards, and they timid
   Beyond their spite. You will have trouble, Caesar:
   My slave was insolent to Cicero
   At my command of late, and the old man
   Resents it bitterly. Nothing of you;
   We disagreed on a point in logic.

Caesar: I will uphold you; but the quarrel is
  One of thousands. Why do you cherish their
  Enmity? Greater tact would let it die.

Cleopatra: Informal fools they are, whose tedious breath
  Fans my rage daily, being impotent.
  Their malice and their praise alike are blunt
  Beyond endurance, even Cicero's.
  Why should I tolerate in them dullness
  A slave would lose his head for? I will not.
  You sent for me and I came. We made no bargain.

Caesar: You find me stupid?

Cleopatra: No, your faults are greater
  As you are greater: only in the highest
  Inaccessible rocks does the vile bird
  Rest; the little ravens plague the fields.

Caesar: How is my son?

Cleopatra: Cesarion is well
  And grows. He is detested in the city—

Caesar: I know, I know. There will be changes here.
  Mark Antony suggests a crown.

Cleopatra: For whom?

Caesar: Demand what you would know.

Cleopatra: I am content.

Caesar: I left him stark and clotted, fit for crows,
  Abandoned in a cave, with all his wounds
  Festering to ugly death—a cave
  Obscure, cold, hideous, in wild country
  Where wolves are sole and fierce inhabitants,
  My legions only held the field—and he

Unable to speak and challenge our mercy,
Which he would not have had: I hated him
As I do loathe the sickness throws me down
Twisting in oblivion. Why do you not speak?

Cleopatra: What should I say?

Caesar: Curse, cry out upon death,
   Hawk your sorrow in the avenues of time
   Where there is none to listen or reply;
   Engrave your indignation on the wind,
   For he is gone—gone, gone, and no entreaty,
   No prayer, sob, love, necessity, no power
   To bring him back: beyond the reach of breath
   He lies in torment who first enjoyed you.

Cleopatra: You are loud against him, even dead; what was
   This absolute quarrel? You say for me?

Caesar: Was he not in your thoughts? Did you not love—

Cleopatra: No more. Your anger was ill-spent, Caesar.
   When he left Alexandria he took
   Less of my anxiety than you would have
   After ten years, should you die tomorrow.
   What ridiculous quirk set you to task
   Dead time with my—my evergreen allegiance?
   When have you known my heart run counter to
   My head? My scrutiny is only you
   And my country, as you at least should know,
   Who answer my demands.

Caesar: I am half-convinced.
   There are no veils in your mind—nor any
   Simplicity in you—but I am disarmed
   By your directness. Gods, had I but known—
   As yet I am not sure—what a deal of pain
   I had been saved. Our union will never
   Pass from complexity—besides, I age

A little—but had this ghost been away,
I might have slept when then I never did.

Cleopatra: Your ingenuity purchased your pain.

Caesar: I am not the open palm either, but
    With you ease is impossible, my dear.
    When Apollodorus brought you to me
    That portentous night in Alexandria,
    Secretly and by darkness into the palace
    Wrapped in a flockbed, a mere mattress, on
    His back, and threw you gently down before me,
    The lips and tongue fertility of Spring
    I found in you, and in your azure eyes
    Imperial lethargy and agate nails.
    But of your penalled veins a labyrinth
    Of emotions without name or number, those
    That throng the child and reconcile him to
    Precarious existence.

Cleopatra: You babble and
    Waste the dense hour. It was jealousy, then,
    That commanded my presence here in Rome.
    I have sometimes wondered how you came thus
    Contrary to your design, Roman opinion,
    Against your every counsel of position.
    So to be led by me.

Caesar: Perhaps. I knew
    What would & would not come of it, in place,
    And ignored.

Cleopatra: I am astonished. Jealousy
    Rots at the heart of the known world's emblem?
    What part have you in the ceremony of love?
    You should know nothing of the infinite hours
    An evening alone contains. For years
    Upon years you have fed at a casual table

Where hundreds came and fed with you, the wives,
　　Even the mothers of your valued friends,
　　And the stale of foreign wars—but none remained.
　　Nor was there ever intimacy, no touch
　　That had a context, lovely in the morning.
　　Decrepit, automatic drive, hairless
　　With brief and foul desire. Monkeys are more
　　But nothing different.

Caesar:　　　　　　　　I have sent men
　　To hell for less. How do you dare to speak
　　Thus? There is a rack will hold a Queen,
　　And wring that arrogance from your torn arms.
　　You are powerless here; being so, but foolish.

Cleopatra:　Yet are we not so weak as we do seem.
　　Should I lift my voice, twenty armed slaves
　　Would throng the chamber, Caesar. Not all your legions
　　And craft could save you.

Caesar:　　　　　　　　They are not such fools:
　　They would be rent like animals, after
　　Watching you carried piecemeal through the streets.

Cleopatra:　What did the Tenth suffer for you in Gaul?
　　Like wise would mine.

Caesar:　　　　　　　I grow forgetful. Yes,
　　I do believe it. And you have great cause
　　To hate me, Cleopatra, as some to love,
　　For freeing Egypt's tribute and securing her
　　To you. If Cneus Pompey is none of it,
　　Yet I drove your sister chained before me
　　Two years ago in triumph here in the city;
　　Thousands of your countrymen have I slaughtered,
　　And bound your priests, robbing your treasuries.
　　But you will not call.

Cleopatra: No, it is not for slaves
   To cut the tallest tree—and yet it is
   By treachery, I think, that you will fall.

Caesar: It is your kindness, not your love, that will
   Not lift your voice against me?

Cleopatra: My kindness?
   Men I have killed in the morning, unable to bear
   Their learnèd eyes upon mine, remembering tongues
   Digesting on the quays my sweet behaviour.
   This I would not allow, and so they lie
   Oblivious.

Caesar: The peace you made with them
   Proclaims a gentle heart.

Cleopatra: Let all this go.
   Do you plan a triumph? The people will
   Bear it hardly, for this war was civil.
   The sons of their great noblemen in chains.
   They will applaud the captives and turn from
   The relentless victor.

Caesar: To the people's tide
   I am the moon, and they will come to flood
   When next I need them. The Senate has named me
   Dictator Perpetual—there is a step,
   But it is "king" I want, the name of "king."
   My dreams are wild until the diadem
   Comes here to rest.

Cleopatra: They are not yet ready.
   Press it when Asia is subdued again.
   What of this triumph?

Caesar: I shall have it but
   To satisfy the army, partly myself.
   It will excite no rancour, for I have pardoned

Many, to some have given offices:
Brutus and Cassius are Praetors.

Cleopatra: Trust not
   The men you spare. Ingratitude is rank
   And thrives upon the earth, most about princes.
   They may remember one day, sword in hand,
   Indignity and defeat in war.

Caesar: Not they.
   Brutus I saved at Munda, and he is
   The last man living to forget a grace.
   Cassius I like not, but his love to me
   Is fixed.

Cleopatra: Whatever your thoughts, go guarded, Caesar.

Caesar: One life is one life only, though it be mine,
   And when it's gone, it's gone forever—once.
   Fear dies with every heart-beat, the coward is
   A momentary prey to death in life.
   The wiser man not recognizes death
   Until he is past the power of recognition
   And easily sleeps.

Cleopatra: I have studied death
   In many guises: it is not to fear,
   But neither a thing to run to, when you might
   So readily forbid its unseasonal
   Approach.

Caesar: I neither invite nor shun, nor will
   Give expectation lodging and a front.—
   I must be gone: I am awaited at
   The Senate. I will come to you tonight.

Cleopatra: To both your Empires, welcome, and farewell.

As Caesar goes, the Narrator speaks:

Narrator: Once a Queen bedded her fixed enemy
　　　　And from that time of heat and hatred came
　　　　A curious legend of love.

Cleopatra:　　　　　　　　O brilliant God
　　　　That over day hast mandate and by night
　　　　Prepares our destiny, even in the edge
　　　　Of darkness our felicity and doom:
　　　　Be thou implacable to him who left
　　　　My lover shredded in the desperate cave
　　　　Far from his fathers and my strength, troops scattered,
　　　　His brother fled, his royal blood too early
　　　　Welling to dust. This is my prayer. Revenge
　　　　In his exaltation this act on Caesar:
　　　　Where he is in State, let his most dear friend,
　　　　Companion to his counsel and his hope,
　　　　Strike even his majesty, a blessèd traitor,
　　　　And let the subtle spirit out—to torture.
　　　　Let Caesar kneel in his blood at the foot
　　　　Of Pompey's statue in the Capitol,
　　　　Suing for mercy that he will not find,
　　　　As Pompey's son, mangled, found none in him.
　　　　Mild as the ravening beaks of vultures be
　　　　His death, patient as storm; and when he stands
　　　　For judgement, Cneus Pompey hold the seat.
　　　　Disaster on disaster, let Caesar's life
　　　　Accumulate destruction toward that time,
　　　　And that time quit my injury forever.

She kneels, and the narrator sings.

Narrator: To meditate upon the Queen
　　　　Has been my strict desire.
　　　　She counted what she gave.
　　　　Giving but wit and the obscene
　　　　Glance, she expected empire.
　　　　And was the flockbed better than the cave?

　　　　Many a lovely monster went
　　　　Triumphantly along

The terrace to the grave.
Lucky to leave, to quit the bent
Back and the forgetful throng.
But was the flockbed better than the cave?

Did she avoid, I say alone,
Compassion at midnight,
The winds that run and rave?
Her foot is even in the tomb
Long before the end of light.
And was the flockbed better than the cave?

Cleopatra: This agony gets truth in me. My life
   I see a chart upon the Roman wall
   That rain disfigures and wind blows away.
   All accident, all paraphrase, I took
   For shining reality, leaves I took
   For the vast oak, the fingers for the arm,
   And am betrayed so, living by translation;
   For a tinsel possibility I am sold,
   Without a house on earth to keep my soul.
   Disaster has been handmaid to my star
   And tricked her to the enemy. What remains
   Will never balance or preserve the lost.
   Pompey has firmer peace than I who live
   To mourn his slow unspeakable decay.
   A casual recovered smile is left me
   Of all that man, those months. The pity there,
   The unmitigated pity, but it is not
   Sufficient to hold me, pacing fled time.
   Antiphonal excitement will I have
   Incessant now, never the single note
   To crown pride's orchestration, but the clash
   Of cymbals and above the roll of drums
   Tinkling of sistra. Dictator Perpetual,
   There is a pause, a light for Cesarion
   To climb by, but I think it will not stay:
   The earless exacerbation of his dream
   Wears Caesar ever outward—he will part

To the forgetful air and leave no name
For us to rule by. What conqueror then?
Faction and murder and Egypt insecure
Again, our treasure summoning. Vile men,
The spoil and pride of empire, will return
To sack, to burn. My flesh and tongue crawl from them.
Let now no *ka* be made, whether of white
Perpetual alabaster or of sycamore,
To be left in a tomb, for I would die
Forever and forever, I would be left
Lying until the earth breaks and reveals,
Courteously dissolved, this terrible beauty
To the cold stars. I beg but a mild thought,
Memory of my son and of this love.
The rest I consecrate to Egypt and
An immaculate dream of her white peace.

Cleopatra dances to the Sun, a dance of love and death; and goes.

Narrator sings: From Pharos I have seen her white
        Standing with Pompey while the moon
        Twice turned and made a silver noon
        Upon the Alexandrian night.
        When air was olive, she but young,
        Ambition died into delight.

        A bird there was that died and then
        Struck from its ashes into life.
        Resentment got continual strife
        And blood upon the marsh and fen.
        Limp in the antique arms of one
        She found her hatred for all men.

        That Queen insulted Cicero,
        Lucan and Horace threw a gibe,
        But Antony and all his tribe
        Cut out the hearts that called her so.
        Wandering upon her terrace
        They go and ask not where they go.

What symbol of degraded death
Will now sustain what she has been?
Not a Tanagra figurine
From out the tumult and the wrath.
Perhaps the sensual eye, the pride
That spent itself before her breath.

Charles Thornbury

Afterword: A Note on the Text and First Performance

For the conference on John Berryman in October 1990, Chuck Nuckles of Concordia College, St. Paul brought together two other actors and directed the premier performance of "Cleopatra." He played the Narrator; Linda Bruning of the Commedia Theatre Company of St. Paul played Cleopatra, and Peter Jensen, Julius Caesar. About a year before the conference, Mr. Nuckles and I read through the two extant, holograph copies of the play, one of which is complete, one unfinished, in the John Berryman Papers, Manuscripts Division, University of Minnesota Libraries, St. Paul, MN. After he did a typescript from the only extant, complete copy of the play, I proofed it and made one major change. I decided to use a combination of the two copies of "Cleopatra." The only complete draft of the play—a holograph script with changes, a title page, and the pages numbered 1 through 26—appears to be Berryman's penultimate draft (how many drafts he wrote before this cannot be determined from the extant papers). The second copy of the play comprises the first 192 lines and is written in a meticulous hand with no changes; the pages are numbered 3 through 15 (pages 1 and 2 perhaps were to be an introduction or preface material). This second copy appears to be nearly half of his final draft (up through Cleopatra's lines, "You are loud against him, even dead; what was / This absolute quarrel? You say for me?").

The text for this edition of "Cleopatra," then, is a combination of the first 192 lines of Berryman's final copy and the remaining 257 lines from the penultimate draft copy. Berryman made most of his changes—approximately thirty-five words, phrases, or lines—in the first 192 lines of the complete draft copy. The final copy, though incomplete, has been admitted as his final intention for that part of the play (he also made several changes, not indicated in the draft copy, as he wrote the final copy). After line 192 the text published here continues with the penultimate draft text. In the remaining 257 lines, Berryman indicated approximately thirty word, phrase, or line changes. It was not possible to observe all the changes he marked because in several instances he did not indicate precisely what the change would be. In the absence of any clear indication, the original word or phrase has been admitted as his final intention.

Contributors

Alan J. Altimont is Assistant Professor of English Literature and Writing, and director of the Literature Program at Saint Edward's University in Austin, Texas. "The End of *Recovery* and the End of Self-Representation" is a version of part of a full-length study, *The Autobiographical Art of John Berryman,* as yet unpublished.

Lea Baechler, of Columbia University, coedited the 1990 edition of Ezra Pound's 1926 *Personae* and has published a number of articles on modern poetry. She is presently finishing a book on twentieth-century American elegies.

Charlotte H. Beck received her Ph.D. in 1972 from the University of Tennessee at Knoxville. Her articles have appeared in various journals and *festschriften,* and her book, *Worlds and Lives: The Poetry of Randall Jarrell,* was published in 1983. She is presently writing a book on the Fugitive legacy, concerning those writers whose literary careers were shaped by their relationships with the Nashville Fugitives. Since 1965 she has been a member of the faculty at Maryville College in Tennessee.

Christopher Benfey is the author of two books on Emily Dickinson as well as the recently published *The Double Life of Stephen Crane.* He teaches at Mount Holyoke College.

Sharon Bryan completed her third collection of poems, *Belongings,* last year. Her first two books, *Salt Air* (1983) and *Objects of Affection* (1987), were both published by Wesleyan University Press. She is currently editing a collection of essays by women poets: *Tradition and the Individual Talent: Women's Perspectives.* She is Associate Professor of English at Memphis State University and editor of the literary magazine *River City.*

John Clendenning is Professor of English at California State University, Northridge. He is the editor of *The Letters of Josiah Royce* (1970) and author of *The Life and Thought of Josiah Royce* (1985). Professor Clendenning is currently writing a book on Stephen Crane.

Roger Forseth (B.A., Carleton College; Ph.D., Northwestern University) is a professor of English at the University of Wisconsin-Superior. He is editor of

Dionysos: The Literature and Addiction Triquarterly and has published articles on Sinclair Lewis, Ernest Hemingway, Eugene O'Neill, and Charles Jackson.

Lewis Hyde is Luce Professor of Arts and Politics at Kenyon College. He is the author of *The Gift* (a book of cultural criticism) and *This Error Is the Sign of Love* (a book of poems). A graduate of the University of Minnesota, he was a student of John Berryman's in 1966.

Richard J. Kelly is a professor and bibliographer in the University of Minnesota Libraries. He is editor of *We Dream of Honour: John Berryman's Letters to His Mother,* author of *John Berryman: A Checklist,* and has written several articles on the poet. He was a student of John Berryman's, at Minnesota, in 1964–65.

Alan K. Lathrop is professor and curator of the Manuscripts Division of the University of Minnesota Libraries, which holds the John Berryman Papers. His articles have appeared in several journals, including the *American Archivist, Minnesota History, Georgia Archive, Journal of Southeast Asian Studies, South Dakota History,* and *Architecture Minnesota.* He is currently editing, for future publication, the diary of a U.S. Army surgeon who served in China and India during World War II.

Philip Levine was a member of the only poetry writing workshop John Berryman ever taught. He is twice winner of the National Book Award in poetry. Long associated with Fresno State University, he retired from there in May 1992. His most recent books are *What Work Is* and *New Selected Poems,* both from 1991.

Joseph Mancini, Jr., Ph.D., L.C.S.W., author of *The Berryman Gestalt: Therapeutic Strategies in the Poetry of John Berryman* (1987), has taught literature, psychology and literature, writing, and men's studies in various universities in the metropolitan areas of Boston and Washington, D.C. Also currently in private practice as a licensed clinical social worker with a Jungian and gestalt orientation, he gives experiential workshops focusing on gender issues from archetypal, sociological, and psychological perspectives.

Paul Mariani is Distinguished Professor of English at the University of Massachusetts, Amherst. His most recent books are *Dream Song: The Life of John Berryman* (1990) and *Salvage Operations: New and Selected Poems* (1990). He is completing a biography of Robert Lowell.

Jerold M. Martin received his B.A. from Indiana University and M.A. from Louisiana State University. He recently completed four years of study as an LSU Alumni Fellow and is currently teaching writing at LSU and working on a dissertation on John Berryman's poetry.

Peter Stitt is the editor of the *Gettysburg Review.* He is the author of *The World's Hieroglyphic Beauty: Five American Poets,* and is the authorized biographer of James Wright.

Charles Thornbury is Professor of English at St. John's University in Minnesota. He has edited and introduced Berryman's *Collected Poems 1937–1971* and published several articles on Berryman's life and poetry. He is working on a critical and literary biography of Berryman.

George F. Wedge is Associate Professor of English at the University of Kansas. He is editor of two literary magazines, *Cottonwood* and *Stiletto*, advisory editor to *Kansas Quarterly* and is on the editorial board of *Dionysos: The Literature and Addiction Triquarterly*.